RELIGION IN THIRD WORLD POLITICS

ISSUES IN THIRD WORLD POLITICS

Series Editor: Vicky Randall, Department of Government,
University of Essex

Current titles:
Heather Deegan: The Middle East and problems of democracy
Jeff Haynes: Religion in Third World politics
Robert Pinkney: Democracy in the Third World

RELIGION IN THIRD WORLD POLITICS

Jeff Haynes

LYNNE RIENNER PUBLISHERS
Boulder, Colorado

To my parents

Published in the United States of America in 1994 by
Lynne Rienner Publishers, Inc.
1800 30th Street, Boulder, Colorado

Library of Congress Cataloging-in-Publication Data
Haynes, Jeffrey.
    Religion in Third World politics / by Jeff Haynes.
        p.   cm. – (Issues in Third World politics)
    Includes bibliographical references and index.
    ISBN 1–55587–456–8 (alk. paper)
    1. Religion and politics – Developing countries.   2. Developing
countries–Religion.   3. Christianity–Developing countries–20th
century.   4. Islam–Developing countries–20th century.   I. Title.
II. Title: Religion in 3rd World politics.   III. Series.
BL65.P7H38   1993
322′.1′09124—dc20   93–11091
                                                                          CIP

5 4 3 2 1

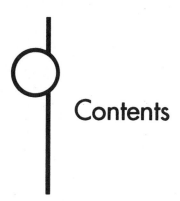

Contents

Series editor's introduction		vii
Acknowledgements		x
	Introduction: the significance of religion in the plural societies of the Third World	1
1	Religion, politics and analysis of Third World development	18
2	Islam and Christianity: the historical expansion and political significance of the global religions	44
3	The political resurgence of Islam in the Third World	64
4	Third World Christianity and politics	95
5	Links between religion and foreign policy in the Third World	122
6	Politics and religion in the Third World: continuity and change	145
	Bibliography	156
	Index	164

Series editor's introduction

When I was invited to edit this series, I thought long and hard about what it should be called. I ended up going back to the well-worn phrase 'Third World' but recognizing that this very term raises problems that both this Introduction and the books in the series would need to address. Its advantage is that to most people it signals something fairly clearcut and recognizable. The expression 'Third World' has come to connote the regions and individual countries of Africa, Asia, the Caribbean, Latin America and the Middle East. It is the politics, in the broadest sense, of this part of the world, and of its relationship with the rest of the world, that constitutes the subject matter of this series.

Yet the notion of a single 'Third World' has always been problematic. When it became clear that the nations so designated were not going to follow a third, 'nonaligned', economic and political route between the capitalist west and the communist world, it was argued that they none the less shared a common predicament. Directly or indirectly they suffered the after-effects of colonization and they came late and on disadvantageous terms into the competitive world economy. Even then there was tremendous variety – in culture, experience of colonial rule, forms and levels of economic activity – between and within Third World regions.

Over time this internal differentiation seems to have grown. On the one hand we have the oil-rich states and the Newly Industrializing Countries (NICs), on the other the World Bank has identified a 'Fourth World' of lower income countries like Bangladesh or Tanzania, distinguished from the lower-middle income countries like Mexico and Malaysia. Then from the later 1980s we have witnessed the disintegration of most of the 'Second World' of state socialist societies – where does that leave the First and the Third?

These developments certainly threaten the coherence of the concept of a

Third World. They must make us wonder whether the concept is any longer plausible or useful in categorizing what are by now well over 100 countries, containing three-quarters of the world's population. Recently writers both on the Right and on the Left have suggested that the notion of a Third World functions primarily as a myth: for the former it is a projection of the guilt of First World liberals while for the latter it evokes for the West a reassuring image of its own opposite, all that it has succeeded in not becoming.

The arguments are not all one way, however. When Nigel Harris writes about the 'end of the Third World' and its dissolution into one world economic system, he is referring to objective economic trends which still have a long way to go and which are by no means automatically accompanied by a decline in Western economic nationalism or cultural chauvinism. Third World countries do still at least some of the time recognize their common status *vis-à-vis* the developed world and the need to stick together, as was apparent at the Rio Earth Summit in June 1992. The fact that some Third World nations may have 'made it' into the developed world, does not negate the existence of the Third World they have left behind. It does, however, undermine the more deterministic arguments of dependency theorists, who have maintained that it is impossible to break out of economic dependence and underdevelopment. The dissolution of the Second World, it could be argued, leaves the confrontation and contrast between First and Third World starker than ever (this might of course indicate the use of a different nomenclature, such as North and South). On the other hand the countries of the old Second World will not be transformed overnight into members of the First and there is a case for retaining a Second World category to refer to countries only recently emerged from a prolonged period of communist rule.

But my purpose here is not to insist on the continuing usefulness of the notion of a Third World so much as to signal the question as part of the agenda I hope that authors in this series will address. It seems to me that there *are* respects in which most of the countries conventionally included in the Third World do continue to share a common predicament and about which it is up to a point legitimate to generalize. But unless we also explore the differences between them, our powers of political explanation will be limited and it may be that it is these differences which now hold answers to the most important and interesting questions we want to ask.

One of the questions which has increasingly begged to be asked but which has hitherto received extraordinarily little sustained attention from social scientists let alone from political scientists is why the role of religion in Third World politics, instead of diminishing as expected, has grown over the last decade or so. In fact, of course, religion has always been important but it took events like the 1979 Iranian Revolution to bring this home. Jeff Haynes' most timely study offers us not only a critical review of the existing literature but his own careful assessment (based largely but not exclusively on considerations of Islam and Christianity, both Liberation Theology and Protestant fundamentalism) of the scope for generalizing about the causes, forms and outcomes of religion's impact on politics in the different regions of the Third World.

Vicky Randall

Acknowledgements

Vicky Randall was an indefatigable series editor, with always useful suggestions and ideas; her enthusiasm for the book helped to bolster my own. Thanks are due to Ted Hewitt and Nazih Ayubi, who read and commented on individual chapters, to Robin Theobald who read the whole thing, to the former Editorial Director of Open University Press, Richard Baggaley, who commissioned the book, and to Richard Delahaye and other staff at Calcutta House library, London Guildhall University, who faced with cheerfulness my seemingly endless demands for inter-library loans.

Introduction: the significance of religion in the plural societies of the Third World

Newspapers, radio and television regularly carry stories in which religion and politics in the Third World appear intertwined. Themes may include internecine clashes or disputes involving Hindus and Moslems in India, or Hindus and Buddhists in Sri Lanka. They may concern Jesuit priest-academics and military men in El Salvador, Islamic guerrillas and communists in Afghanistan, different branches of Islam in Iraq or Syria, and Christians and Muslims in Nigeria and elsewhere in Africa. Such conflicts reflect a religious dimension in Third World politics which has frequently been played down or treated as an archaic survival by scholarly analyses (Levine 1986: 95; Brown 1989; Mews 1989a: vii, 1). In other words, there has been little general academic awareness of the importance of religion in most studies of politics in the Third World. Indeed, until recently it was generally considered in Western academic circles that religion was a declining force in politics in general. The conventional view was summed up by C. Wright Mills over thirty years ago: 'Neither preachers nor the religious laity matter, [they could] be readily agreed with and safely ignored' (Wright Mills 1959: 150).

It was three discrete events in the late 1970s that forced the politics of religion in the Third World to the forefront of both academic and governmental concerns. These were Iran's Islamic revolution of 1978–80, the civil war between communists and Islamists in Afghanistan from 1978, and the establishment of the Sandinista government in Nicaragua in 1979, following the overthrow of the dictator Somoza. Sandinista leaders included radical Christians whose ideas were moulded by the concerns of liberation theology: social justice, equity and political transformation. These events were, however, only the most overt manifestations of renewed signs of the prominence of religion in the politics of diverse countries and regions. As a result, a renewed focus on the interactions between politics, theology and culture was essential in order to gain information and understanding of a Third World which stubbornly refused to conform to Western stereotypical expectations.

What seems to have changed fundamentally during the period since Wright Mills wrote has three interrelated aspects. First, and most obviously, what is now commonly known as the Third World or the developing countries[1] emerged as a culturally fragmented, frequently politically unstable, economically diverse group of states, with burgeoning populations. Collectively, they had no particular affinity with the international status quo which they were obliged to accept upon assuming political independence.

Second, ordinary people in the Third World found themselves caught by the desires of their governments to modernize their societies along Western lines while at the same time attempting to retain their long held cultural and religious beliefs at a time of almost unprecedented political, economic and technological change (Foster-Carter 1985: 207). Historically, such developments were, of course, by no means confined to the Third World. In what is now known as the 'developed world' or 'the West', a parallel development had taken place since the eighteenth century or earlier, which resulted in people being faced with massive and seemingly inexplicable sudden changes in their lives. During this period of industrialization and state centralization, they naturally struggled to make sense of what was happening to them. Not infrequently, in pre-modern Europe as much as in the contemporary Third World, the explanations they came up with had a strongly religious form (Alexander 1982; Lannon 1982). What seems to have happened in many parts of the Third World is that both the state and religious bodies enlarged their spheres of operation (Mews 1989a: vii). Sometimes, as the cases of, for example, Iran, El Salvador, Guatemala and Pakistan show, the result was a kind of political condominium of joint control over society. In others, the process was confrontational: for example, in Nicaragua, Nigeria, Saudi Arabia and Syria, religious organizations clashed with state authorities over the question of 'Who wields greater power?' In both sets of examples, the likelihood of state and religion coming into contention with each other was increased as, in the post-1945 era (the *de facto* modern age), states everywhere increased their realms of involvement, frequently taking up formerly exclusively religious issues, including moral and philosophical concerns (Robertson and Chirico 1985: 224).

Third, modern communications and ease of travel have, in a very real way, 'shrunk' the world: what happens in Romania today will be known tomorrow in Nigeria. The result has been a kind of globalization of issues, with ideologues and groups learning from others in a process of shrewd imitation with variations imposed to suit changes in circumstances. Such a process was highlighted during the 1990–1 Gulf War. Because of Iraq's status as a country with large numbers of Muslims (even though different Islamic groups were in political contention), and because of the ability of television, radio and newspapers to penetrate and spread information and ideas to every area of the globe very quickly, there were spontaneous demonstrations of support for Saddam Hussein in virtually every country with a substantial Muslim population (Azzam 1991: 474). The Gulf crisis not only affirmed to many Muslims their previous suspicions of America's enmity towards Islam; in addition, displays of solidarity frequently developed into anti-government riots, especially if the ruling regime was perceived to have failed in its professed aim of increasing its citizens' collective well-being. Thus international events could be the instigator of (or at least the excuse for) anti-government outbursts at home which, as we shall see, were frequently portrayed in terms of 'Islamists versus secular governments'.[2] The non-Muslim interpretation of the 1990–1 Gulf War was as a United Nations policing exercise to prevent one aggressive state redrawing unilaterally the international boundaries of another. Muslim states' governments generally adhered to this legalistic interpretation of Iraq's aggression, yet many ordinary Muslims did not deem it inherently wrong for Iraq to try to incorporate Kuwait because the latter was seen as a colonially created state which had once been part of Iraq.

A further manifestation of the international dimension of the Gulf War was that it was seen by many as a modern form of the medieval Crusades, when Christians sought to liberate the so-called 'Holy Land' from the Muslim Turks. The demise of the Cold War involving the USA and the Soviet Union at the beginning of the 1990s left military strategists in the West searching for a new enemy. They came up with the 'fundamentalist Muslims' of North Africa and the Middle East; a contemporary version of the Crusades pitting Christian knights against Muslim warriors in new international conflict. National interests draped in the mantle of religion became a foreign policy concern. This interpretation of the post-Cold War period is given credence by the results of a Gallup Poll survey in Britain at the end of 1989 (i.e. *before* the Gulf War), which found that 37 per cent of those questioned thought an international conflict between Christians and Muslims (i.e. between the North Atlantic region and the Middle East) to be 'likely' in the 1990s (Modood 1990: 143).

The three interrelated aspects of the religionization of politics are most clearly manifested in the contemporary phenomenon that is often erroneously and simplistically referred to in the West as 'Muslim fundamentalism'. This appellation is simplistic because if 'fundamentalism' refers to the doctrine of scriptural inerrancy, 'then all Muslims are fundamentalists' (Perry 1991: 129) as the Quran is deemed to be literally the Word of God. It is erroneous because there are significant variations in both the aims and programmes of the different political groups lumped together as 'fundamentalist'. Yet, generally, a very striking feature of most of the contemporary Muslim world in recent times is the growth of a militant, political Islam, of which the Iranian revolution of 1978–80 and the electoral success of the Islamic Salvation Front (FIS) in Algeria in 1991 were only the best known examples. The growth of political Islam focused attention on a more widespread contemporary religio-political development: the emergence and growth of 'revivalist', 'neo-traditionalist' or 'fundamentalist' versions of the monotheistic religions: Islam, Judaism and Christianity.

In Iran, Algeria, Jordan, Pakistan, Somalia and Sudan, Islamists gained positions of political power in the 1980s or early 1990s. Yet, since as long ago as 1932, successive Saudi Arabian rulers have allowed a political role for the *ulama* (i.e. Islamic religious teachers). This indicates that the emergence of Islamic groups into positions of political power is by no means a contemporary phenomenon; yet, significantly, the Saudi ruling elite itself came under pressure from Islamic militants from the 1970s for not being 'Islamic' enough. Within the context of a recent global, cultural Islamicization, both religio-political movements and often quite secularized governments attempt to use religious doctrine as means of, respectively, challenge or legitimation.

It is not the case, we should note in passing before dealing with the issue more substantively later, that Christian and Islamic 'fundamentalists' necessarily share much in common. Indeed, in some cases groups cleaving to a militant Islamic world view have more in common with quasi-Marxist liberation theology ideas than with conservative Christian 'fundamentalists' (Munson 1988: 33; Robertson 1988: 133; Hussein Razi 1990: 86). Whether militant ideas of contemporary Islam are to be considered as ideologically related to Christian liberation theology is a question worthy of investigation; at this point I merely note that the language of popular religious liberationism appears to be something each has in common with the other.

Explanations for the phenomenal growth and increasing political prominence of forms of militant Islam frequently, and necessarily, highlight two developments. The first is the apparent crisis of identity experienced by those caught up in the great population migrations of the past 30 years, which has placed them in alien environments, often exposing them to the traumas of city life for the first time. The second is popular frustration at the increasing economic hardships – sometimes despite the apparent mitigating effects of significant oil revenues – which most ordinary people suffer. Such frustration may well have political results, especially in the crowded population centres. In Algeria, for example, it is estimated that half the young people of working age are jobless; such people appear to be the main supporters of the militant Islamic FIS (*The Guardian*, 28 January 1992).

Such religious-ideological reorientation was rarely predicted. Those who had foreseen the Shah of Iran's downfall tended to assume that the impetus would be secular and perhaps socialist (Foster-Carter 1985: 209). In the event, secular, socially progressive forces in Iranian society received short shrift from what turned out to be a militant theocracy. Yet, following the death of Khomeini in 1989 there were signs of a weakening of the regime's determination to Islamicize fully the state and society, given the increasing difficulties of the regime in the areas of economics, technology and foreign policy, areas in which mutually beneficial interaction with the West was necessary from a rational perspective. On the other hand, conservative adherents of a traditionalist vision of Judaism consolidated their hold in Israel until the June 1992 general election removed them from power. The Shamir government's attitude towards doing a deal with the largely Muslim Palestinians was bolstered by the support of the religious conservatives, a development which could only hinder the chances of peace breaking out in the Middle East. What appeared to be the dividing factor between the two regimes was that of popular support: Iran's government back-pedalled in the light of deteriorating economic conditions; whereas the Israelis stuck to a hard line *as a direct result* of popular pressure. But over time public opinion shifted significantly in Israel in the wake of 'war weariness', economic disarray, growing social dissatisfaction and international pressure, especially from the USA.

Both Islam and Judaism are 'ways of life' in which followers may see little or no division between the spiritual and the secular. Christianity, on the other hand, has a long history of separateness between 'religion' and 'politics'. Yet the spread of radical types of Christianity in recent times has not been without political impact. In much of Latin America and the Caribbean, as well as in parts of Asia (South Korea, the Philippines), Africa (Nigeria, South Africa) and the Pacific Rim (Fiji), conservative Protestantism (frequently evangelical and/or pentecostal) made extensive gains, usually at the expense of the Catholic Church. Occasionally such changes were aided and abetted – if not precipitated – by US foreign policy aims and objectives. This is not to say that there was something manufactured in the observed swing from Catholicism towards conservative Protestant sects. It is merely to note at this stage, before a closer examination in Chapter 4, that during a period of worldwide retreat from communism and revolutionary socialism, the development and growth of a free-market oriented, politically, morally and socially conservative Protestantism paralleled the rise of Reaganism in the USA and Thatcherism in Britain. Religious-conservative Protestant movements are fiercely anti-communist as well as sometimes being vehicles of government repression. In a number of Latin American states the proponents of religious-conservative ideas – usually US missionaries, big landowners, rich business people and senior military personnel – confront, sometimes literally, those individuals and movements – including priests, trade unionists and ecologists – associated with the socially progressive liberation theology.

Religion and Western academic political theorizing

One result of the increasing interaction of religion and politics was the decreasing utility of explanations of political change grounded in Western understandings of those changes, such as political development/modernization and dependency/underdevelopment analyses. Very little attention was paid to religion in virtually all the theoretical work done on Third World political change, and in the early 1990s it is still difficult to locate a major work on the politics of development that bothers to devote a chapter to this topic. Yet if religion is a highly significant aspect of politics in a large number of Third World states, and the underpinning argument of this book is that it certainly is, then how are we to begin explaining why it has been given little serious attention in attempts to construct theoretical explanations of political change?

The main explanation why religion (or other cultural phenomena such as ethnicity or caste for that matter) were relatively ignored in explanations of Third World political behaviour was that analysis was dominated, from the late 1950s, first by the modernization or political development paradigm and later by dependency/underdevelopment, neo-Marxist and other 'radical' perspectives (Manor 1991). In both sets of explanations religion and other cultural phenomena were depicted as epiphenomena. They were regarded as remnants of tradition which would inevitably and invariably decline in significance as cultural rationality and national integration developed. As long as political change was depicted as a process of transition to Western-style modernization (or as failure to so do due to structural factors), however erratic and problematical that process was, then religion and ethnicity seemed to be both marginal and temporary features of politics. Socio-political and economic 'development', whether via liberal or socialist models, would see them off as significant features of Third World societies.

Samuel Huntington, spurred by the problematic of a Third World that resolutely failed to conform to Western stereotypes, was one of the first political scientists to articulate a more careful assessment of the allegedly clear-cut division between modernity and tradition (Randall and Theobald 1985: 178). He pointed out that not only was tradition often treated as an apparently residual concept, i.e. everything that is not modern is *de facto* traditional, but also that there may be a *number* of traditions in any society (Randall and Theobald 1985: 35). Following Huntington, communalistic phenomena such as ethnicity, caste and clientelism were reassessed and reinterpreted in their relations with 'modern' institutions such as the state and political parties. The main contribution of this 'modernization revision-ism' was to add a concern with indigenous social structures and culture to assessments of Third World political development.

The insistence at looking at what *actually* was going on in Third World countries, with a focus upon political institutions as potential determinants of change, was a welcome advance on the sterile and ideal formulations of earlier analyses. Rather than events following theory as the early modern-ization school anticipated, it became clear that developments in the real world would of necessity dictate changes in that theory. The 1960s and 1970s were decades of political upheaval throughout much of the Third World. Huntington considered a lessening of distance between classes and rapid economic development – because they create a crisis of the public (old) order – as sources of instability that contribute to revolutions (Huntington 1968: 265–73). Davies (1971) posited that the optimum con-dition for social unrest exists when a sustained period of improvement in material conditions is followed by a sudden and sharp reversal. He notes the importance of expectations in people's minds, yet fails to relate such expectations to governmental legitimacy. This is not to say that revolution will necessarily occur. But it is to argue that the importance of religion in politics and vice versa over the past 20 years or so in the Middle East, Africa, the Caribbean, Asia and Latin America is causally connected to the impact of widespread economic regression, following general economic growth in the 1960s. The socially and politically explosive effects of swiftly growing populations, increasing unemployment and urbanization dovetailed with a crisis of governmental legitimacy and authority. The effect was compounded by the swifty rising world costs of petroleum products in the 1970s, which very seriously affected many Third World states' development chances.

The mistake in modernization revisionism analyses was to see ethnicity, caste, clientelism and (when it was mentioned at all) religion simply as manifestations of tradition. The impacts on communalistic issues of the insertion of Third World societies via colonialism into the modern international system were downplayed or ignored completely. The effects of class and/or social structures within the context of colonial and postcolonial economic policies made such 'traditional' factors as caste, ethnicity, clientelism and religion (i.e. *cultural* components of politics) change their forms and functions over time. As Newman (1991: 452) asserts,

> In the course of modernization ethnic [and for that matter, religious] political identities and institutions are repeatedly created and recreated anew, a process that constantly destroys the old ethnic loyalties while creating new ethnic ideologies, institutions, and constituencies.

In other words, it is insufficient to view modernization as merely reactivating and reinserting such 'traditional' concepts as religion or ethnicity into the political framework without taking account of their dynamic nature. An aim of this book is to see things in a more analytically complex way than hitherto, and in the process to stress the role of peoples, cultures, states and governments in the growth of what may be called political religions.

Religion, ethnicity and secular ideologies

Generally, religious institutions became indigenized, and politics became localized, following the departure of European colonists.[3] Secular ideologies, invariably drawn from the developed countries' experiences, including nationalism, socialism, 'state-building' and so on, were tolerated (rarely if ever enthusiastically endorsed) by populations if two interlinked factors were present. As long as governments were viewed as both authoritative and legitimate they were accepted (though rarely loved) by their citizens. From the 1970s, however, government legitimacy often plummeted in the wake of corruption, economic failure and political repression. People turned to others to champion their interests. Ethnicity and religion intertwined in a cultural worldview which, as in the case of the Sikhs and their demand for a state of 'Khalistan', utilized potent forms of pressure within and upon political systems to try to gain political ends.

It is, of course, often difficult to separate the concepts of ethnicity and religion. Both are often essential cultural components of a nation's self-identity. For example, it would be very difficult to isolate the different cultural components of what it means to be a Sikh, a Tibetan, an Israeli, a Somali or a Tajik. Ethnicity, caste and clientelism as politicized phenomena attracted much scholarly attention from the late 1970s, in response to empirical and theoretical circumstances (Newman 1991: 451). We shall examine this development, and its relationship with religion, more closely in Chapter 1. For now we merely need to note the increasing importance of ethnicity in politics from the late 1970s, often interacting with religion as politically salient features.

Whereas ethnicity may be defined as the shared characteristics of a racial or cultural group, this tells us little about religion *per se*. It is clear that no consensus exists as to what religion *is;* theologians, sociologists and anthropologists all define it differently (Laitin 1978: 570). Anthropologists regard religion as one component of the cultural aspects of social life, while sociologists seek its social rather than political significance. The theological approach to religion closely examines the doctrine, in its 'purest' form, of the charismatic founder of the religion, whether it be Moses in Judaism, Jesus in Christianity or Muhammad in Islam. The original faith not only announces the doctrine, but also details how to live a moral life conforming to the religious conceptualization. This guidance obviously has potential consequences for the organization of political life and values (Laitin 1978: 571). In this book 'religion' will refer to formal religious organizations and their practices, to groups sponsored or inspired by such religious organizations and, finally, to general models of appropriate or proper behaviour that helps to organize everyday life. 'Politics', on the other hand, includes both formal political institutions and the relations of power in an organized setting. Of particular concern from a political viewpoint are issues of authority, legitimacy, power and equity.

Pure religious doctrine of centuries ago, Laitin (1978: 571) observes, was 'a product of its times, and often of a particular social class with particular social needs.' The interaction between the original doctrine and the social, political and economic conditions of the time yields what he calls 'the practical religion', which may have an 'independent effect on political life, often quite different from the political or economic intentions of the original propagating group' (Laitin 1978: 571). Frequently, however, the original doctrine, whether it be Jesus', Moses', Muhammad's or Buddha's, delivers a social message with independent effects on the course of history. Thus, we need to bear in mind *interpretations* of religious doctrine which may instil in separate groups *ostensibly following the same religious guidance* differing, perhaps mutually irreconcilable, versions of received religious teachings.

The differing interpretations and political ramifications of religious teachings become transformed by space as well as by time. The local Christianity of Galilee, the teachings of Jesus, a social radical, became the religion of the city-state of Rome, which by imperial extension and demographic expansion became the Christianity of North Africa, of Western Europe and, later, of the Americas and beyond. Similarly, Muhammad's divinely inspired teachings involved not only the dissemination of a sacred message but also the political standing of the Quaraysh lineage in Mecca. His religious teachings were further transformed as the Islamic religion spread by conquest, trade and social osmosis to the Arab world and surrounding areas, and beyond to Africa and to South and East Asia. In the same way, although on a smaller geographical scale, the philosophy of Prince Gautama (the Buddha), moulded by the characteristics of Northern India of 2500 years ago, underwent change, transformed during its spread to Tibet, Burma, Sri Lanka, Thailand and elsewhere. The foregoing examples highlight how the very nature of religion, including the interpretations of religious truths, changes when it is exposed to new cultural dimensions, over space and time.

In this book we are particularly concerned with the two global religions: Islam and Christianity. We need to understand them as dynamic, culturally amorphous theologies which *mean different things to different peoples at different times*. Through the course of this book we shall need to take into account fully the socio-political, economic and cultural conditions of the state, nation or peoples in question, to understand how religion is transformed to meet the needs and demands of adherents, being in the process strongly influenced by contemporary social conditions.

Laitin (1978) usefully identifies three independent sources of religious influence which have effects on political life. These are: the original, 'pure' religious doctrine; the 'practical' religion, which emerges out of the interaction of the doctrine and people's interpretations of it; and the 'practical religion of the converted', i.e. the religion's interaction with the cultural conditions of the community of converts from a different culture. He argues that the effects of all three levels can exist simultaneously.

Laitin's schema both clarifies and obfuscates the effects of religious–political interaction. It clarifies it to the extent that it highlights the fact that religious realities in any society are a function of both the distance that society is from the birthplace of the religion and its cultural characteristics. He points to a potentially most fruitful area of comparison, i.e. the creation of models of the impact of world religions on local cultures in a systematic manner. However, he obfuscates the issue by failing to underline that such changes are continuing, dynamic features of religious–cultural interactions in several ways. The first is that as ruling elites failed to 'deliver' the developmental goods in the overwhelming majority of Third World states, their own legitimacy was called into question by religious and/or ethnic leaders, who often framed their criticisms in religious doctrinal or sub-nationalist terms. As we shall see, such leaders' motivations were religious, political or personal; frequently, however, concerns were mixed. Such calls came in the midst of the failure of modernization to improve generally the poor's living standards. Further, in contradistinction to the modernization revisionists, it is clear that there is no obvious correlation between economic and social modernization and the emergence of more stable, democratic political systems, and that modernization does not necessarily lead to greater equality or to a general improvement in the human condition. Finally, Laitin fails to highlight (or even to expect in the future) that 'religion' in its myriad forms would become an alternative to the failed certainties of the secular global 'religions', communism, socialism, liberal democracy and capitalism.

In the 1990s there is a *global* religious revival: from the previously officially secular states of the East European former communist world, through the developed countries of Western Europe, North America and elsewhere, to large swathes of the Third World: religious concerns now feature highly on many people's, groups' and governments' agendas. The argument is not that there has suddenly been an outbreak of religious belief in the sense of a widespread reversion to 'pure' religious doctrine alone. Rather, in the context of political authoritarianism, failed modernization and ideological dead ends, people often view sympathetically the purveyors of religious dogma and their messages of salvation, many of which have a 'this-world' impact.

Authority, legitimacy, power and equity in the Third World

I am not arguing that many Third World peoples have necessarily come to disbelieve former secular ideological certainties. It is clear, however, from the continuing political salience of caste, ethnicity and clientelism that people's world views are generally local in context rather than moulded by state ideologies of nationalism, statism or socialism. Rather, the argument is that in the context of failed modernization and inadequate government people are highly susceptible to radical alternatives which hold out the promise of transforming this world. Such a process is universalized because while many people in developing countries have become materially poorer over the past 20 years, they have acquired access to different religious ideologies and teachings. The huge numerical increase in the numbers of Protestants in Latin America and in followers of radical versions of Islam is partly because of the increased dissemination of ideas through the media of video and audio cassettes, pamphlets and books, missionary activity, pilgrimages and visits to different societies where new ideas may be absorbed. Thus global religious doctrines may be spread. The effect upon national societies depends crucially on a number of factors, including governments' legitimacy and ability to deal with threats to their rule, the unity or disunity of religio-political opponents and the popularity of their religious message, the geographical proximity of the state to the source of new religious ideas, and the residual status and strength of religion within the society.

Such concerns interact with the classic issues of politics: power, authority, legitimacy and equity. Huntington (1968) argued that the communal violence, military coups and secession attempts which characterized the politics of many developing countries in the 1960s were effects of the early stages of economic development, a process that would continue. Social inequalities would tend to be exacerbated, and newly aroused expectations not fulfilled quickly. Frustrated social mobilization would be converted into increasing pressure for *political* participation. The problem, according to Huntington, was that political institutions – whether traditional or modern accretions – were not strong enough to accommodate or withstand such pressure: 'Social and economic change [would] extend political consciousness, multiply political demands, [and] broaden political participation' (Huntington quoted in Diamond *et al.* 1990: 19). The result was that political institutions either broke down or decayed. Thus before political development could occur a measure of political stability would need to be secured. A key factor here is political institutionalization, i.e. the capacity of government 'to absorb, reconcile and act upon the diverse pressures and demands to which it is subjected' (Randall and Theobald 1985: 68). To succeed in its task it needs to establish or maintain its legitimacy.

Legitimacy is of crucial concern to political stability, not only in the Third World but everywhere. In political terms, it has two separate, but linked, meanings. First, it refers to a 'set of norms and values relating to politics that are sufficiently shared to make a political system possible' (Razi 1990: 70). The content and sources of the norms and values are also of concern, particularly since institutionalization is not possible in the absence of shared values. Second, it refers to the degree to which politically salient sections of the population perceive that their rulers are ruling according to the aforementioned norms. In other words, as long as 'the articulate members of a population are by and large satisfied with the government's actions in the areas of identity, participation, distribution, equality, and sovereignty according to the norms they believe in . . . there is no crisis of legitimacy' (Razi 1990: 70). The significant issue is not *whether* inequalities exist or the degree of political participation *per se* but whether the degree to which such features exist is considered just or unjust in terms of the shared values. Regimes 'that lack deep legitimacy depend more precariously on current performance and are vulnerable to collapse in periods of economic and social distress' (Diamond *et al.* 1990: 10). This has been a particular problem for many Third World regimes, given the widespread tendency to experience an interaction of low legitimacy and low effectiveness. As Diamond *et al.* put it:

Because of the combination of widespread poverty and the strains imposed by modernization, regimes that begin with low legitimacy also find it difficult to perform effectively, and regimes that lack effectiveness, especially in economic growth, find it difficult to build legitimacy.

(Diamond *et al.* 1990: 10)

While not immune to problems of recession, inflation and corruption, the more successful Third World democracies in the 1980s and early 1990s, including Botswana, Brazil, Senegal, Thailand[4] and Turkey, did not experience serious (or at least insurmountable) problems associated with state challenges resulting from inadequate legitimacy. Yet, as we shall see, 'democracy plus "reasonable" economic growth' is not necessarily sufficient to guarantee the absence of challenges to governmental legitimacy, usually expressed through religious, ethnic or regional political manifestations. For example, India, with an average rate of GDP growth of about 4.5 per cent per annum in the 1980s (i.e. significantly higher than population increase), nevertheless experienced a number of serious communal upheavals involving interactions of cultural, religious, ethnic and regional concerns, which threatened to tear apart the fabric of Indian statehood (Diamond *et al.* 1990: 12).

A second dimension of legitimacy is authority. Authority, i.e. legal power or right, may derive from one of three sources: from office, character or prestige. This characterization follows that developed by Max Weber, who 'emphasized the difference between the legitimate and non-legitimate domination of one person or group over others' (Hart 1985: 631). When the wielding of power is regarded as having social legitimacy, those experiencing that power accept it as appropriate. In the absence of social legitimacy, however, those aspiring to dominate may of necessity rely on force. In the long term, non-legitimate domination is likely both to be unstable and unconducive to maintenance of social order. Weber identifies three ways of generating and sustaining legitimate domination: tradition, charisma and rational-legal authority. The latter predominates in developed countries and 'is the power of office' (Hart 1985: 631). Its importance is linked to the growth of bureaucracy, where 'power is exercised according to written rules and regulations' which are generally obeyed (Hart 1985: 631).

Religious leaders are not usually vested with rational-legal power, because religious authority and civil authority are nearly always kept separate. Rather they may have either (or both) traditional or charismatic authority. For example, Ayatollah Khomeini had both an authority deriving from his character and ability to stimulate the masses to action (charisma) and also a traditional legitimacy based on his standing as an Islamic scholar and leader. Later, he also gained a rational-legal authority deriving from his position as Iran's head of state. Such a three-pronged manifestation of authority is unusual. Much more frequently religious leaders' authority is based on a combination of charisma and traditional authority. This may be especially salient politically when an incumbent government loses its legitimacy or its authority or both. An argument of this book is that people have turned to religious leaders as sources of authority precisely because of the absence of legitimacy and hence authority on the part of civil, secular leaders in the context of the failed expectations of modernization.

Before I summarize the arguments of the book, I need to distinguish between several different categories of movements and ideas within the global religious renaissance. The first type, which I shall call *religio-political*, includes those, not exclusively in the Islamic world, whose leaders utilize religious ideologies, often invoking God's 'pure' doctrine, to attack the socio-political legitimacy and economic performance of incumbent governments. Thus militant Islamist movements, such as the Islamic Republican Party in Iran, Algeria's Islamic Salvation Front, al-Nahdha in Tunisia and others in Jordan, Egypt, Afghanistan, Morocco, Indonesia and elsewhere, fall into this category. We should note, however, that while such groups share a number of characteristics they are also often separated by different programmes, theological interpretations and the means to gain power, whether through armed force, the ballot box or infiltration of government. Whichever tactical choice is selected reflects differing social, cultural, geographical, strategic, national and international characteristics and orientations.

Commonly, however, the aim is to set up an 'Islamic state', with laws derived from the precepts of the Quran, the Sharia and the Sunnah (i.e. the sayings and practices of the prophet Muhammad, including all those deeds he approved of). Such movements are not conservative. Rather, they seek to reinterpret Islam in a modern context. They are revolutionary in their social, economic and political aims, which include a fundamental reorientation of the nature and legitimacy of the state to establish polities with no *de jure* separation between government and religion. In another respect, however, it is clear that both Islamist opposition movements *and* governments are atavistic in their perceptions of the position and standing of women in their societies. In the context provided by economic failure, urbanization and the spread of 'Western' ideas, the role of women in society is closely scrutinized by both Islamicists and their more politicized counterparts, the Islamists. Even though there is little in the Quran which unequivocally indicates that women should be under men's dominance, Islamists, in asserting that 'women's place is in the home' (and not, by extension, in the workplace), may gain the support of the burgeoning numbers of unemployed youths who throng the population centres of the Arab world. In 1992 three states claim to be based on Islamist principles: Saudi Arabia, governed according to Sharia law since 1932; Iran since 1979; and Sudan since March 1991,[5] when the military government of General Omar Hassan al-Bashir introduced a code of punishment based on Sharia law. Yet these were only some of the states claiming to be Islamist or Islamist-leaning. Among others were Mauritania, Afghanistan, Pakistan, several of the former soviet central Asian republics and, to an extent, Jordan and Lebanon.

A second form of overtly political religion is to be found within Christian Third World societies in South America, Haiti, the Philippines, South Africa and elsewhere. It is frequently referred to as 'liberation theology'. It shares with opposition Islamicist groups a concern with equity, anti-imperialism and general radical political change, i.e. the need for structural transformation over charity. As we shall see, however, the shared concerns with popular participation and the creation of broadly representative governments must be understood within the quite different cultures, religious messages and geographical positions of the Islamic and Roman Catholic centres.

The second type of religious orientation is *religious revivalism*. Followers are dedicated to society's moral re-awakening and at times have a national political dimension. Such groups include conservative Protestant sects and churches which seek to reform and produce 'new' Christians. Sects of this type, often labelled 'fundamentalist' by their adherents, are to be found in Europe, North and Latin America, Sub-Saharan Africa and the Pacific Rim. The aim is not to establish a Christian *state*, but rather to establish communities of right-minded people to do God's will on earth. This is not to say that they wish to stay out of politics. Fundamentalist Christians made a big impact upon politics in the USA in the 1980s and 1990s with their campaigns about religious teaching in schools, while 'born again' Christians became rulers of El Salvador and Honduras in the 1980s (O'Shaughnessy 1990: 93*ff*.). Throughout South America as a whole Protestantism spread quickly in the 1980s, posing a challenge to the ascendancy of the Catholic Church. In addition, United States foreign policy aims dovetailed neatly with such leaders' anti-Communism. In Nigeria growing numbers of self-proclaimed Christian fundamentalists became of political salience in the context of serious clashes with Islamists.

The third type, which I shall call *syncretic hybrids*, are amalgams of Christian or Islamic religious beliefs and traditional practices. Examples are to be found in Latin America, Sub-Saharan Africa, Asia and the Pacific Rim. Such groups may have a nationalist orientation which questions the whole concept of, for example, 'Christian civilization' as progress, and seeks to highlight the pre-Christian belief structure. Such groups may or may not be politicized. The crucial factors are the legitimacy, authority and economic performance of incumbent governments. In Sub-Saharan Africa such groups are to be found in Mozambique, Uganda and elsewhere. They utilize pre-Christian beliefs in magic in association with Christian teachings, while in the Philippines syncretic hybrid sects may be virulently anti-communist. Often complementary to the syncretic hybrids are manifestations of millenarianism, i.e. a second coming or new kingdom of God. Forms of millenarianism may be extremely diverse and may be associated with Christianity, Islam or other religions. One highly visible expression is the growth, in colonies and former colonies following periods of proselytising by missionaries, especially over the past 20 years, of new indigenous churches and sects. Sometimes these regard themselves as the true church, from which the 'white man's church' has strayed.

Summary of this book's concerns

This book is generally concerned with the relation between religion and politics in the Third World, especially within the contexts of power, authority, legitimacy, democracy, economic growth and the international spread of ideas. There are four central issues involved. The first is that religion has always been 'political', and that change within doctrinal development is both normal and continuous, a function of culture and geography. In Chapter 1 we shall look at this from differing theoretical perspectives. It is only in Western or communist derived development paradigms that religion and politics have been (artificially) separated. Liberal political development analyses and 'radical' dependency ideas made religion epiphenomenal to their analyses. In the context of Third World countries where neo-Marxists gained political power, such as in several Indian states, we shall consider ways in which they tried to rationalize 'atavistic' religion with their radical secular ideologies.

Chapter 2 examines the growth and political impact of the global religions, i.e. Christianity and Islam. It considers their global spread in the wake of conquest and trade and their impact upon local people and their political institutions. It argues that, within the context of the global imperialism of the nineteenth and early twentieth centuries, Christianity especially became an integral part of the rulers' tools for legitimacy and authority. Once the decolonization process began in earnest in the Middle East after the First World War, religion and politics were drawn closer together as indigenous cultural identities began to predominate. A parallel, but chronologically later, process occurred in South America where the Roman Catholic church's monolithic dominance was challenged both by the spread of Protestantism from the north and by the impact of liberation theology, derived from a mixture of secular neo-Marxism and biblical religious radicalism.

Second, religious groups and motivations were seen as less evolved alternatives to politics for 'traditional' people who were waiting to be secularized as they became more 'modern'. As this book will demonstrate, religious ideas have a ready audience even among those deemed 'modern'. What conditions make for change in religion and combine to give religious ideas a ready audience at any given historical moment? Chapters 3 and 4 look at this issue from the perspective of, respectively, Islam and Christianity. The third chapter is concerned with the growth and ideas of Islamist groups and ideas. They began to become politically salient after the Second World War, although, as we shall see, modern groups were in some respects the descendants of earlier organizations which had fought Christianity or Western imperialism in a series of *jihads* (holy wars). We need to identify ways in which Islamic groups share characteristics as well as the ways in which they differ. Such an examination will help us to understand the political impacts of groups in different countries. Chapter 4 will examine Christian ideas and movements, in particular those associated with liberation theological ideas and those of the more conservative Protestant groups. We will see that in the contexts, shared by many Islamicist movements, of low legitimacy and low authority of often unelected governments, such groups form an alternative ideological referent to those championed by government, including nationalism, liberal democracy and socialism.

Third, religious groups utilize religious themes in their attacks against incumbent governments. Religious leaders have enlarged their constituencies as a direct result of the failure of governments to oversee general economic development. The former have assumed the mantle of legitimate authorities for many; this is not an atavistic move but reflects change in religion and culture *vis-à-vis* governments. Finally, the increasing political salience of religion is a direct result of urbanization, swiftly growing populations and the communications revolution of the past 20 years. Yet why do people participate in such groups; why not just revert to fatalism? The answer, it is argued, lies in an understanding of how change in the structure of popular life intersects and combines with religiously derived messages and organizational forms. In these respects, throughout the book the globalization of religion is stressed. The fifth chapter looks at the impact of religious ideas upon the goals of foreign policy. For example, Pakistan, Libya, Iran and the USA all had religious or quasi-religious goals of foreign policy, goals which were in addition to the usual foreign policy goals of national interest, economic prosperity, diplomatic advance and prestige enhancement. The book concludes with an assessment of the political salience of religion in Third World domestic and international politics and speculates as to its future importance.

Not everywhere nor on every occasion was there a link between religion and politics. Yet, as this book will make clear, the intertwining of concerns and interactions between the religious and the political – both domestically and internationally – should make the long-neglected areas of religion and culture of paramount interest to anyone concerned with the politics of the Third World in the 1990s.

Notes

1 Those areas of the world which were generally until the 1950s or later under the direct political control of Western powers, including Belgium, Britain, France, the Netherlands and Portugal. Other areas, such as Latin America and some states in the Middle East, gained independence earlier.
2 An Islamicist is a Muslim who believes in the superiority of Islamic culture, law and learning, without necessarily taking such beliefs to the political arena. An Islamist, on the other hand, is one who seeks to increase the Islamization of a Muslim society by political means. The ways chosen to achieve such a goal may be by either constitutional or non-constitutional means.
3 In places, however, the picture was not as clear-cut as this may suggest: In Latin America, as in much of Soviet Central Asia and in parts of Sub-Saharan Africa, colonists did not depart, but instead became absorbed into the political culture. Religion and religious institutions reflected this.

4 An outbreak of serious political opposition to an unelected Thai prime minister's
   rule in May 1992 was a clear demonstration that economic growth is not sufficient on its own to ensure rulers' legitimacy and stability, especially at a time of
   global agitation for democracy.
5 The attempt to set up an Islamic state in Sudan was despite the fact that a size-
   able minority of Sudanese are non-Muslims, i.e. Christians or animists. Much of
   the current political conflict in Sudan is due to the Islamists' desire to impose an
   Islamic state on non-Muslims.

Religion, politics and analysis of Third World development

Alexis de Tocqueville, commenting on religion in America in the first half of the nineteenth century, noted how central it was to the country's culture and politics: 'Eighteenth century philosophers had a very simple explanation for the general weakening of beliefs. Religious zeal, they said, was bound to die down as enlightenment and freedom spread. It is tiresome that the facts do not fit this theory at all' (de Tocqueville 1969: 295). The view which de Tocqueville associated with philosophers of an earlier age generally remains conventional wisdom: as societies industrialize, urbanize and are led by secular leaders, religion will increasingly appear as an anachronism, as a remnant from the past, doomed to privatization and even, ultimately, disappearance. Most analyses of Third World political developments took such premises for granted until very recently.

Such assumptions of religion's stasis and passivity hinder rather than aid our understanding, because they obscure *the sources and dynamics of change within religion and their effects on politics*. Examination of discrete political events alone makes it likely that one will misunderstand the nature of religio-political interaction. At issue is the continual structuring and re-structuring of the relationship between the two spheres. Of importance in this respect are the aims, aspirations and fears derived from and grounded within religious beliefs, which often reflect people's world views in the Third World better than the secular ideologies of nationalism, socialism and capitalism do. In this book, we are concerned with interactions of religion and politics in a number of contexts. The first is that of popular religious movements which challenge or lobby incumbent governments, almost invariably because of political or economic discontent. Examples include radical Islam in pre-revolutionary Iran, Algeria, Tunisia, Egypt, Nigeria and elsewhere; and radical Christian base communities in Latin America. The second involves the co-optation or manipulation of religion and its ideas for the purposes of bolstering state power. Examples include post-revolutionary Iran, Saudi Arabia, Sudan, Sandinista-led Nicaragua, Aristide-led Haiti and Israel (in the sense of 'greater Israel' and the connotations of state expansion for the peoples of the occupied territories and Lebanon). The third is that of the phenomenon of the explosive growth of conservative Christian doctrines, originally in the United States, and spreading to Latin America, South-East Asia (South Korea), the Pacific Rim (the Philippines) and Sub-Saharan Africa (e.g. Ghana and Nigeria). Shared world views and ideologies, rooted in religious beliefs, may help to strengthen pre-existing links between local conservative politicians and the military, on the one hand, and between such interests and US foreign policy makers, on the other. A final context is in the sphere of foreign policy. It is usually considered that all states (regardless of size, geographical position, proclaimed ideology and so on) seek broadly similar goals: national security, economic prosperity, diplomatic advancement and prestige enhancement (Waltz 1979). The issue which interests us is: how far do foreign policy aims reflect state religious orientations in, for example, Saudi Arabia, Iran, Libya, Pakistan or the USA? Do they complement or take precedence over traditional, secular objectives of foreign policy?

Before proceeding to an examination of the above-mentioned issues, we need to begin by looking at the two existing paradigms or 'grand theories' of analysis of Third World politics, the modernization/political development and the dependency/underdevelopment/neo-Marxist frameworks. Over the past 30 years or so both have uniformly and consistently neglected religion when analysing both state–society relations and international relations in the Third World. We can then create a more satisfactory analytical framework for comparing religio-political ideas and movements, before ending this chapter with an examination of the characteristics of movements known as 'religious fundamentalist', which are of great importance in any examination of the interactions of religion and politics in the Third World.

Paradigms of Third World politics and religion

The vast majority of the countries which now collectively constitute the Third World underwent at some time the experience of colonial rule. By the 1990s, however, virtually no such colonies remained. Most, including some with large populations and extant religious schisms (e.g. India, Indonesia and Nigeria), became independent after 1945. In South Asia there was a 'rush to independence' shortly after that date, while in Africa there was a similar movement towards independent statehood around the year 1960 (Goldthorpe 1984: 39). Others have been politically independent for much longer: Spanish and Portuguese colonies in Latin America achieved independence in the first quarter of the nineteenth century; the former in 1810, while Brazil effectively asserted its independence from Portugal in 1822. In some countries, however, political independence was attained by

European communities which continued to dominate populations of non-European descent. In this way a colonial situation was both internalized and until very recently 'frozen' in, for example, South Africa; at an earlier period the independence of Brazil and other South American countries may be seen in a somewhat similar light. To this day, there is a socio-political hierarchy in much of South America and the Caribbean – even in socialist Cuba – in which one's skin colour is often an accurate guide to one's status. This situation is a legacy of colonialism.

During the past two centuries it was overwhelmingly Western Europeans from Belgium, Britain, France, Germany, Italy, the Netherlands and Portugal who were the international colonizers; individuals and governments within the USA and Russia were busily subjugating indigenous people nearer to home in order to build centralized states. To many Europeans, the spreading of Christianity was an important element of the extending of 'Western civilization' to supposedly godless, benighted native populations. At earlier periods, however, and in differing parts of the globe, it was Islam and Buddhism which were expanding and internationalizing. To proselytise among non-believers, to convert them to the colonizers' religion by force or by the force of argument, was the aim of each.

Two of the most important monotheistic religions, Christianity and Islam, made substantial headway, in differing historical periods, in most areas of the globe; as we shall see, this process continues, albeit within the context of a largely decolonized international environment. Before we examine the impact of the legacy of the two religions we need to establish the ways in which religion and politics in the Third World are regarded by the two main 'schools' of explanation: the political development/modernization and the underdevelopment/dependency/neo-Marxist. From the 1950s each enjoyed prolonged periods of paradigmatic predominance and sought to explain, and to a degree predict, political behaviour in the newly independent states of the Third World.

The emergence of the Third World, the decline of war-weakened European powers and the contemporaneous rivalry between the nuclear weapons-endowed superpowers, the United States and the Soviet Union, emphasized the changed nature of the international system after 1945. Before the Second World War there had been a few European colonizers and a large number of colonized areas. The colonizers were not especially interested in the nature and characteristics of the areas that they ruled, despite the diversity of political and social systems, other than in terms of quiescence at their rule and maximization of economic gains. Following the emergence of the USA on to the international scene at the end of the nineteenth century, US social scientists were encouraged, often through direct government funding, to develop an interest in the Third World, increasingly the target of US influence and policy in the context of the Cold War. As Randall and Theobald (1985: 12–13) put it: 'There was perhaps initially less pressure on political science than on sociologists and economists because of the early prevailing assumption . . . of a relatively unproblematic chain of causation from cultural modernisation to economic development to democracy.' Thus, perceived shared characteristics such as poverty, technological backwardness and a preponderance of 'tradition' over 'modernity' conjoined to result in a general state of what would now be called 'underdevelopment' among (the now more than 130) Third World states; such assumed similarities were thought to be of far greater analytical salience than were any differences. It was deemed relatively unproblematic to trace the development of societies in an undifferentiated chain of cause and effect which had apparently reached its most developed state in the liberal democracies of Western Europe and the USA: the process was known as 'modernization'. 'They will become like us in time, we only have to describe the pace of what's happening,' may be a caricature but it was not that far from the prevailing assumptions of the 1950s and 1960s. As a result, it is appropriate to look at some of the major themes of the 'modernization' and 'dependency' approaches to Third World political and economic development in order to appreciate why religion and other cultural factors were ignored.

The process known variously as 'modernization' or 'Westernization' involves two main emphases. One is that developing states are interested in increasing their wealth by enlarging their own productive capacities. A second, related to the first, involves increasing differentiation and complexity in available roles in developing societies (Foster-Carter 1985: 103; Randall and Theobald 1985: 19). One of the most well-known accounts of the problems and probability of Third World development, written from a 'modernization' perspective and published in 1959, is *The Stages of Economic Growth: a Non-Communist Manifesto*, by the American economic historian Walt Rostow. Rostow helped to popularize the idea of a 'take-off' into self-sustaining economic growth as being the key stage of the development process. His theory of economic growth was based upon the concept of a five-stage process through which, he argued, all developing societies must pass, in order to attain the 'promised land' of a stable liberal democratic system along the lines of the United States or Britain. The first of these he described as the *traditional* stage. At this point it is very difficult to expand production beyond a limited ceiling, because of the existence of a pre-Newtonian science and technology, a basically agricultural economy, and a rigidly ascriptive social structure, usually based on kinship.

The second stage, *preconditions for take-off*, is triggered off by some kind of external impulse (although Rostow is vague about specifying precisely which), manifested in changes which begin across a whole range of institutions. These preconditions originally emerged in Western Europe 'when the insights of modern science began to be translated into both agricultural and industrial production' (Randall and Theobald 1985: 19–20). At this juncture the economy becomes less self-sufficient and localized, as trade and improved communications facilitate the growth of both national and international economies (Foster-Carter 1985: 104). These processes are socially and politically related to the emergence of an elite group, able and willing to reinvest their wealth rather than use it solely for immediate personal consumption. These developments proceed gradually until the threshold of the third stage, 'take-off', is attained. Two characteristics of this stage are crucial. First, investment as a proportion of national income rises to at least 10 per cent, thus ensuring both that increases in per capita output outstrip population growth and that industrial output increases appreciably. Second, as a result, political and social institutions are reshaped in order to permit the pursuit of growth to take root. The 'take-off' stage lasts, typically, about 20 years. Rostow attempted to date the take-off of those countries which had reached that developmental stage: Britain (1783–1803), the USA (1843–60), Japan (1878–1900), Russia (1900–14), and, more controversially, India and China (from 1950).

The last two stages of Rostow's putative scenario can be dealt with briefly: by definition any society that has reached such a position is no longer underdeveloped. Stage four is the *drive to maturity*, a period of consolidation. By this time, modern science and technology are extended to most if not all branches of the economy, which thus acquires a wide range of leading sectors. The rate of investment remains high, at between 10 and 20 per cent of national income. Political reform continues, and the economy is able to compete internationally. The conclusion of the five-stage development process is reached in the *age of mass consumption*, which involves further consolidation and advance. Such is the productive power of the society by this stage that three broad strategic choices of orientation are available. Wealth can be concentrated in individual consumption, as in the USA; or channelled into a welfare state as in Western Europe; or used to build up global power and influence, which is how Rostow characterizes the USSR (Foster-Carter 1985: 104).

An important feature of Rostow's development scenario is that, whereas for the agriculturally based societies of the Third World the initial stimulus to modernization arrives from outside through the example set by the industrialized countries, the basic problem for them of taking off is totally internal to the economies concerned (Randall and Theobald 1985: 21). Essentially it is to produce enough individuals with entrepreneurial abilities. This is in line with Weber's analysis that there was something unique about the development of Protestantism in North-West Europe which led to the evolution of capitalism.

Rostow's five-stage programme for development and its consolidation attracted criticisms. He failed to stress the diversity of Third World countries, a diversity which makes comparative analysis extremely problematic. His major conceptual weakness was in failing to emphasize *inter-* as well as *intra-*societal connections, i.e. relationships between as well as within societies, especially those between the industrially developed countries and the Third World. In addition, and germane to the theme of this volume, Rostow failed to make any mention of the role of religion in the development process, an oversight made understandable by the apparently declining political salience of religion generally at the time he was writing.

More generally, analyses located within the modernization paradigm share various assumptions related to the idea that manifestations of cultural identity, including religion, are merely remnants of tradition. These would necessarily decline in significance as cultural rationality and national integration developed. Thus, as long as political change was depicted as a process of transition to modernization, however erratic and problematical that process was, then religion seemed to be both a marginal and declining feature of politics: to modernize is to secularize. In other words, it is implicit in modernization analysis that 'traditional society' modernizes in such a way as to become more like the West (i.e. secular) and less like pre-existing Third World societies (i.e. religiously based). Yet as we shall see, rather than contemporary religio-political manifestation being merely a uniformly primordial response to the often bewildering pace and range of change in the late twentieth century, it encompasses a number of distinct meanings dependent on the religion, the society and the ruling regime affected.

The lack of concern with religion in modernization treatments of the politics of 'pre-take off' societies is underlined by John Kautsky, in *The Political Consequences of Modernization*, published in 1972. Kautsky claims that, although religion and politics *may* be linked in many Third World countries, as he is

> centrally concerned with [political] conflict, I shall not deal with communal conflicts based on religious, ethnic, or linguistic differences. . . . I ignore them . . . because they *originated before, and to some extent continue to exist apart from, the impact of modernization on politics* [my emphasis].
>
> (Kautsky 1972: 3)

Religion in Kautsky's view is to be seen in the context of the Third World's politico-economic development as primordial, as a bar towards swift 'modernization'. By definition that involved the secularization of politics between competing, undifferentiated groups such as 'bureaucracies', 'classes' or 'strata' (such as the aristocracy, peasants, the military), as in the developed countries.

The second paradigmatic alternative to the political development or modernization 'school' is known variably as 'dependency', 'neo-Marxist' or 'underdevelopment' analysis. An early and influential analysis of this kind, *Capitalism and Underdevelopment in Latin America*, was written by the then American-based German Andre Gunder Frank in 1971. His key term, 'the development of underdevelopment', was the radical counterpoint of Rostow's 'take-off'. Like Rostow and other 'modernization' writers, however, Frank ignored the interaction of religion and politics in his essentially class-based treatment of Latin America's history of failure to develop economically, politically or socially. This is an astounding omission when one bears in mind the role, historically, of Roman Catholicism in the region.

It is understandable when we note that Frank's analytical focus was the international capitalist system.

Both methodologically and politically, Frank's starting point is radically different from Rostow's. Frank perceives national economies as structural elements in a global capitalist system, rather than taking individual societies as the unit of analysis. This is because the whole global system, according to Frank, is unevenly structured in a whole chain of 'metropolis–satellite' relations. This chain links the entire system (Foster-Carter 1985: 107; Randall and Theobald 1985: 106–7). As a result, for Frank, the modernization scenario is to be wholly rejected because it does not correspond to historical or contemporary reality. It is impossible to find anywhere in the world today a society which exhibits the characteristics of Rostow's 'traditional' stage. The reason, Frank asserts, is that such 'traditional' societies have long since disintegrated because of their incorporation into the global capitalist economy. Such a view necessarily highlights the asymmetrically interdependent nature of the 'metropolis–satellite' relationship, a relationship which Rostow does not investigate.

Frank argues that the development of the industrialized countries from the fifteenth century was a direct result of their economic, and later political, dominance of today's underdeveloped countries, a huge majority of which were colonies. The process sucked them into a long-term structurally disadvantageous relationship which resulted in the development of some countries and the current underdevelopment of Latin America, and by extension other Third World regions. This is the foundation of Frank's argument: that the development of the industrialized states was only made possible (and continues to be) by the underdevelopment of the Third World.

Frank argues that satellites can only develop when their ties with the metropolis are weakened, citing, *inter alia*, Paraguay (in the 1930s) and Japan (before 1939) as examples (Foster-Carter 1985: 108). Self-sufficiency and inward-oriented development strategies are appropriate, indeed essential. Such a situation, whether coming about through economic recession or through war, reduces the chain of metropolis control. When the period of disequilibrium is passed, however, the metropolis reasserts control, in contemporary times through the penetration of multinational corporations. Frank asserts that the regions which are most underdeveloped today are those which had the closest links with the metropolis in the past. He cites the example of Brazil's impoverished north-east, which was formally a major sugar cane growing area. Its current poverty and accompanying backwardness are not in the least 'traditional', as formally the area was the most flourishing part of Brazil. Once the demand for sugar was filled elsewhere, however, the region lapsed into the poverty which it continues to exhibit.

Frank's model is externalist, bilinear and stagnationist; his approach is on the macroeconomic level of the global capitalist system, in complete contrast to those of the modernization paradigm. In the latter the international economic dimension was practically absent. To Frank and other analysts of the same persuasion such as Samir Amin or Walter Rodney, decisive politico-economic change comes from outside the Third World. Metropolis and satellite pursue different structural roles. The Third World's role is unchanging as supplier of (underpriced) raw materials to the metropolis. The route out of this lies in disengagement from the global capitalist system via self-sufficiency, socialism and increased trade with progressive states. Because the dependency school's focus is unswervingly upon the 'international capitalist system', the domestic political dimension is severely downgraded.

In summary, both 'schools' of analysis, despite their contending and contrasting analyses and conclusions, serve to marginalize the effect of religion and other cultural factors on politics (and vice versa). The question is, why were such factors omitted from attempts to analyse and understand? The answer lies in the way that political development scholars were preoccupied with issues such as institutional transformation and the impact of 'agents of modernization' on indigenous Third World communities. They highlighted the marginalization of 'tradition' by modern state structures which would transform political, social and economic realities. Neo-Marxist and other 'radical' analysts, on the other hand, emphasized the baneful effects of imperialism and class divisions while downplaying or ignoring cultural factors, such as religion and ethnicity. Scholars of both persuasions saw religion as anachronistic and dysfunctional to the modernization process.

Political analysis goes through periods of paradigmatic hegemony, only to be overturned by the inauguration and acceptance of a successor. The dominance of political development or modernization theory in the 1950s and for much of the 1960s was followed by a period of paradigmatic domination of underdevelopment or dependency theory in the late 1960s and 1970s. In the 1980s, such paradigmatic domination – purporting to explain Third World politics in their entirety despite clear signs that such treatments were unproductive – came to an end: general, 'grand theory' political analysis of the Third World was replaced by a plethora of case studies and newly tentative comparisons. Yet there was still little or no apparent awareness of religion's *centrality* as a manifestation of political identity in much of the Third World (Brown 1989: 1).

In the 1980s, a number of books, monographs and articles appeared concerned with religion–politics interactions in many parts of the world, including the Third World. They were generally of the case study type, and did not try to identify and analyse characteristics and developments which transcended state, regional and other political boundaries. Yet, for the first time, there appeared to be some convergence of interests between those concerned with cultural effects – including religion – and the development of the state; these were the areas deemed to be most deserving of future study. This underlined a fundamental truth, too frequently overlooked since the early days of analysis of politico-economic development in the Third World: mono-causal, deterministic and unilinear explanations of development do not significantly advance our understanding of the politics of development in the Third World. As Brown (1989: 4) notes: 'The nature of development is seen to be too complex for that.'

Nevertheless, in the early 1990s it continued to be very difficult to locate a major general work on the politics of Third World development or theoretical treatments of developing states' political change that devotes a chapter to religious factors. Religion was regarded as merely one of a number of minor impediments to effective state integration, uniformly conservative and often a drawback to the development of modern societies and centralized states. Yet the geographic spread of Buddhism, Christianity and Islam was via political domination and, less importantly, trade. Societies that they infiltrated were over time transformed socially, culturally, politically and economically. This is not to suggest that the impacts were uniform, but rather to note that *virtually all Third World Societies were transformed by the impact of hegemonic, externally imposed religions.* In other words, religion and politics were inextricably linked, radical if not revolutionary in impact, spread by the sword and by trade. The most recent wave of external political domination – that of Western European powers in the nineteenth and early twentieth centuries – had the effect of converting millions of people to Christianity. Those that were already followers of socially and culturally hegemonic religions (Islam and Buddhism) were not generally converted to the new religion, even though Muslims' hegemonic political status was often ended. New recruits generally came from traditional religions; acceptance of Christianity was the first step towards 'civilization'.

In the post-independence period, i.e. after 1945, the Christian-capitalist separation of state and church was deemed to be of fundamental importance in the development of modern centralized states. Third World rulers concentrated primarily on remaining in power and officially, but certainly secondarily, on building socially cohesive, economically successful polities. Religious, communal and regional issues were obviously unwelcome, regarded as 'divisive' and inappropriate during the phase of state-building. National leaders hoped that as citizens became 'modernized' they would drop their 'primordial' allegiances, become 'developed' and follow secular ideologies of nationalism, state or 'African' socialism and, thus, aid state consolidation and centralization. This holds true even if the rulers were neo-Marxists: in the Indian states of West Bengal and Kerala communist parties ruled not through emphasizing class struggle but via the creation of multi-class, rural–urban coalitions (Das Gupta 1990: 240).

At the end of the 1970s, the Iranian revolution, the civil war in Afghanistan and the triumph of the Sandinistas in Nicaragua independently underlined in different ways the salience of religion to politics in the Third World. Whereas the Leninist national front organizational model traditionally enjoyed pre-eminence as a supposed explanatory variable for successful revolution, the Shia militancy demonstrated so effectively in Iran arguably provided a more appropriate basic model for other Muslim contexts

– including Sunni ones – which were by no means beholden to the dictates of the Shia holy men (Foltz 1990: 61). The successful Marxist-led coup in Afghanistan in 1978 led to a civil war, with Shiite Islamic radicals – aided by Iran's theocratic government – in the forefront of the opposition to the revolutionary regime. Events in Algeria in 1992, such as attacks on security forces by Islamists, bear witness to the radicalization of Algerian volunteers who fought on the side of the Afghan mojahiden. The position of the Sandinista government in Nicaragua was progressively weakened by the opposition of the conservative Catholic Church establishment and of the Pope. At the same time, however, a number of socially progressive Catholic priests helped to bolster support for the regime at the grass roots. Despite their apparent dissimilarities, these and other events reflected religion's crucial role in the 'political expression of unresolved issues, ill concealed by the fabric of normal politics and not articulated by political institutions' (Mitra 1991: 55). It may be added that they were not explicable through the foci of modernization or underdevelopment analyses.

Religion, secularity and ideology

The remarks at the end of the last section raise three important questions. First, how geographically widespread is the juxtaposition or interaction of religion in politics in the Third World? Second, just *what* distinguishes religio-political movements from other ideologically motivated groups? Third, *how* do religious and secular concerns in a political context differ? The first question is obviously difficult to answer with any degree of precision. Given the winner-takes-all nature of most Third World countries' competitive politics (when they have any, that is), it is only the victors who attract much international attention. Since the 1970s, throughout the Muslim world (i.e. the swathe of more than 30 states from Morocco in the west to Indonesia in the east), Islam has generally become the ideology of ruling elites, of the chief opposition parties, or of both. With the exception of the atypical case of the Vatican City, there currently exist no Christian (or for that matter Buddhist or Hindu) governments in the world. There are no Christian governments because from the seventeenth century (symbolized by the Treaty of Westphalia of 1648, which greatly diminished the Pope's political powers and formalized secular rulers') church and state were separated in Christianity's heartland, Western Europe, the birthplace of the nation state. As a result, unlike in the Islamic world, there is no model for opposition movements or rulers to aspire to, no Christianized polity to seek to emulate.

In Christian countries, then, there is a tradition of separation of church and state which precludes the formation of theocratic polities. Yet, as we shall see in Chapter 4, there are a number of political manifestations and movements which take as their ideological referent aspects of Christian belief. Thus while there may be no Christian political parties in an ideological sense in the Third World, various forms of organization, especially at local level, are underpinned by sometimes conflicting religious dynamisms which are uniformly rooted in differing aspects of Christian beliefs. Other world religions, such as Buddhism, Judaism and Hinduism, are politically important in a number of countries, including India, Israel, Burma (since 1989, Myanma), Tibet (which was a theocracy until the early 1950s), Sri Lanka and Thailand.

The argument is that throughout much of the Third World – as in the former communist states of Eastern Europe and in the West – there has been a *de facto* resurgence of religion since the late 1960s or early 1970s, often with an accompanying effect on both domestic and international politics. In both the West and Eastern Europe religion has gained increased social (and in places, such as Poland in the early 1980s, political) salience because of the failure of industrialization and the tarnished icons of Marx and Mammon to bring full happiness and satisfaction to millions of people. In the Third World, religion has gained significance politically partly as a result of the failure of secular development programmes to lead to sustained improvements in most people's well-being and partly as a result of the lack of legitimacy and accountability of secular rulers. It is, however, difficult to quantify the resurgence of religion as a factor in politics. Nevertheless, the growing number of books, monographs, articles and academic conference papers that try to explain religio-political resurgence, the increasing numbers of newspaper stories alluding to such a growth, the rout of communism as an ideology of the poor and dispossessed, and the frequent melding of nationalism and religion in a powerful ideological cocktail, all point to a rise in importance of religio-political movements and ideas throughout the Third World (Mews 1989a; Sahliyeh 1990; Moyser 1991).

To help justify such a conclusion we need to be clear as to what religion *is*, and how it differs from ideology in general. In particular, what are the dividing lines between the 'religious' and the 'secular'? What are the characteristics of a religio-political movement? How does it differ from a secular political movement?

The term 'religion' is used in this book as a multi-faceted concept with three distinct, yet interrelated, meanings. First, the term includes religious establishments (including priests and officials) and groups sponsored by religious organizations (such as the Islamic Salvation Front (FIS) in Algeria or Ahmed Niasse's Party of God (*hizboullahi*) in Senegal). Second, spiritually, the term pertains to models of social and individual behaviour that help to organize everyday life: it is to do with the idea of *transcendence*, i.e. it is associated with supernatural realities; with *sacredness*, i.e. as a system of language and practice that organizes the world in terms of what is deemed sacred; and, finally, it is to do with *ultimacy*, i.e. religion relates people to the ultimate conditions of their existence (Moyser 1991: 9–10). Thus religion encompasses religious establishments, groups sponsored by religious organizations, spiritual belief patterns and models of behaviour that help to organize everyday life. Religious concerns often overlap with other cultural issues, which together reinforce ethnic consciousness. Yet it does not do so in all cases, as examinations of the interaction between religion and politics in, for example, Central America, Nigeria and Afghanistan indicate.

We should not see contemporary religious concerns in the Third World as a result of colonialism, but rather as a development of pre-existing belief patterns which were moulded but not destroyed by the European influx. In pre-colonial societies generally,

> The traditional, or pre-modern, relationship between religion and politics was one in which the two were closely integrated, one with the other. Religious beliefs and practices underpinned and entered into the heart of the political process, supporting and sustaining the exercise of power. But, by this very token, political concerns also extended throughout the religious sphere. The two formed, in effect, one co-terminous set of beliefs and actions. It was a system in which social and political life was touched at virtually all points by religious considerations.
>
> (Moyser 1991: 12)

Thus in pre-modern societies religion was closely affiliated to, if not inseparable from, politics. In other words, it validated politics. Rulers were not only political heads: they were also religious leaders, a symbol of 'their' people's health and welfare (Mbiti 1969: 182). The coming of the Europeans and the creation of colonies usually meant, on the one hand, the at least partial reduction of such rulers' political and spiritual power, while, on the other hand, it led to a partial secularization and separation of politics from religious matters. This was not always unequivocally the case (e.g. the Muslim sultans of Sokoto in northern Nigeria retained both religious and political significance), but in areas not dominated by Islam the introduction of European-created political systems was juxtaposed with (or preceded by) an influx of Christian missionaries. In the process, Christianity became inseparable from secular political power in the minds of the colonized. Yet the point to make here is not that the European Christian colonizers changed Third World areas so radically, but rather the opposite: the colonial period was a hiatus; the 'traditional' may have been changed, but it was not transformed. Thus, after the brief period of colonial rule (only about 50 years in some cases) the post-colonial state was grafted on to an essentially pre-colonial socio-political order in which popular representation was much more reflected in the positions and status of local leaders than it was in the figures of official representatives of the people in parliament in the capital city.

What this amounts to is that there are not separate secular and religious compartments in most Third World people's world views. Moreover, secular ideologies rarely (if ever) have the same significance, meaning and impact in the Third World as in the West. In the West Marxism, socialism, liberalism, conservatism and so on have broadly agreed meanings and implications for political action. Secular ideologies were transplanted – rather than developing *in situ*, as it were – into the Third World by putative ideologues who almost without exception underwent some form of secularized (i.e. Western) education, usually to first degree level or beyond, and usually overseas. The crucial point is that transplanted secular ideologies *did not take firm root* in the societies of the Third World.

In the Muslim world the international effects of the Iranian revolution included the dissemination of an Islamist ideology which partially transcended the Shiite–Sunni division. It did this by injecting a form of politicization which took as its *leitmotiv* the rallying cry of anti-imperialism, non-alignment and 'Third World first'. Thus it was possible to see elements of secular ideology melding with religious beliefs and concerns to produce radical Islamist religio-political movements. For example, the anti-imperialist, 'leftist', Iranian theocratic government confronted the pro-West, 'rightist', monarchical regime in Saudi Arabia over ideological issues. Such a process was not confined to the Muslim world: in Christian Nicaragua, the anti-imperialist, 'leftist', Sandinista regime was challenged by the pro-West, 'rightist', Contras, aided and abetted by the 'Christian' government of the United States of America. In a sense, important concerns of Iranian revolutionary dogma were also those of Christian liberation theology. The ideas and ideals of revolutionary Islam, on the one hand, and of liberation theology, on the other, helped to provide a set of beliefs which people could relate to, grounded as they were in pre-existing belief patterns. This is not to argue that Shiite radicalism and Christian liberation theology have anything much in common other than a stated ideal of a better future for the underdog. By the same token, followers of pentecostal religions, whether in the USA, Central America, Nigeria of Fiji, share certain beliefs of a conservative kind (especially anti-communism and anti-secularism), which mean that such movements have considerable impact in the political realm.

Generally, the characteristics of a religio-political movement would include:

- the seeking of a transformation of the prevailing socio-political situation;
- the search for power – either within government or by the attainment of more informal positions of influence – by leaders of the movement;
- the formulation and attempted introduction of a political programme which seeks to put into practice salient facets of the religious ideology that underpins the movement's *raison d'être*;
- the employment of religious myths and symbols by the religio-political movement to influence the process by which public resources are allocated, and, perhaps, to seek control of that process;
- the espousal of both religious goals and secular, sometimes class-based, demands.

Religio-political movements differ from secular political organizations in one important way. Secular political movements may seek the same goals as religio-political movements but do so without the benefit of allusion to religious beliefs, which are very important to many people. It is no co-incidence that religio-political movements in much of the Third World have gained converts while support for secular political organizations (other than nationalist ones) has generally declined. In other words, secularized political groups, by denying what is to many people of supreme import-ance, have come to be regarded by many as of only limited relevance to their own lives. This is especially the case with movements (e.g. pan-Arabism and pan-Africanism) that seek to mobilize people across inter-national boundaries without concern for local issues.

The concept of secularity pertains in its widest sense to the idea of things not spiritual, not concerned with religion. The notion of secularization may be understood to be either anti-religion or neutral towards it (Martin 1969: 9). Contrary to the earlier conventional wisdom of political analysis, it would be incorrect to see the secularization of a society as an inevit-able end-result of modernization, given the way that some modernized, increasingly industrialized societies (e.g. Iran, Saudi Arabia, Brazil) are also highly religious. This is to argue that in Iran, Saudi Arabia, Pakistan and elsewhere a process of ideological secularization has been reversed: the basic values and belief systems used to evaluate the political realm and to give it meaning have become couched in religious terms (Moyser 1991: 14–15).

Hadden and Shupe (1986) argue for the analytical salience of a cyclical theory of secularization which sees the re-emergence of religious ideologies periodically. This-wordly, non-religious answers to the basic questions of life leave a void; they become to many both alienating and unsatisfying. Periodically, then, religious ideas are received by those who are alienated and dispossessed (especially the young), and may become mobilizing ideo-logies. The argument here is that as Third World societies have become increasingly urbanized, buffeted by forces beyond their control (such as values created and perpetuated by Western multinational corporations), many people have (re)turned to religion for an answer to questions which cannot be satisfactorily answered in any other way.

This points to a number of dimensions which need to be focused upon simultaneously in order to understand fully the interaction of religion and politics in the Third World. Given the numbers of states concerned and the historical, cultural, social, geographic and political variations between them there is in fact little to be gained in making the term 'Third World' serve as an analytical concept. It is used in the current context to divide – albeit crudely – the developed, industrialized countries from the rest. We are not concerned with the newly politically pluralistic states of the formerly communist Eastern Europe for reasons of space, and thus do not have to tackle the thorny issue of whether or not they are to be included in the Third World. Indeed, a search for parsimonious models to explain *all* political and religious interactions within such complexity is almost certainly doomed to failure. At the same time, however, there are certain similarities which make comparative analysis and attempts at conceptualization fruitful.

According to Mitra (1987: 3),

> The political discourse of a third world society may be characterized
> by the predominance of the *primordial* factors such as caste, tribe,
> language and ethnicity, without the benefit of a set of general, legit-
> imate rules for the mediation of conflict [emphasis added].

It is correct to argue that Third World societies have rarely – if ever –
evolved generally acceptable rules for the mediation of societal conflict.
This is hardly surprising given the diversity which Mitra alludes to, coupled
with their relatively recent formation. In Britain, for example, it took 300
years to introduce full democracy. Even today all schismatic tendencies
(e.g. Scottish and Welsh nationalism) are not eradicated. In the light of
growing racial, ethnic, linguistic and religious tensions in Western and
Central Europe it is surely incorrect to refer to the 'primordial' nature of
cultural factors. Moreover, to describe culture as 'primordial' is to imply
that such factors have not changed since their inception, despite the colonization, independence, statehood, economic disappointment and so on that
Third World societies have experienced. It is a contention of this book that
cultural factors – including religion – are not in the least primordial but
rather dynamic stimuli and reflectors of political and social change. To understand fully religion's role in political discourse we need to focus upon and
be aware of the 'theatrical' and 'imaginary' dimensions of politics. As Manor
(1991b: 11) puts it, 'The theatrical dimension is the result of initiatives
undertaken by political actors – in or out of power – while the imaginary
dimension mainly refers to the construction which is put on politics in the
popular mind.'

In one sense, it is an oversimplification to assert, as Manor does, that
there is a uniformity of political views held by those who are not political
actors at the state level. Regional, ethnic, gender, religious, economic and
environmental differences between people certainly lead them to regard politics in differing ways. At the same time, however, we can agree that the
rulers and the ruled see things differently, they have different priorities.
Cultural differences in each of the Third World's 130 or more states mean
that the precise nature of the theatrical and imaginary is different in each
state setting, yet the arena and concerns of politics do not differ much.
Political discourse, in the usual settings of economic scarcity and dominance by a small – usually unelected and unrepresentative – elite, is about the
same things. Whereas rulers wish to rule as effectively, cheaply and free of
challenges as possible, individuals organized in opposition groupings are
concerned with the creation (or re-creation) of a civil society which, reflecting cultural conflicts and ideological differences with their leaders, sets
out to transform reality. Religion, far from being 'a static system of symbols, shared by members of a group or society' (van der Veer 1987: 284),
is usually a vehicle for these intensely *political* challenges, which reflect the
differences between the theatrical and the imaginary. In short, the political
dimension is both wider and richer in the Third World than in the West.

Modes of analysis must be more flexible than the familiar paradigms have been to take account of this.

It is, moreover, very difficult to apply Western interpretations of the concepts of legitimacy and consensus in Third World settings. This is because there are competing and often cross-cutting sectional or communal loyalties (religious, ethnic, cultural). These interact with 'highly complicated ideological values, operating structures, modes of operations and relationships' (Samudavanija 1991: 19) which are apparent in the relationship between ruling elites and society in general, as well as between urban and rural people more particularly. Ruling elites invariably pursue three, frequently contradictory, goals at the same time, within the context of state building: their own security and position of rule, popular participation (often in order to gain bilateral foreign financial aid) and economic development (to bolster their domestic and international positions). Leaders of European polities during their formative periods of state building had it much easier by comparison. Demands on Third World rulers have increased three-fold when compared to those on the rulers of the early absolutist period in Europe, who at a comparative stage of political development did not have to take into account either participation or development concerns (Samudavanija 1991).

This leads to a second, related idea: that in 'Third World societies, cultures and polities, incongruous or contradictory elements tend to coexist uneasily in disequilibrium, in curious hybrids' (Manor 1991: 5). This is the case when we consider the role of religion in Third World politics. Politicians and religious organizations may demonstrate incongruities in a number of ways: in thought, behaviour and actions. Educated, urban, apparently modernized people may lobby and struggle for the creation of religiously 'correct' societies and social values which – legally, socially, politically and even economically – owe their organizing precepts to the ideas of Arabia of 1300 years ago or to those ideals and commands found in the Bible. Support may be garnered from the urban alienated or the rural dispossessed: very different class positions may coalesce within the confines of a religio-political movement. Ideas, actors and goals change from time to time, but they seldom, if ever, dichotomize in the way that scholars working in either modernization or dependency traditions appear to expect. In other words, societies and polities seldom if ever undergo thoroughgoing transformations.

Religious 'fundamentalism' in the Third World

Of the most obvious political salience is the development of the disparate phenomena, commonly but erroneously grouped together and labelled 'religious fundamentalism'. The way that 'religious fundamentalisms' are regarded is a further example of the desire of Western scholars to lump things together unwarrantedly for analytic convenience. 'Fundamentalism' is in fact an Anglo-Saxon term, especially applied to those, such as Protestants or Muslims, who hold that the Bible, the Quran or other holy books must be accepted and interpreted literally (Montgomery Watt 1990: 2). The nearest French equivalent is *integrisme*, which refers to a similar tendency within Roman Catholicism. Thus 'fundamentalist' regimes and aspiring political movements are nearly always Muslim or Protestant.

Christian (i.e. Protestant) fundamentalism grew up in the USA at the beginning of the twentieth century. Modern Islamic resurgence dates from just before the Second World War, although there are parallel examples of anti-imperialist, anti-Western movements (*jihads*) throughout the Muslim world of a hundred years ago. Generally, however, the arrival and consolidation of contemporary religious militancy is rooted in the failed promise of modernity. Our era is one where God was in danger of being superseded by a gospel of technical progress and economic growth, a process identified earlier as 'modernization'. Yet all this is very confusing: the pace of change in this century (and especially over the past 50 years) has been very swift, with traditional habits, beliefs and cultures under constant pressure to adapt. In an increasingly materialist world one's individual worth is increasingly measured according to standards of wealth and status, and hence power.

David Martin argues that fundamentalism is a misleading term as it over-laps conservative versions of various religions. In the case of Protestant fundamentalism of the kind found especially in the United States, it

> is tied historically, and by definition, to certain dogmatic fundamen-
> tals of Christianity and to the inerrancy of Scripture. Typically it
> embraces a package of dogma, scriptural inerrancy, and moral con-
> servatism, which may or may not be tied up with active political
> conservatism. Often the political conservatism is just a passive potential
> lying inside a cultural conservatism, which becomes active . . . when
> liberals of every stripe begin to exercise a mixture of political and
> cultural domination.
>
> (Martin 1990a: 129)

The result of cultural and economic confusion was to provide fertile ground for the growth of religious militancy and conservatism (which *may* be the same thing). It was also conducive to the creation of political movements which may or may not be hegemonic in Gramsci's meaning of the term. To the Christian Protestant conservative in the Unite States, Honduras or Guatemala the appropriate world view might involve quasi-memories of a time when all was right with the world, when communism and other leftist ideologies were rejected and social instability was relatively absent. Socially – and basking in the rosy glow of nostalgia – it was characterized by the intimate gathering around the family hearth, when a clear sense of what is right and would be rewarded, and what is wrong and would be punished, was present. Underpinning this was a mystical belief in some-thing bigger than ourselves. Significantly, however, owing to different perceptions of the roles of the state, of religion and of civil society in the

Christian world there not have been political movements aiming for the creation of a theocracy, but a complex interaction between state, the established church and 'grass roots' political movements. We shall examine these conceptual issues in Chapter 4.

A second form of conservative Protestantism, especially popular in many Third World regions, may be contrasted with the species of North American fundamentalism referred to above, where adherence to the fundamentals and a pronounced moral conservatism are the most important characteristics. Pentecostalism is the most active and expansive version of Christianity *and* the most theologically conservative, being based on a non-critical, non-questioning perception of the Bible. This form of Protestantism is marked by such characteristics as exorcism, glossolalia (i.e. speaking in 'tongues'), healing by touch and various other alleged manifestations of spiritual powers given by God to suitable individuals. This particular movement, when found in Latin America, the Pacific Rim and Africa, is generally a form of syncretism. This is a blending and fusing of pre- or non-Christian beliefs with a Christian interpretation of a varied series of abnormal phenomena, for the most part caused by spiritual beings acting upon especially sensitive persons or mediums, rather than conservative fundamentalist Protestantism *per se* (Martin 1990a: 131). On occasions, however, as in Central America, there is a shared focus of interest in political conservatism: US conservative Protestant missionaries frequently share a goal, that of the ensconcement of conservative political regimes, with local pentecostalists and frequently the US State Department and the Central Intelligence Agency as well.

Although we may usefully identify a species or two of Christian fundamentalism (with a discernible impact upon politics), the process is less easy within the realms of Islam. To the radical and militant Islamic groups the reformist vision centres on a programme of rigorous moral reform enforced in unbelievers by a government of the 'chosen', laying down rules and laws as to how life should be lived. Yet within Islam there are doctrinal schisms that colour the vision. Sunnite radicals and militants may accept the Quran literally, though in some cases with qualifications, but they also have other distinctive features which colour the way they regard and carry out politics. Due to developments in the past, Shiites do not accept the status quo in the same way that most Sunnis do. Yet, as we shall see, this division between the two main strands of Islam is itself being undermined by a political radicalism which transcends such demarcations and involves secular concerns to do with class and power.

It is of course difficult to enforce a static code, especially if it derives from another historical era. This is a major, perhaps even insurmountable, problem. The late Ayatollah Khomeini's *Explication by Problems* contains more than 3000 rulings on the conduct of daily life, including everything from laws of inheritance to matters of personal cleanliness and how to slaughter animals correctly. But the growing manifestations of discontent in Iran in the early 1990s – centring on economic failure, political authoritarianism and a failure of the state to deliver the development 'goods' – highlighted the fragility of the hegemony of politico-religious dogma if it was not accompanied by sustained improvements in societal well-being.

The term 'religious fundamentalism' is in fact little more than a label of convenience used to describe and explain religious-based developments, often of quite different qualitative forms. According to Goldthorpe (1984: 9, 226):

> The establishment of new values may encounter severe resistance from groups adhering to older values which are no longer appropriate, a resistance which may be called 'fundamentalism'. . . . There is a reaction against the materialism that seems inherent in economic development and the secularism that pervades modernisation. In recent times that reaction . . . has taken the form of religious fundamentalism and the re-assertion of a traditional faith not as one denomination among others but as the dominant form of religion in a whole society.

Goldthorpe sees 'new values' as taking over, completely displacing old concerns. To him, modernization, strongly implying secularization, is fought against by reactionaries, anxious to deny the possibility or even desirability of progress. They utilize 'traditional' faith as their vehicle. Thus Goldthorpe sees fundamentalism as inherently reactionary. Richard Swift (1990) shows more confusion in his attempts to explain and describe religious fundamentalism. He argues that

> The fundamentalist is by and large a reactionary but not a conservative in any traditional meaning of the word. A conservative wants to conserve what is: be it the existing system of privileges, a set of political boundaries or a local neighbourhood or forest. While fundamentalists venerate the authority and wisdom of the past, it is a past already lost under the assaults of the modern world. Their program is to regain this lost past. The present state of affairs must be entirely overturned to achieve their aims. They use the vocabulary of revolution but hark back to a mythical golden age that must be recovered in order to set things right.
>
> (Swift 1990: 4)

Swift argues that religious fundamentalists aim to reassert old truths and former certainties: a reversion to the past is justified by contemporary concerns. There are several problems with this formulation. The first is that the types of movements often dubbed 'fundamentalist' arc not exclusively modern phenomena. Movements of religious revival (which usually connote both political and spiritual defiance) have erupted throughout history. Yet the radical populist or revolutionary ideas and movements that Swift alludes to do share something in common, something which more often than not transcends doctrinal differences between religions. In the erosion of the modern secular verisimilitudes and ideologies, religion may be used by both the incumbent state and aspiring national leaders to focus and lead supporters. For this reason it is inadequate to claim that 'fundamentalist' religious movements are simply reactionary, implying that adherents wish to *revert to past social and cultural conditions*. It is literally impossible to 'return' to seventh-century Arabian realities or for that matter the conditions of 2000 years ago in Palestine, as one may infer from Swift that Islamic or Christian 'fundamentalists' wish to do. There is a third factor. Most of the 'fundamentalist' religious groups seek social and political change in order to improve the lot of adherents: they wish to tie the undesirability of Western-derived political and social changes (such as democracy and sexual equality) to the words of their holy books. This is as true for Islamic (male) radicals in Pakistan, who often wish to deny the legitimate struggle of women for political, economic and social equality with men, as it is for Christian fundamentalists in El Salvador, Honduras or for that matter the United States. They wish to keep their own gender privileges during a period of rapid social change, instability or upheaval. The former Prime Minister of Pakistan, Benazir Bhutto, was a political victim of the extremely reactionary nature of male-dominated Pakistani society, which uses the Quran to strengthen and justify women's domination by men. Something of the same was apparent in the electoral triumphs of the FIS in Algeria in the late 1980s and early 1990s. This is not to argue that there are no female religious zealots, but rather to assert that the ideas held by most males in this context are partly derived from their fears of losing social predominance.

Religion and the globalization of ideas

A political Islamic resurgence is, of course, a prominent feature of the contemporary international scene, especially in the Middle East, Southern Asia and North Africa. To some it is synonymous with, even axiomatic of, the notion of terrorism (Capitanchik 1986: 116). Headline-catching issues in the late 1980s and early 1990s, such as the Rushdie affair, the Lockerbie bombing, and the kidnapping and incarceration of Western hostages in Lebanon, focused attention on Islamist groups and goals. Yet terrorism is not simply mindless violence but rather, when all else has failed, an instrument utilized in the struggle for political power. It may be employed by those on the ideological extremes of the political spectrum, by national minorities or by religious groups (Laquer 1984).

Obviously, extreme (or extremist) tactics to accomplish political objectives are not by any means the province solely of Muslims, but may be resorted to by a number of ethnic and religious groups. Fifty years ago, for example, the recent Prime Minister of Israel, Yitzhak Shamir, was a known terrorist, wanted by the British authorities for serious crimes perpetrated for a religio-political goal: the establishment of the state of Israel as a homeland for the Jews, who had been persecuted both in Nazi Germany and for hundreds of years in parts of Europe. More recently, Basque extremists sought political self-determination in a no-holds-barred struggle with the Spanish state; the 'troubles' (often a euphemism for terrorist acts) in Northern Ireland are rooted in a sectarian divide between Catholics and Protestants; Croats and Serbs as well as Serbs and Muslims perpetrate cruelties against each other in the name of nationalist autonomy, as do Muslim Azeris and Christian Armenians.

What unites these otherwise disparate groups is a desire to achieve state power. This may be in the context of an ethnic–religious group's desire for self-government (e.g. Croats, Slovenes, Kurds, Serbs, Macedonians), or in a religious challenge to the status quo which transcends ethnicity (e.g. Sikhs and Hindus in India or Muslims in Nigeria and Burma). Generally, religion, ethnicity and other cultural attributes are interlinked in forms which Doornbos (1991: 64) dichotomizes as either 'liberating' (i.e. seeking self-expression within a restrictive environment) or 'chauvinistic' (i.e. aiming for hegemony over all other groups). While one is aware of what Doornbos is getting at here, the division is not analytically or conceptually very useful. It rests on a highly subjective, idealized dichotomy involving progressive or reactionary manifestations of group interest, reminiscent of the perennial 'terrorist or freedom fighter' debate.

Mitra (1991: 757) argues that 'the role of religion in politics is influenced by the specific kind of state and society relation that obtains in a given historical conjuncture. . . . [The latter] may be conducive towards the growth of a particular form of religious movement.' In one sense this is correct: the nature of government rule may result in the emergence of religiously oriented political movements. In another it is unnecessarily reductionist: it implies that only one manifestation of religio-politics will result at any single juncture. The reality is more complex than this and reflects the differing ideological positions obtaining in any given society at any given point.

Religion is merely one of a set of interacting beliefs to which people adhere. As with ethnicity, religion is a complex set of beliefs and motivations which draws upon both 'tradition' and 'modernity'. Where a form of Christianity is the hegemonic religion, as in South America and parts of Sub-Saharan Africa, Asia and the Pacific Rim, individuals and groups often express political preferences in a religious framework. In this context, such ideas may be deeply conservative, tied to the objectives of dominant social groups. The same development is observable in Muslim societies, where state preferences for modernization, rationality and sometimes secularization are contextualized by the overriding aim: regime continuity. In both cases, the theatrical dimension (i.e. the result of initiatives undertaken by political actors) juxtaposes itself (and in analysis should be linked) with the construction put on politics in people's minds (i.e. the imaginary dimension). Yet popular objectives are not necessarily the same as elite aspirations. The latter seek rule continuity; the former seek economic development, the upholding of religion and its values, perhaps political participation and, above all, to be left alone by government.

This situation is not new. What is novel is a growing scholarly awareness that the secularized ideologies of the political centre (e.g. communism, socialism and in some contexts centralized state-nationalism) are not by and large the mobilizing precepts of ordinary Third World people. Religion, ethnicity, caste and clientelism are of much more relevance to many people. Increasingly, belief in redemption or salvation through God, increasingly expressed as a *political* choice, is apparent. In the present context three politico-religious strands may be highlighted.

First, syncretic religions may be an important element in mobilizing previously politically powerless people to organize resistance against those seeking to attack their communities. Examples may be found in a number of geographic locations, although Christianity is usually a common referent. For example, the Maoist revolutionaries of Sendero Luminoso (Shining Path) in Peru use mysticism and allusions to pre-Christian gods to gain recruits for their aim of a violent overthrow of the constitutional government in order to build a Maoist polity (Dietz 1990: 122). In Mozambique, the inability of the state to deal with a long-running military and political challenge to its position left hundreds of thousands of people dead and millions of displaced persons. Local people formed the *naparamas*, a 20,000 strong independent peasant militia galvanized by a mixture of Catholicism and traditional religious beliefs, to fight South African-backed Renamo terrorists with spears and other simple weapons, believing themselves to be protected by magic. From 1989, Renamo was driven from large areas of the north of Mozambique by the *naparamas*, allowing refugees to return to their homes and farms (Brittain 1991). A final example involves a 'volatile mix of cargo cult worship and Catholic missionary zeal [which] infuses the strange secession of Bougainville, a Pacific island [geographically close to New Guinea] that has returned to the past' (Fathers 1991). In each of these examples central government's political failures were not suffered with apathy and fatalism; rather people organized themselves in community-oriented ways, by allusions to the power of pre-colonial deities, which served as potent symbols of resistance.

Second, in the Muslim world politics has been transformed by a general Islamic resurgence over the past two decades or so. It is pertinent to remind ourselves that what Islamization means to the ordinary people in the towns and cities and in the rural areas is not necessarily the same thing as it means to leaders and activists of Islamist groups. In other words, the theatrical and imaginary dimensions are also relevant when focusing on opposition groups; we must not focus exclusively upon the utterances and activities of militant leaders and ideologues while ignoring more moderate groups. As Esposito (1990: 6) notes:

There are often as many differences as similarities in Muslim interpretations of the nature of the state, Islamic law, the status of women and minorities as there are sharp differences regarding the methods to be employed for the realization and implementation of an Islamic order or system of government. *Thus, there is today, as in the past, a rich diversity of interpretations and applications of Islam* [emphasis added].

The most striking example of the political impact of Islamic resurgence is undoubtedly that of Iran, where religion was utilized to lead a class-based revolt. The downfall of that modernizing autocrat, the Shah, was largely the result of an upsurge of Islamic-oriented militancy that led to the establishment of a theocratic state under clerical leadership in 1979. The implication of both Goldthorpe's and Swift's related arguments is that a 'reassertion' of Islamic 'fundamentalist' militancy in Iran was little more than an atavistic response to the Shah's attempt to modernize the society. Yet the events that saw the Shah toppled and exiled in Iran are generally known as a revolution. Thus reaction and revolution are one and the same! As we shall see in Chapter 3, domestically the Iranian revolution was qualitatively more than a desire for a reversion to earlier social norms which the Shah had displaced in his drive for modernization. Internationally its inspirational character affected Muslim thinking and organizations and challenged incumbent governments from Morocco to Malaysia, from India to Indonesia, and from Tunisia to Trinidad. Yet although the contemporary global Islamic reassertion certainly has as one of its chief inspirations the revolution in Iran, the exemplary effect was tempered by local variations of government, culture and environment. In short, the Iranian revolution should be seen as an important example of a more widespread reaction to the secular ideologies (communism, socialism, statism and so on) which manifestly failed to improve the living standards of millions of people in Third World societies after a generation or more of independence, in a period of immense social and cultural change.

The international impact of the Iranian revolution was not uniform in another sense: manifestations of Islamic reassertion or reaffirmation are not necessarily revolutionary. However, in recent times the mutually advantageous relationship between governments and leaders of status quo accepting Islamic groups have been threatened by the development of Islam as an ideology of opposition. Those wishing for an enhanced role for Islam may or may not wish to change the government by their actions; they may be content to enforce Islam's social code without an impact upon national politics.

Before we deal with the issue more fully in Chapter 3, it may be useful to note at this point that in every Muslim society (i.e. one in which Islam is followed by a substantial proportion of the population, say a third or more) different political or ideological manifestations of Islam will be discernible. Three broad types of Islamic orientation may be identified: traditionalist, mainstream and radical. The first wishes to preserve Islamic culture and norms, but without taking this to the political arena. The second seeks the creation of a society utilizing the best elements in the Islamic and Western traditions; in other words, the mainstream Muslim is quite happy to adopt and use the fruits of Western technology but, at the same time, wishes to preserve a social position, often based on gender, which allows him to 'rule the roost' at home, at work and in government. The third, and this strand is by no means necessarily dominant, seeks a pure (or purist's) Islamic society (modelled on Saudi Arabia's or Iran's) without Western accretions. In other words, modernist groups with social, political and cultural goals influenced by reformist or sometimes revolutionary notions have been formed. Challenges to the status quo from Islamic radicals tend to be both generational and class- or group-oriented, occasioned by the state's failure to deliver the development goods over time, and directed as much against the status quo accepting Islamic leaders as against the state's official representatives. The potential of what we shall call radical Islam (i.e. those desiring social and/or political change through constitutional or non-constitutional means) to attract followers should not be underestimated. An uncountable but extremely large number of Muslims associate themselves with the ideas of radical Islam, which may or may not encompass the idea of an Islamic state.

We need to take into account that the hegemonic or state ideology may call itself 'Islamic'. Such nomenclature may also describe opposition political programmes and ideas, which challenge such regimes and the religious establishment (e.g. in Saudi Arabia) about a claimed *lack* of Islamic piety. Thus Islam may be a vehicle of either challenge or domination. In both cases Islam is utilized as a religio-political doctrine which adopts religious symbolism and ideas, claiming divine support. This is not to argue that all Islamist groups aim for a violent overthrow of the ruling elite and pre-existing political structure. Such groups may be radical, mainstream or traditional: their programmes will reflect their differing aims and aspirations. Within Islam's parameters one may discern different strands which themselves may be in contention *with each other* for state power and social predominance. Differing means to gain preponderant influence will be utilized as deemed appropriate.

This is also true of our third strand, i.e. non-syncretist Christian beliefs which have spread to parts of the Third World from the USA. There are several manifestations of this outside the mainstream Protestant and Catholic churches and their accompanying belief systems. The first two are dedicated to religious revivalism, and make up what may be called the Christian 'religio-political right wing'. They seek justification and guidance from the pages of the Bible, which is judged to be the literal Word of God. Fundamentalist Protestantism is tied to the 'fundamentals' of Bible interpretation. The movement's stronghold is in the south, midwest and western states of the USA. Its anti-communist ideas are perpetrated by US missionaries, who often find ready support among sections of the military and the wealthy, especially in Latin America. Another is pentecostalism, which may or may not be fundamentalist. Adherents do, however, generally share a conservative political outlook, differing from fundamentalist Protestantism by a much greater emphasis on the spiritual powers of the Holy Spirit. Pentecostals may be 'politically disinterested' as in Chile or more involved in politics as in Central America (Marishane 1991: 75).

Another example of Third World Christianity that has had an impact upon politics is socially progressive liberation theology, which is of political importance not only in Latin America, but also in parts of the Caribbean and Sub-Saharan Africa. There is a clear ideological division between, on the one hand, Christian fundamentalists and pentecostals and, on the other, liberation theologists. It would not be too great an exaggeration to say that, in Latin America in recent times, politics has been chiefly played out within the context of this religio-political divide.

The degree of political salience of each religious strand – Christian syncretisms, fundamentalist Christianity, liberation theology or interpretations of Islam – will depend upon: the nature of state–society relations within a polity, the manifestations and contexts of the theatrical and imaginary dimensions of politics, the existence of other mobilizing ideas (such as ethnicity or class) and the extent and characteristics of external penetration of the domestic arena. A combination of some or all of these produces certain types of religio-political interests. As we noted earlier, religion has always been political. Yet it has only been within the past 20 years or so that religion has become such a common vehicle for political opposition or domination in the Third World. Why is this? Why does religion dominate politics in so many countries? Why do people follow religious dogmatists? It is insufficient to state that religio-political salience is the result of an absence of alternative avenues of mobilization or merely a consequence of economic disappointment. Political pluralism has been almost universal in South America for up to a decade, yet this is the region in which religio-politics is particularly pronounced. Moreover, there is not a straightforward correlation between economic decline or disappointment and the burgeoning of politico-religions. To understand religion's dynamism and expansion in the context of politics, we must begin with an examination of the growth and internationalization of the world religions, Islam and Christianity. This will allow us to see recent developments in historical perspective and to note the position and character of these religions in Third World state–society contexts over time. This will be followed in Chapter 3 by an examination and assessment of Islamist groups, and in Chapter 4 by an analysis of the role of Christianity in Third World politics.

In summary, the worldwide advance of Western, secular values, owing to the increasing ease of global communications as the twentieth century proceeded, led to opposition from both Islamic and Christian groups which attempted to erect different cultural and religious values. To this consideration must be added another, related one: the widespread reaction against the materialism that was inherent in economic development and the secularism that pervaded modernization. In recent times that reaction, in Iran, Algeria, Sudan and so on, took the form of a militant Islamic reassertion or resurgence. The precise characteristics in each country reflected the nature of civil society as well as the theatrical and imaginary dimensions of politics. Frequently, *both* governments and opposition groups sought to adopt the banner of Islam, as evidence of their political or cultural correctness. As we shall see, however, the role that Islam plays in contemporary politics and society is a multi-faceted one that defies simple analysis: in Iran and, to an extent, Libya the Islamic resurgence had a clear revolutionary impact; on the other hand, long established Islamic states, such as Saudi Arabia, have themselves been under attack from people who see the state as not 'Islamic' enough, indeed as reactionary; finally, there is a number of states (e.g. Malaysia, Indonesia, the Philippines) where Islamic groups challenge the state as part of a general attack on Westernization (Voll and von der Mehden 1990: 100). It would not be going too far to say that in all regions of the world where significant numbers of Muslims live, Islam is a factor to be reckoned with, utilized by either governments or oppositions for their own political or social ends.

Four concerns establish the parameters of analysis. First, religion has always been political. Normal and continuous doctrinal change has an impact upon political questions of the day: what combination of conditions make for change in religion, which then has an impact upon politics? Second, religious beliefs are not held only by so-called 'traditional' or 'unmodernized' people and groups (i.e. rural dwellers), but also finds followers among those described as 'modernized' (i.e. educated, sophisticated urbanites). Why is this? Third, religious leaders and dogmatists utilize doctrinal themes as vehicles for political attacks upon incumbent governments. Why are they listened to? Finally, what gives religio-political concerns a ready audience at any given time?

What we shall be concerned with in the following pages is the growth and political salience of resurgent religion in the Third World over the past 50 years. The widespread reaction to the failure of modernization led to the expansion of political theologies. Both Islamic and Christian varieties often appear as curious admixtures of reaction and radical reform, although some, for example Christian liberation theology, are revolutionary. Taken together they involve attempts to utilize religious symbolism and teachings to bolster the position of groups – whether ruling elites or opposition formations – which perceive that their positions are under threat. Thus the inherent conservatism of both the Islamic *ulama* and the dominant groups in Central America – usually an alliance of the military and large-scale landowners – leads them to deal with attacks on their politico-economic positions by a reversion or at least allusion to traditional religious teachings and practices. As we shall see, however, such generalizations, unless qualified, tend to mask a variety of approaches which reflect the different political, economic and social realities of the interactions of religion and politics in the various parts of the Third World.

2

Islam and Christianity: the historical expansion and political significance of the global religions

Division, expansionism and the 'Golden Age' of Islam

Despite the existence of religio-political movements among many disparate peoples, it is the current global Islamic revival, with its genesis in the debacle (for the Arabs) of the 1967 Arab–Israeli war, which focused attention on Muslims as terrorists and revolutionaries. Racist stereotypes abound: the 'Arab oil sheik' of the 20 years ago has been replaced by the Kalashnikov-wielding, bomb-planting 'Arab-Muslim terrorist' in Western perceptions. A result has been an upsurge in the 1990s of anti-Arab and anti-Muslim sentiments in France, Germany and other European countries, paralleled by a corresponding anti-Western sentiment in many Muslim countries (even before the 1990–1 Gulf War). These developments were also reflective of attempts to rule through interpretations of Islamic law, the *sharia*, in Algeria, Iran, Pakistan, Saudi Arabia, Sudan and, most recently, Somalia. Elsewhere, in Egypt, Indonesia, Jordan, Malaysia, Morocco, Nigeria, Saudi Arabia, Senegal, Trinidad and Tunisia, Islamist oppositions challenge incumbent governments. Their general aim is for increased, although rarely clearly defined, Islamization of their respective societies. The cumulative result of such challenges to the status quo has been to increase dramatically Islam's political profile.

The current concern with Muslim violence has prompted a search by Western analysts for 'some explanation in the beliefs, values and ethics of . . . Islam, and in a combination of the history, culture and contemporary conditions of the Middle East', to help explain the resort to unacceptable forms of political struggle (Capitanchik 1986: 116). Explanatory accounts tend simplistically to equate modern Islamic resurgence with violence and

revolution, without acknowledging the vast majority of 'Islamically committed Muslims who belong to the moderate mainstream of society rather
than a radicalized minority' (Esposito 1990: 4). In other words, a triadic
distinction must be drawn between those (the vast majority) who would
like to see a return to (often vaguely defined) 'Islamic values', but who
would not resort to political violence to achieve their aims; a middle strata
which may argue and lobby for Islamization without resorting to extra-
constitutional measures; and the small numbers of zealots or fanatics who
believe that any means – including political violence – are justified by the
end, the creation of an Islamic state.

It is not the case that Islam has only recently developed a political orientation. From its inception in the seventh century it developed as a religio-
political community, albeit with different, and rival, Shia and Sunni
interpretations (Newman 1991: 469). Islam's holy book, the Quran, depicts
Islam as a belief system encompassing both faith and politics, with
Muhammad its founder and prophet. In 622, Muhammad emigrated from
Mecca to Medina (both in present day Saudi Arabia), where he was able to
establish a state based upon his prophetic message received from God
(Capitanchik 1986: 117–18). The community which Muhammad established,
the *umma*, was important enough to warrant the dating of the Islamic
calendar from its inception in 622 rather than from 610, the year of God's
first revelation to Muhammad. Under his leadership, the Muslims established their dominance over much of the Arabian heartland, resulting in the
welding of the disparate Arab tribes into a single polity with common institutions and a common ideology, a unity which endured until Muhammad's
death in 632.

Muhammad's death was the prelude to the establishment of the caliphate
period (632–1258), during which Islamic ideology and institutions as they
are understood today by Muslims were formed and developed. This period
is of especial importance in the context of the rule of the first caliph (*kalifa*),
since it is the period to which Islamic activists today turn for guidance in
attempting to define the Islamic character of the modern state (Capitanchik
1986: 118).

Muhammad died without either naming a successor or establishing any
mechanism for the selection of one. Following a brief period of uncer-
tainty, however, his companions chose as their leader one of Muhammad's
associates, Abu Bakr, the father of the Prophet's youngest wife, Aishah.
Abu Bakr adopted the title of caliph (successor) to Muhammad, the Prophet
of God, which endowed in him both political and military leadership of
the community. During his brief caliphate (632–4), Abu Bakr had to deal
with a number of tribal revolts which followed Muhammad's death. His
campaign was so successful that in crushing tribal revolt he was able to
consolidate Muslim rule over the entire Arabian peninsular.

The split in Islam between Shia and Sunni sects came 20 years after
Muhammad's death in 632. A line of caliphs took Muhammad's place as his
deputies and successors. The first four (known as the 'rightly guided') were

selected from among Muhammad's personal associates; from then on the position became hereditary. Given that the caliph's was a powerful position, implying both political and spiritual status, it is perhaps unsurprising that there was a lack of consensus in the Muslim community over the issue of succession. Some insisted that Ali, the husband of Muhammad's daughter Fatima, was the true successor. The murder of the reigning caliph was the beginning of a civil war in 656, which resulted in the open split between the party of Ali (in Arabic, *shia* means party or sect), who was also assassinated, and the main branch (*sunna*, Arabic for custom or practice). The struggle for domination between the two groups lasted until 680, when the battle of Kerbala resulted in Sunni domination and the defeat of the supporters of Ali, led by his son Hussein (Kirk 1959: 21).

The victor of the battle of Kerbala, Yazid, went on to solidify the Ummayyad dynasty in Damascus, which was recognized by the politically dominant Sunnis, while the subservient minority of Shia recognized the line of caliphs through Hussein's lineage. This inglorious end to Hussein's attempt to gain the caliphate led to the rise of a movement of political protest centred on the martyred family of Muhammad, providing the pattern for the Shia strand of Islam. To the latter, the traditional martyrdom story of Hussein symbolized the Shia relationship to political activity. The violent deaths that father and son both suffered instilled in Shias an admiration for martyrdom and in some a deep desire to emulate their sacrifice. The goal for Shias is to establish righteous rule and social justice through martyrdom and protest 'under the political leadership of the imam, hence the fundamental political and legal difference between the majority Sunni stream of Islam and the minority Shi'a denomination' (Capitanchik 1986: 121–2).

Until recently, Shias interpreted this tale as an allegorical representation of the plight of their community: they would suffer and be martyred at the hands of the Sunnis until the Twelfth Iman, or caliph, a heaven-sent Messiah, intervened on their behalf to establish Shia dominance over the Sunnis. This interpretation always reinforced the political passivity of the Shias – until the 1970s, when the story of the martyrdom of Hussein was re-created. Ayatollah Khomeini, addressing Iranians, and Musa al Sadr, active among the Shias of Lebanon, argued that the willingness of Hussein and his 70 followers to challenge Yazid's powerful army should serve as a model for how Shias should actively stand up and combat oppression and political marginalization (Newman 1991: 460). The reinterpretation of the Hussein incident helped, first, to establish a theological justification for the participation of the devout in the secular political arena. Second, it created a political myth fed by religious symbolism that structured political perceptions in Lebanon. When Musa al Sadr disappeared under mysterious circumstances in Libya, or when Ayatollah Khomeini assumed significant political powers in Iran, their lives took on new meanings for their constituencies (respectively Lebanese and Iranian Shias) as modern manifestations of the Twelfth (Hidden) Imam (Newman 1991: 469).

With the death of Ali and the rise of the Umayyads, the 'Golden Age' of Islam was brought to a close; the deaths of Ali and Hussein occasioned the split of the Muslim *umma* (Muslim community), which created a perennial legitimacy crisis in Muslim leadership. Yet despite the 'centrifugal forces operating on the Muslim body, many of the Islamic ideas of rule and legitimacy from the "Golden Age" survived as cornerstones common to all Muslim polities through the centuries' (Faksh 1990: 28). These are: the absolute unity of God (*tawhid*) with the establishment of divinely inspired laws as a minimum prerequisite of a legitimate government; the necessity for a caliph to maintain the unity and viability of the community; the implementation of the rules of the Quran and the Sunnah as the pattern of life for the *umma*; and, finally, the process of the *shura*, i.e. consultation among the leaders of the *umma* (Faksh 1990: 29–30). These cornerstones are the contemporary goals of Islamists wherever they may be. What is needed for a correct Islamic society is the adoption of divinely inspired laws under the leadership of an authoritative figure who rules by consent.

The establishment of the imperial caliphate, first under the Umayyads and then under the Abbasids, was followed by a period of extreme division in the body of the *umma*. It also marked the beginning of the transformation of the Islamic concepts of rule and legitimacy to fit new conditions. Because the Ummayyad caliphs could no longer claim legitimacy derived from close personal association with the Prophet or rule what had become an empire with an embryonic administration, they had to devise ways of governing which adapted the general concepts developed during the time of Muhammad and his rightly guided caliphs. As a result, the nature of the caliphate 'changed from a religio-political leadership based on the consent of the *umma* to a dynastic imperial-administrative leadership based on military strength' (Faksh 1990: 31). The *ulama* were allowed broad authority on matters of implementing and defining Islamic law because they were prepared to accept the caliph's dual role as defender of the *umma* and as symbol of unity.

The Umayyad dynasty was displaced by the Abbasids, a rival branch of the Arab clan of the Quraysh, aided by non-Arab elements who were subject to socio-political discrimination under the Umayyads. The centre of power moved to Baghdad (present-day Iraq), with the Abbasid caliphate coming under the influence of Persian-Sasanian traditions. The result was that the caliph was promoted as an absolute monarchic figure who ruled by divine mandate. This was an alien concept in relation to the Arab-Muslim grass roots leadership style under Muhammad and the early caliphs, and counter to Arab traditions of the chief being *primus inter pares*. Although these developments ran contrary to the Islamic concept of *sharia* supremacy, the *ulama* acquiesced in the new caliphal absolutism on the grounds that the caliphal court provided a political and administrative cadre necessary to maintain an orderly society. Within such a society the *ulama* could ensure adherence to *sharia* if the caliphs would not.

By the middle of the tenth century AD the Abbasid empire was disintegrating, with the position of the caliph considerably undermined and coming under the influence of first Iranian and later Turkish elements. The caliph became a mere symbol of Islamic unity; practical political power was held locally by governors or *amirs*. The *ulama* sought to legitimize the development of local power-holders by arguing that if they preserved public interests, defended and maintained the institutions of Islam in their areas, and recognized the religious authority of the caliph, they were acceptable. Thus the *ulama* sought to define the *amirs'* legitimacy to rule as long as they accepted (at least ostensibly) the superiority of the *sharia* and the *ulama*. Yet, as Faksh (1990: 33) notes, these 'limits were merely a facade of legal constructs that hardly squared with the actual situation'.

Following the Mongol invasion and the demise of the Abbasid caliphate in 1258, the Damascene jurist Ibn Jama'a (died AD 1333) characterized the new situation as follows:

> The sovereign has a right to govern until another and stronger shall oust him from power and rule in his stead. The latter will rule by the same title and will have to be acknowledged on the same grounds; for a government, however objectionable, is better than no government at all, and between two evils we must choose the lesser.
>
> (quoted in Faksh 1990: 33)

Thus according to Ibn Jama'a both usurpation (*istila*) and tyranny (*istibdad*) were justified: a government that rules by force, but protects Muslims and applies the *sharia*, is better than none. The situation was to remain essentially the same until the nineteenth-century reawakening, which came as a result of the Western Christian offensive. This gave rise to Islamic reformist movements, such as the Wahhabi movement in eighteenth-century Arabia and others in the West African region in the nineteenth century, advocating a revival of Islamic traditions of governance based on the four general concepts of legitimate rule in Islam: *tawhid* (absolute unity of God), *khilafah* (caliphate), *shura* (consultation among the leaders of the *umma*) and *sharia* (the religious law). Such reformist movements aimed generally to establish popular, responsive governments which would strengthen Muslim polities against Western influences and attack. As we shall see, the nineteenth-century reformists' responses to external and internal threats, i.e. to look back to the 'Golden Age' of Muhammad and the early Islamic community for guidance, were also those of a section of Islamists in the contemporary period. We shall turn to modern Islamist groups in the next chapter. We shall see then that their response to perceived inadequacies of state rule is dependent upon the nature and characteristics of the society within which they are located. In other words, Islamist groups may be seeking the same goals (*sharia*, strong consensual leadership) wherever they may be, but their precise nature varies owing to a number of factors. Thus we need to look at Islam's geographic expansion over time in order to understand the nature and characteristics of extant reformist groups. This will be followed by an examination of the spread of Christianity to appreciate the variations within it.

The spread of Islam by conquest and trade

The process of creating a Middle Eastern Islamic civilisation took 600 years, from the beginning of the seventh to the beginning of the thirteenth century AD. On the eve of the Islamic era Middle Eastern society was organized in numerous local, parochial communities built around factional, lineage, tribal and village groups. The results of some 600 years of Islam included the formation of new political and social elites and identities, the organization of new religious communities and the generation, out of the elements of the past, of a new cultural style. One important result of all this was that the Muslims of the Middle East created a number of international empires between the thirteenth and sixteenth centuries. During that time Islam's relation to the West was not that of an inferior; on the contrary, until the sixteenth century, continental Europeans feared invasions by Muslims from the East. Muslim martial prowess was matched by technological skills; until the seventeenth or eighteenth century Europe was synonymous with backwardness. Ironically, one of the legacies of Muslim inventiveness and civilization was the Renaissance in Western Europe, which marked the transition from the so-called Middle Ages to the modern world and led to the process of global domination in the nineteenth century (Modood 1990: 145).

Muslim advances (and retreats) were not restricted to Europe, of course. By the time of the Muslim flight from Western Europe at the end of the fifteenth century, Islam had established itself as the dominant socio-religious factor in the Middle East and North Africa, and was of growing significance in parts of Sub-Saharan Africa and in Central and Southern Asia. This

> spread of Muslim power and the mass conversions which accompanied it brought into Islam a wide range of beliefs, superstitions, religious practices and social customs of the new Muslims and of conquered peoples such as the Hindus, such that Islam was no longer the simple, rational, anti-idolatrous, egalitarian faith that had made history.
>
> (Modood 1990: 146)

As time went on, however, the mixing of Muslim and non-Muslim elements led to the diminution and later demise of Islam's political superiority. For example, Muslim power in India in the eighteenth century was threatened by the rising political militancy of both Hindu Marathas and Sikhs, while in the nineteenth century Europeans brought to an end the *jihads* of West and Central Africa and thus Islam's political dominance. By that time virtually the entire Muslim world had begun to come under the sway of European dominance and imperialism. From this time on, the West and its norms had a great effect upon Muslim thought. To many Muslims, modernist reform came to mean acceptance of existing political realities and adoption of a Western framework of ideas, albeit within the context and parameters of syncretic, culturally relevant ideas.

Islam spread from the Middle East via North to Sub-Saharan Africa in two ways: first, by a series of *jihad*s in the seventh and eighth centuries; second, by trade in commodities and people (Kaba 1976: 38). Slavery continued for a millenium, from the ninth to the nineteenth centuries on the eastern seaboard of Africa, beginning before and ending after the Western Europe and Americas centred trade on the west coast, which brought Christianity, to join the pre-existing Islam, to that region (Fisher and Fisher 1971: 1–2). Overall, the spread took about twelve centuries, until by the nineteenth century Islam had spread throughout much of the continent (Agyeman 1984: 8).

The diffusion of Islam into Sub-Saharan Africa was multi-directional. When they existed it followed pre-existing trade routes, such as the North African and Indian Ocean ways, which were used before the Arabs' encroachment. The expansion of Islam from Egypt to Morocco in the seventh century, and from Morocco to West Africa in the tenth, was eased by the existence of such conduits. Yet, as we have already noted, this is not to argue that Islam's spread was necessarily by peaceful means. For example, in West Africa the process of Islamization dates from the eleventh century, following the fall of the kingdom of Ghana to the Almoravids in 1076. The fall of Ghana to Muslims had two important effects on the advance of Islam in West Africa. First, it was important politically and psychologically because, until this time, Ghana was one of the most important African states. Second, it led to the conversion of the elite, and to the subsequent dominance by Muslims of many societies, especially in West Africa. From this time on it was West Africans themselves who spread Islam. This led to the African Islamized kingdoms of Mali, Songhai and Hausa (in present-day Northern Nigeria), and to the civilization of Timbuktu (present-day Mali) in the fifteenth and sixteenth centuries. A Moroccan invasion of 1591 destroyed the empire of Songhai, and the descendants of the invading army became the ruling elite in the Niger region. By the end of the eighteenth century, however, the once great Muslim kingdoms of the western Sahara had disintegrated into a plethora of small states (Lapidus 1988: 495).

Islamic revival movements from Mauritania to Sudan, encompassing present-day Senegal, Guinea, Mali, northern Nigeria, Niger, and Burkina Faso between the sixteenth and nineteenth centuries AD, 'gave Muslim civilization an impetus which continued during the (European) colonial era' (Kaba 1976: 38). A militant tradition grew up of determination to turn small colonies into Muslim states by defeating corrupt Muslim rulers, conquering the pagan populations, converting them to Islam and ruling them according to Muslim law. The West African *jihad*s at this time were led by Muslim teachers or scholars, taking inspiration variously from earlier militant reformers and from the pilgrimage to Mecca and Medina which brought them into contact with reformist circles. Although great numbers of people were converted to Islam in this process, the speed of conversion was slow and the change in institutions and beliefs variable and patchy. 'The result was not the formation of a uniform Islamic culture but of a plethora of local variations of Islamic practice' (Lapidus 1988: 522), which went through three stages of conversion: first, local Africans accepted elements of Islamic culture and practice, such as clothes, food and some religious concepts; second, more formal conversion was accomplished, with the *ulama* accepted as the sole representatives of God's will; finally, West African Muslims recognized the principles of Islamic law, accepted the five pillars of Islam and Islamized their cultures. But the time of the consolidation of Muslim thought, law and culture coincided with European expansionism, as the French and the British began to assert their own domination. The *jihad*s were finally suppressed by the British and the French at the end of the nineteenth century, part of the process of the colonization of West Africa (Lapidus 1988: 522–3).

There was a contrasting situation in East Africa. Paradoxical as it may seem, although there were extensive pre-Islamic contacts between the East African coastal people and those of Arabia, Islam remained largely a coastal phenomenon not affecting African cultures in the hinterland significantly. This was because Islam largely remained the religion of foreigners: Arabs, Persians, Indians and Swahili merchants who were generally culturally oriented towards the Arab world. The result was that the spread of Islam among indigenous East Africans was not facilitated, with Islamization in East Africa between the eighth and nineteenth centuries never reaching the scale in West Africa. In central Africa there was even less Islamic progress as its late introduction came up against the rapid spread of European Christianity; a result was that the former's influence was minimized. By the 1980s, for example, only 0.3 per cent (about 23,000 people) of Zambia's population of seven million were estimated to be Muslims (Ammah 1984: 19).

In sum, the spread of Islam throughout Africa became fragmented and diluted the further it got from its Middle Eastern heartland. The Islamization of North Africa resulted in rule by Arabs from the seventh century. In West Africa Islamic rule developed during the period of the Arabs' political dominance, between the seventh and twelfth centuries; after this time it was local Africans who continued with Islamic proselytization. A thousand years of slave trading in East Africa served by and large to distance local people from the religion of their tormentors, while in Central and Southern Africa the expansionism of European Christianity served to minimize the impact of Islam. Yet such was the hold that Islam took on sociopolitical organization and local culture in North and much of West Africa over the course of a millenium that attempts at Christian conversions in those areas in the nineteenth century were remarkably unsuccessful.

A second geographical focus of Islam's international expansion was northern India from the early thirteenth century, although there had been a Muslim presence in the country since the seventh century on the Malabar coast. Hindus have historically formed the majority community in India (currently some 83 per cent or 650 million), although it is a very heterogeneous majority divided by linguistic and caste cleavages. Currently, some 11 per cent (88 million) of Indians are Muslims. The largest mass conversions of Hindus – usually by force – took place after the Muslim conquest of Bengal in the thirteenth and fourteenth centuries (Vanhanen 1991: 46). As Ghosh (1987: 1–2) puts it: 'Arabs, the Turks, the Afghans and the Mughals invaded India in hordes from 1206 onwards, reducing temples to rubble, putting hundreds of thousands to the sword, and forcibly converting the survivors to Islam.'

During much of India's history there has not been a single centralized government. Instead, there were hundreds of small princedoms or statelets, and a pattern of local government involving representative committees (*panchayats*, literally 'councils of five'). A typical vacuum of leadership at the centre made it possible for Muslim rulers from Central Asia and Persia (Iran) to establish great imperial powers, including the Mughal dynasties that ruled the country from the sixteenth to nineteenth centuries, before giving way to the British. Both the Mughals and their British successors formed alliances with local rulers. As a result traditional Hinduism was left largely untouched. There followed long periods of peaceful coexistence between Muslims and Hindus, although from the eighteenth century onwards, coinciding with European penetration, communal disturbances were recorded. In the early twentieth century the number of disturbances increased, with nearly 1200 recorded dead during the 1924–40 period. Since the founding of Pakistan in 1947, itself a result of Muslim disquiet at the perceived Hinduization of the Indian nationalist movement, relations between the majority Hindus and minority Muslims have at times been tense or even worse. During the 1980s and early 1990s elements of the two religions clashed as both Hindus and Muslims sought to assert themselves. For ultra-nationalist Hindus the issue was the complete Hinduization of India, while the Muslims tended to be on the defensive rather than stimulated to revolt by international Islamic resurgence. During the 1980s on average over 450 Indians a year lost their lives in communal disturbances between Hindus and Muslims (Rajgopal 1987: 16).

In addition, the Muslims of Kashmir (the only Indian state in which the Muslims are in a majority, at a ratio of 2 : 1 to Hindus) sought increased political and economic links with Pakistan which, together with Sikh separatism, posed two of the more serious ethnic and communal troubles in the early 1990s. Yet, overall, Islam remained very much secondary to Hinduism in India. To a certain extent the situation historically was reminiscent of what happened at the same time in East Africa: Islam was by and large the religion and culture of invaders or those forcibly converted, of dominant political and economic figures whose motivation was more one of power accumulation than religious conversion for spiritual reasons.

A third major area of Islamic expansion was South-East Asia. Local Indo-Malay societies were not strictly parallel in form to Middle Eastern and South Asian Islamic empires. South-East Asia had a similar heritage of an agrarian and commercial economic base and a history of state regimes legitimized by way of high religious culture, but political fragmentation rather than imperial unity was the rule. South-East Asia was never conquered by Muslim tribal peoples. Nor were indigenous regimes able to achieve political unity. Indo-Malay polities evolved from within. The coastal and regional states of Malaya, Sumatra and the principalities of Java took on an Islamic identity, but they were derived historically from pre-Islamic states. Characteristically, Indo-Malay Muslim states depended heavily upon symbolic and cultural attachments to implement their rule. While Islam was woven into the symbolism of state authority, legitimation still depended upon the heritage of Hindu and Buddhist concepts. Even as compared with Mughal India, the non-Islamic cultural aspect of the political system was strongly pronounced.

The Muslim religious communities of South-East Asia also tended to be decentralized: religious life was built, locally, around individual teachers and holy men, the *ulama* schools were institutionally weak, and there were no significant tribal communities. In Indonesia, the mass of villagers considered themselves Muslims but were not strongly influenced by Islamic rituals, concepts, laws, ethics or institutions. They followed a customary religious and social life that had existed prior to the establishment of Islam and assimilated Islam into this pre-existing culture. Islam in Indonesia was manifest as identity rather than as social organization (Lapidus 1988: 547).

Thus, South-East Asian Islamic societies differed from the Middle Eastern in that there was little state participation in the organization of Muslim religious life; the village *ulama* were wholly independent. The ordinary people believed that a saviour or just ruler would eventually overthrow the state order to create a truly Islamic society. In both India and South-East Asia the initiative passed to numerous independent religious reformers who would struggle among themselves and with foreign and non-Islamic forces to shape the Islamic destiny of the area in the modern era (Lapidus 1988: 547). The several types of Islamic societies – in the Middle East, Africa, and South and South-East Asia – can be analysed in terms of a pattern of institutional arrangements which involved state, parochial and Muslim religious institutions. In each case the pattern of relations describes a variant form of Muslim society. Different Islamic societies can be analysed by way of looking at their characteristic constellation of state, religious and local communal institutions. As Muslim societies entered the modern era they were to be drastically changed by internal reorganization and by the impact of European imperialism and the world commercial economy. Nevertheless, the inherited patterns would be a powerful force in the shaping of Islam-influenced societies in the modern era.

Christianity: from European to world religion

In contrast to Islam, there has been within Christianity a more or less clear-cut separation of power between church and state, especially in Western

Europe. This situation developed over time, with an important symbolic watershed being the 1648 Treaty of Westphalia. This agreement not only brought to an end the Thirty Years War between Protestants and Catholics, but also saw the end of religious wars which had followed in the wake of the Reformation. The Westphalian settlement established the rule that it was for secular political leaders to decide which religion would be favoured in their polity. What this amounted to was that the emerging states of Western Europe tended to be more or less religious monopolies of one religion or another, as well as increasingly the homes of self-conscious national groups. Autocratic rulers saw religious conformity as an essential underpinning of their rule, necessary to maintain the existing social and political order in their favour.

The tendency towards rulers' absolutism and the growth of nationalism were both greatly affected by the French Revolution of 1789. In France itself, the Catholic Church, which had retained much of its wealth, social influence and political power after the 1648 Treaty, came under attack from the radicals and revolutionaries. The division between them and the Church was not bridged during the nineteenth century: by the end of that period the rise of socialism and communism helped to diminish further the Church's influence in the political battles fought between socialists, social democrats, liberals and conservatives in Western Europe. While this simplifies a complex situation (for example, the Church retained much power in Spain, Italy, Ireland and elsewhere), the overall effect of the growth of nationalism and secular political mobilization was effectively to diminish over time in many places the Church's political power in relation to secular rulers and their parties.

Islam's first expansion was in an earlier epoch than Christianity's. It was not until the fifteenth century – following the so-called 'Dark Ages' after the Romans' decline as imperialists – that first Roman Catholics and then Protestants began their religious expansionism. The first area of Christianity's expansionism in the Third World via European imperialism was in South America. As with Muslims elsewhere the motives were a mixture of religious conversion, civilizing of perceived primitive communities and commercial gain. The Spanish *conquistadores*' reasons for venturing to the 'New World' of the Americas from the late fifteenth century was first plunder and second saving souls for Christ (Pendle 1976: 38). Dominican, Franciscan or other Catholic friars accompanied expeditions. When a city was founded it was given a religious name and a priestly blessing; a church soon followed. The *Conquistadores* were the advance agents (*adelantados*) of both the Catholic Church and the Crown. Their secular head was the King whose authority was the same both in Spain and Spanish America. This illustrates how at this time secular and spiritual authority tended to be synonymous with the person of the monarch.

As Herring (1968: 169) noted 25 years ago: 'The last Spanish flag has long since been hauled down, but the Cross is still silhouetted against the sky from Mexico to Argentina.' The swift religious conquest of the New

World and other Spanish colonies, such as the Philippines, from the early sixteenth century was inextricably linked with both political and military domination. At this time, Spanish Catholicism was still a belligerent faith. When Christopher Columbus visited Queen Isabella before embarking on his first voyage to the Americas in 1492, their meeting took place at an armed camp outside the southern Spanish city of Granada, which was the last Muslim stronghold in the Iberian peninsular (Pendle 1976: 56). This centre of Islam in Europe fell to Spanish crusaders in that same year. As Christianity achieved unchallenged dominance in Europe, it was not surprising that the Church's power at home was reflected in developments in the New World. 'In the early period of colonial organization in Latin America religious figures were at least as numerous as the civilian officials sent out by the Spanish Crown' (Pendle 1976: 57). Religious figures soon operated side by side with secular rulers. Due to Papal concession, the Church, under the king's authority, served his purpose by helping to control the Spanish population. The chosen method was the Inquisition, tribunals organized for the discovery, repression and punishment of heresy or unbelief. Every foray into the interior of the Continent led to the king's dominions being increased because missionary outposts soon became Spanish settlements. The first task, however, was to consolidate their position by gaining souls for Christ. In the Spanish settlement, churches were swiftly erected, but quickly proved to be too small for the large congregations which sought to attend Christian services. Often they spilled out into the yard.

Local Indians flocked to be baptised, 'apparently accepting without much inconvenience the new priests who replaced their own' (Pendle 1976: 57). As with the spread of Islam internationally, Christianity in Latin America was grafted on to pre-existing local religions. Sometimes this happened literally: in Cuzco and Mexico City, for example, Christian churches were built on the foundations of Indian pre-Christian temples. A spiritual fusion was clear in the syncretic nature of Latin American Christianity. At the present time, local Guatemalan Indians perform pre-Christian rites on the steps of their church – then enter it to pray to the Christian God. According to Pendle (1976: 57), 'At one Guatemalan village the Indians will light candles in the church and then climb a nearby hill to offer candles, alcohol, and even crosses to the god of their forefathers.' Guatemalan villagers even rioted in 1960 when they believed a Christian priest had arrived to dismantle their shrine to a local god, San Pascual, the 'Lord of Crops and Protector of Flocks'. Such unusual toleration on the part of Christian missionaries was for two reasons. First, they were more concerned with the 'numbers game' than with anything else: once a convert had been baptized he or she could be added to the tally of 'Christians' and, like modern-day salesmen and women whose overriding aim is to sign up a purchaser for their products without concern with the ability to pay, the numbers of converts were more important than the quality of their belief. Second, the missionaries probably realized that if they insisted on eradicating pre-existing religious beliefs they would find themselves with no converts at all.

There was a practical, as well as spiritual, benefit to local people in converting to Christianity. The clergy were often the protectors of local Indians against the rapacity of Spanish mercenaries. One of the most dedicated and influential of Spanish priests was Bartolome de Las Casas. He was born in 1474 and following ordination at the age of 40 in 1514 he dedicated his life to the welfare of the Indians. He was largely instrumental in securing the promulgation of the New Laws of the Indies in 1542, following his entreaties to the Spanish king. Despite the passing of these Laws, however, their impact was diminished due to the geographical distance between Spain and the New World.

The period of the worst treatment of the Andean Indians was remembered as the 'Black Legend'. The Indians were forced under a system of slave labour (the *mita*) to work all week in the mines; they were only released on Sundays to pray. Throughout Spanish America, the Indians were severely oppressed, despite Las Casas' and others' efforts to ameliorate their plight. As Henriquez Urena (1949: 37) put it: 'It would be a delusion to imagine that the Conquest was anything but a tragedy for the natives.' When Latin America's republics eventually gained their independence from first Spain then Portugal in the early decades of the nineteenth century, the exploitation of the Indians continued. A similar situation existed in the other main area of Spanish conquest: the Philippines. As we shall see, nothing has changed in the 175 years since then: in many regions even now the second-class citizenship of the local Indians has not ended, and has proved to be an impetus for radical and revolutionary political movements, such as Sendero Luminoso in Peru or the Filipino New People's Army, some of which have been associated with radical or revolution-minded clergy.

Christianity is still far and away the most important religion in Latin America, but since the 1960s the Christian Church locally has divided into three: between Catholics inspired by the socially progressive ideas of liberation theology and conservative co-religionists, on the one hand, and between Catholics as a group and the fast growing Protestant evangelical sects, on the other. The political salience of the three-way division has been aided and abetted by local and foreign Protestant fundamentalists as well as by politically left-wing regimes such as that of the Sandinistas in Nicaragua. A second (although not necessarily secondary) context is that of the interlinked civil strife or war common in Central America in the 1980s and United States foreign policy goals in the region at that time. We shall look at the domestic and international contexts of the fragmentation of Christianity in Latin America in Chapters 4 and 5 respectively.

Christianity, in the form of mainstream Protestantism, was also the religion of a further wave of European imperialism in the nineteenth century, which saw substantial areas of tropical Africa and Asia brought under European control. At this time not only new tropical areas but also lands in the temperate zones of North America, Australia, New Zealand and Southern Africa were opened up to white settler farmers. These developments were made possible by technological innovations, particularly the railway, the steamship and, later, the internal combustion engine; and by some important medical discoveries, especially quinine which could control malaria, thus enabling Europeans to survive in mosquito-infested tropical areas.

European political and economic control of colonies was also facilitated by the spread of the Christian missions. Just like in sixteenth-century Latin America, Christian missions in Sub-Saharan Africa were integrally involved in European expansion in ways that went far beyond the preaching of the gospel. Christian missionaries founded branches of the churches that had sent them, which were long dominated by European men and women until these were replaced by local, Europeanized people, locally born and ordained (Goldthorpe 1984: 51). Europeans found it necessary to concern themselves with the physical, as well as the spiritual, needs of 'their' people. In association with mission stations there developed hospitals and dispensaries, soon followed by schools for training nurses and other medical personnel. Schools were essential for the general spread of literacy, indispensable as that was for membership of the church, while higher and more specialized education was required for the training of local African clergy and catechists. Schools needed books and other equipment, so that the missions' activities extended into commerce and small-scale industry as they initiated and controlled printing works, bookshops and workshops where materials such as school furniture were manufactured. Furthermore, in some areas it came to be felt that people's material standard of living had to be raised if they were to be able to care as Christians should for their children and other dependants in a house with minimum sanitary and hygienic arrangements, such as soap and mosquito nets. Some missions accordingly developed an industrial or manufacturing side, training men as skilled craftsmen, and introducing cash crops to enable people to earn money for Bibles, clothes and school fees. Thus in Africa a large mission station was often like a small town. It might have a hospital, school(s), perhaps a theology college, workshops, a bookshop and houses of foreign ministries and native converts, all centred on a church (Goldthorpe 1984: 51–2; Livingstone 1917). Some had walls around them for security, which helped to establish them as refuges for those who needed protection. In sum, mission stations were settled communities with an economic base, different from the surrounding areas and acting as agents of change in the life of those areas.

Despite the opportunities extended to local people by the establishment of a Christian mission, missionaries did not always make themselves popular with local Africans. Their concern for the latter's welfare necessarily meant that the missionaries were deeply committed to changing many aspects of local cultures. Local deities were condemned as false gods, to be abjured by the convert along with customs and practices which from a Christian point of view were immoral. Forms of dress and dancing, for example, were often judged indecent, as transgressing the Victorian moral bounds of the time. Most important, however, was African resentment of the occupancy of positions of authority in the Church exclusively by Europeans. Different Churches had different approaches to this problem. Roman Catholic missions established schools from which a few young men with the necessary intelligence and vocation might pass into theological training, to be eventually ordained. Once ordained, there were no (formal) distinctions between European and African priests, although at best covert racism led to Africans being regarded as inferior by Europeans within the Church. Some Protestant missions also took higher education and the training of (local) clergy seriously. Among Anglicans, however, there was a distinction between the mission, financed by donations from Britain, and the so-called 'Native Anglican Church', locally supported. Even though the living standards of expatriate Anglican missionaries were frugal, African Anglican clergymen and their families were even poorer materially. This caused widespread ill-feeling within the Church. Other Protestant denominations were slower to ordain local men; this gave the appearance that they were trying to keep control of Church affairs as a European prerogative.

The growing resentment of European domination by Africans extended to the Christian missions and missionaries. One result was the establishment of African independent churches in many parts of the Sub-Saharan African region from the late nineteenth century. Pioneer studies of African independent churches were carried out by a Swedish missionary, Bengt Sundkler, in the late 1930s and early 1940s. He found that there were about 800 such sects in South Africa alone at this time. Thirty years later the figure had risen to about 3000. In addition there were more than '500 separate church bodies of independents in West Africa and 500 in Central Africa, [and] about 300 in East Africa' (Parrinder 1976: 149).

Sundkler's *Bantu Prophets in South Africa* (1948) was one of the earliest and most thorough studies of the South African independent churches. In it he distinguished two main types, Ethiopian and Zionist. Ethiopian sects were either direct or indirect offshoots of white mission churches, whose forms of organization and doctrines of biblical interpretation they followed on the whole very closely. They tended to be African churches which left the missions chiefly on racial grounds (Parrinder 1976: 158); their essential character was encapsulated by the notion that Africans could lead and run churches as well as Europeans. In other words, most of the Ethiopian churches stressed a nationalist or at least a proto-nationalist outlook.

Ethiopia, even though it is now merely one state of Africa's more than 50, was regarded as synonymous with Africa as a whole; biblical references to Ethiopia were cited in support of claims for the antiquity of an African church. Some of these churches had links with so-called 'Negro sects' in the United States, ties strengthened in some cases by the Jamaican-born black American leader, Marcus Garvey, who travelled widely in the 1920s and 1930s spreading the idea of independent black churches as a means to liberation. Garvey was regarded as an important prophet by the Rastafarians, militant Jamaican descendants of West African slaves, who regarded the Ethiopian emperor, Haile Selassie ('Ras Tafari'), who ruled from 1932 to 1974, as a living god. From the founding of the sect in the 1930s, Rastafarians sought for a meaningful creed distinct from the teachings of white colonial Christians (Hall 1985: 269–96). The Ethiopian African churches paralleled the development of Rastafarianism in Jamaica with one major distinction: the essential aim of the African independent black churches was to be both African *and* Christian; Christian in the essentials of doctrine and practice with only minor modifications to accommodate the first aim, that of being self-governing and independent of white control.

The Zionist sects, on the other hand, were syncretist, i.e. involving a fusion or blending of religious ideas. They were first 'inspired by a Zion church in Zion City, Illinois, USA, which taught divine healing, triple immersion, and the near second advent of Christ' (Parrinder 1976: 159). The Zionist sects emphasized healing by faith, speaking in tongues in ecstasy, rites of purification and taboos on blood, pork and alcohol in accordance with Old Testament teachings. While the Ethiopians kept close to the pattern of church worship and life of their parent missions, the Zionists were much more 'African' and syncretistic, like prophetic movements everywhere, even when they made conscious efforts to reject anything 'heathen'. Traditional drum-based music, dancing, possession, purification, sacred dress and ritual avoidance all figured largely in their life. Throughout much of present day Sub-Saharan Africa Zionist sects have evolved into pentecostalist churches.

In general, the rise of African independent churches involved a mixture of social, political and religious factors. Commonly both types, Ethiopian and Zionist, stressed national feeling, struggles for authority and leadership, disagreements over finance, breaches of church discipline and the desire to allow polygamy. The independents in the early twentieth century and, as we shall see, currently came into conflict with their governments, who frequently viewed them, sometimes justifiably, with unease as political, even nationalist movements, even though their aims were principally religious.

According to Wilson (1985: 297), such sects 'are born in primitive societies in reply to social change and to deterioration in the traditional culture'. Such a characterization omits to mention that social changes were induced by the coming of Europeans to Africa and were, at least in part, a reaction to the inability of Africans to climb the church hierarchy because of the colour of their skins. Before the twentieth century moves had begun for African church self-government, and it is noteworthy that from the beginning they were not only linked with freedom from foreign control but also aimed at the evangelization of Africa by modern methods. Second, more recently the plethora of sects which have been identified in Africa have been by and large a reaction to the general political and economic retrogression in that continent since the breakdown of the optimism which greeted independence 30 years ago.

Indigenous religious movements (variously called schisms, secessionists, separatist sects or independent churches) were and continue to be a feature in all parts of Sub-Saharan Africa. One of the most politically important was founded in central Africa in the early years of the twentieth century. In 1921 in the then Belgian Congo (now Zaire) a Baptist, Simon Kimbangu, began to see visions and apparently found he had the power of healing. He quickly attracted a large following, to the detriment of the Roman Catholic missions and work on the railway and plantations (Desanti 1971: 7). Then other, similar (although lesser) prophets emerged. Both Roman Catholic and Protestant Church leaders were seriously disturbed at such a potentially serious development. The Belgian colonial government took fright at civil disturbances; Kimbangu was arrested and imprisoned for 30 years, until he died, still incarcerated, in 1951. Missionary hostility notwithstanding, his movement continued to grow throughout the period of Belgian rule. His 'Church of Christ on Earth through the Prophet Simon Kimbangu' (CCEPSK) was persecuted but non-violent, and was unrecognized until 1959. Since Zaire's independence in 1960, the CCEPSK has grown in numbers, with some three million adherents, and in standing under the leadership of Kimbangu's sons, one of whom was elected a deputy to the Zairean parliament and served as Minister of Labour in Patrice Lumumba's short-lived post-colonial government (Desanti 1971: 16).

Independent church movements also sprang up in Angola and Mozambique at about the same time as Kimbangu's CCESPK. As with the latter, they were often suppressed as being vehicles for political revolution. In Malawi, John Chilembwe, who was influenced by the National Baptist Convention (a black civil rights movement) in the USA, returned to Nyasaland (pre-independence Malawi) with a number of black Americans to found the Providence Industrial Mission (PIM). After they left in 1906, Chilembwe's mission became a centre for African militancy, and in 1915 he led an unsuccessful armed uprising in the Shire Highlands during which he was killed. Chilembwe's movement was one of several in Nyasaland at this time. Watch Tower, associated with Jehovah's Witnesses in the USA, spread widely in Nyasaland and in other areas of colonial Africa, becoming almost wholly independent of the parent sect. It acquired a militantly anti-white tone in which the coming millenium was viewed chiefly in terms of liberation from white rule (Shepperson 1954: 234–6).

Chilembwe's PIM, as well as the Jehovah's Witnesses in Africa generally, are examples of what John Milton Yinger (1967: 482) calls 'attack cults'. According to Yinger, such organizations arise within 'groups caught in conditions of severe disprivilege' following either conquest by a militarily and industrially more advanced society, or domination by a more powerful segment of their own society. The religion of the conqueror, though often strongly promoted by missionary activity, is embedded in the whole social system of the dominant group and thus unacceptable to the subordinate groups. Among the latter, too, despite traditional tribal differences, people find themselves caught up in common situations, so that unifying themes are needed. Despite the ending of the colonial era, the Jehovah's Witnesses maintain a substantial number of lay missionaries in Africa and elsewhere, and have been persecuted by state authorities for their beliefs (Wilson 1985: 309).

East Africa also had its share of independent churches and religious movements, many of which stressed the unjustness of the relationship between Africans and Europeans. One of these was the African Orthodox Church, founded in Uganda in 1929 by two young Anglican teachers, Reuben Spartas Mukasa amd Obadaiah Basajjakitalo. Its rationale is well captured in the following: 'A church established for all right-thinking Africans, men who wish to be free in their own house, not always being thought of as boys' (Goldthorpe 1984: 220). In Kenya, African churches grew up in association with the independent schools movement among the Kikuyu of Kenya, which was in turn a part of the reaction to harsh conquest and white settlement. That reaction had its political aspects in the African nationalist parties and movements which arose during the period from 1920 onwards, most of them to be suppressed by the colonial administration in a conflict that eventually took the form of an armed revolt and guerilla movement to which Europeans gave the name of 'Mau Mau' (Parrinder 1976: 155–6). Its aim was to free the land from foreign occupation. It was also a defender of pre-European cultural norms, notably the odious practice of female circumcision, which led it into conflict with the Kenya Missionary Council. Whereas the Kenyan colonial administration regarded Mau Mau as yet another religious movement, modernization theory-influenced interpretations in the 1960s characterized it as an African nationalist political movement and rejected explanations rooted in religious beliefs (see Rosberg and Nottingham 1966). The point is that it is very difficult to disentangle the religious, political, educational and military aspects of Mau Mau, a broad movement of revolt among the Kikuyu against white settlement. In an important sense it was a proto-nationalist movement which utilized cultural symbolism, including religious, in its political struggle against white domination.

African independent churches have been dealt with at some length, because of their importance in the context of proto-nationalist stirrings in the early years of the twentieth century. In effect, many of them were examples of an African liberation theology which stressed the necessity for black people to build their self-pride and dignity in the context of years of European colonial rule. In many accounts the explanatory emphasis was on the particular circumstances of the religious movement in question. In the South African context, for example, Bengt Sundkler attributed the rise of independent African churches to particular features of life there, including the colour bar, residential segregation, the land question and the Dutch Reformed Churches' twin leitmotifs of 'geen gelijkstelling' (no equality in church or state) and 'net vir Blankes' (for Europeans only), figuratively written on many church doors (Goldthorpe 1984: 224–5). In short, then, the characteristics of White-dominated political arrangements often led to the establishment of black African-directed religious movements, one of the few areas of meaningful organization that was possible in the circumstances.

Even though the racist severity and political exclusiveness of South African apartheid was not replicated completely elsewhere (although the conditions of white dominance in Southern Rhodesia (Zimbabwe) ran it a close second), it does seem to be the case that the more pronounced the European domination and the more rigid the colour bar, the greater the tendency to form separatist religious movements. Yet it is too much of a simplification to see breakaway Christian movements in Africa solely within the secular context of the struggle for political independence. It was also the case that the forms of religious worship sanctioned by European-dominated churches were perceived by many indigenes as inappropriate to African realities, fashioned within different social, cultural and political settings from those of Europe. The initiatives of white church leaders did not 'fit' well with the construction put on religion in the minds of ordinary Africans. This was quite apart from the issue of leadership of the churches.

The position of the Catholic Church in Latin America was different for three reasons. First, independence from Spain or Portugal was uniformly won by the early years of the twentieth century. Second, as a result of liberation from European rule, local cultures and Catholicism were virtually untouched by enlightenment definitions of the individual. In other words, the philosophical ideas emanating from eighteenth-century France, such as the belief in reason and human progress and a questioning of tradition and authority, largely passed the societies of South America by. This situation depended 'on the existence of a popular religious culture that was the antithesis [of] modernity' (Linden 1991: 120). Third, it was only well into the twentieth century that establishment Catholicism came under serious attack from two sources: Protestantism and liberation theology. These developments had a major impact upon the religion–politics equation.

In some senses the situation within the Muslim world(s) was like that of the Catholic environment. As we saw earlier, unlike in Christian-influenced states, there was never a separation between state and religion in Muslim polities. There could be no reformist, breakaway rivals to Islam because it was regarded as the unchangeable word of God, so any religious challenges would be regarded as heretical. Thus Islam remained omnipotent in areas where it dominated. Even when local variations (e.g. Sufism) arose, they developed within parameters broadly acceptable to the *ulama*. At the same time control by the Ottoman Empire (Middle East) or by Western Europeans (Africa, South and South-East Asia) meant that large swathes of Muslim territory were politically controlled by either nominal or non-Muslims. At the same time the *ulama* retained their spiritual power, which ensured the continuity of religious belief. Often Europeans deemed it both expedient and politically rational not to challenge Islam as it provided a pre-existing social cement that could be utilized wholesale for the transference of European rule, if not values. This was particularly important in the north of Nigeria, where Lord Lugard's famous notion of 'indirect rule' owed its success to the fact that it tampered not at all with local social and cultural norms. The political effects of not challenging Islam's social and cultural predominance are highly relevant to the religion-derived instability which pertains in contemporary Nigeria.

Generally, however, by the time of the emergence of the independent Third World from 1945 religion was perceived by leaders as something to be ignored or tolerated. It was considered as primordial and reactionary. Frequently the secular state – as in India, Nigeria, Indonesia and so on – did not provide any formal role for religion in public affairs, even though religious beliefs established the parameters of society and culture. One reason for the attempted exclusion of religion is that many post-independence Third World states featured a number of religions within their boundaries. To establish the formal hegemony of one would obviously have incurred the enmity of those excluded. At the same time, as we have already made abundantly clear, over time such states were generally and obviously unsuccessful in excluding religion from the political agenda. In the Muslim heartland – the Middle East – the overwhelming majority of rulers attempted to rule either through a secular party or via their absolutist authority, utilizing Islam and a pliant *ulama* for symbolic effect when necessary. Unusually in the Third World, Islam was not challenged in the Middle East by other religions. We now turn to an examination of the political conditions occasioned by widespread secular rule within the context of frequently deeply religious societies, and the resulting challenges from a multi-faceted resurgent Islam.

The political resurgence of Islam in the Third World

By the 1980s, Islam was the chief vehicle of political opposition in North Africa and the Middle East, regardless of official state ideology, political system or leadership. Whether in communist Afghanistan, socialist Algeria, revolutionary Libya, secular Tunisia, pro-Western Egypt, divided Lebanon or puritanical Saudi Arabia, the generalization holds true. Elsewhere, in states as diverse as Turkey, India, Indonesia, Malaysia and Trinidad, Islamic groups strained the relationship between governments and governed. In addition, Islam was the *leitmotif* of rebellions in Burma, Chad, Ethiopia, Thailand and the Philippines. In the context of international relations, Islamic issues helped to justify and fuel conflicts between Iran and Iraq, Iraq and Saudi Arabia, Iran and Saudi Arabia, Israel and Arab states collectively, and Pakistan and India over the status of Kashmir.

Islam, then, is an important political factor in virtually all Muslim societies. Yet, it does not take the same form everywhere. What unites otherwise disparate groups is, on the one hand, partial or total rejection of Western values, lifestyles, legal systems and ideologies and, on the other, a desire for strict(er) observance of Islamic codes of personal conduct and demands for the enforcement of the *sharia*. Generally there is dissatisfaction with the political and economic status quo and the common political and economic corruption of ruling elites. The goal of all Islamic movements may be some form of 'Islamic state'. Yet there is no consensus as to the nature and characteristics of such a state. The Quran does not provide clear guidelines in this respect: indeed there is very little in the Quran and other Islamic sources on how to form states, run governments and manage organizations (Ayubi 1991: 4).

A second problem concerns the mechanisms of state–society relationships. Just *what* would an Islamic state look like? How should it be administered and given direction when no blueprint exists? What should be the form of rule? Should it be a dictatorship ruling by decree, or some form of democratic polity with popular representation? How are decisions to be made? To whom is the government responsible? Perhaps most fundamentally of all, given the idea that Islam promotes the idea of a community of believers (*ummah*) which knows no state or national boundaries, are not the terms 'Islam' and 'state' contradictory?

Reflecting ideological, national and doctrinal differences, there is no consensus beyond generalities among Muslim scholars or *Islamists themselves* as to the nature, characteristics and parameters of an 'Islamic state'. Divisions have been reflected, as Sardar (1985: 128) notes, in the inability to create 'a modern mechanism by which the all-important principles of Shura or consultation can be put into practice in an Islamic society'. It may be agreed in the abstract that an Islamic state should be a form of democratic polity, headed by leaders who take fully into account popular demands and desires. They should aim to create a politically and socially open society in which individuals may enjoy freedom of religion, of culture and of social development. Abd al-Rahman Azzam (1979: 113) makes consultation an important, if not pivotal, aspect of the Islamic state, while Muhammad Asad (1980: 33) considers that it should have as essential tenets justice, freedom and equality. Yet concrete problems remain. By what means should an aspiring Islamic state work towards a just and equitable order? How may strong yet caring political leadership emerge? In what ways can a socially responsible administration evolve?

For millions of Muslims in, for example, Egypt, Iraq, Jordan, Lebanon and Syria, political life over the past 80 years has been conducted in independent states. During this time the constitutional basis of political systems and sovereign legal authority has rested on the Western notion of popular sovereignty. In other words, at least officially, the modern secularized state has been both the legitimate foundation of political life and the focus of group identity. At the same time, most Muslims remain faithful to conservative, Islamic world views, regardless of social position, educational level, place of habitation or frequency of international travel (Sivan 1985: 183–4).

The only revolutionary Islamic state is Iran, a country dominated by Shia Muslims. Yet to Sunnis Shia Islam is regarded as a Persian religion (Tibi 1990: 18). As a result, Iran is perhaps unlikely to be the role model for Arab Sunni Muslims, the vast majority in Middle Eastern states. At the same time, however, it should be noted that the anti-Western, militant ideology of Iran's government does strike a chord with some ideologically similar groups (e.g. in Sudan and Nigeria), even if the latter are Sunni groups. The first post-revolutionary leader of Iran, Ayatollah Khomeini, summarized the essential nature of the Shia Islamic state by emphasizing its uniqueness when compared to Western or other recognized (e.g. communist) conceptions: 'The Islamic state bears no resemblance to any existing system of government' (quoted in Sardar 1985: 127). To Khomeini the 'Islamic state' has two main characteristics: it is not despotic, in the sense that it may not be ruled by authoritarian means; and it is a constitutional state, in that the leaders 'are bound by the rules and conditions laid down by the Qu'ran and the Sunnah' (quoted in Sardar 1985: 127). Yet, as we have noted, one of the main problems for the Islamization of polity is just how to translate less than precise guidelines to the modern complex political arena.

Sunni scholars have also concerned themselves with the question of an Islamic state in the modern age. One of the most influential was the Syrian, Muhammad Rashid Rida, who died in 1935. His ideas had a profound influence on such Islamic movements as the Muslim Brotherhood and the Jamaat-i-Islami. Rida's conception of an acceptable Islamic state did not differ profoundly from Ayatollah Khomeini's. It was also predicated on two essential preconditions: the restoration of rule by an Islamic leader and the paramountcy of the *sharia*. On the principle of sovereignty, Rida argued that once regular and formal consultation between ruler and ruled was established then the modern Islamic state would *ipso facto* be a democratic one. This was because the political leader would be both elected from and advised by a Council of Jurists – themselves representing all groups of Muslims – and modelled on the Electoral Council established by Umar to find his successor following the death of the first Caliph of Islam, Abu Bakr, in 634 (see Chapter 2). Thus the head of the state would be both a religious and a political leader, the chief of all Muslims. Popular support would be forthcoming as long as his decisions conformed to the principles of Islam. As a further check on absolutist power, Rida asserted that the *ulama* (the jurists of Islam) would ensure that democracy prevailed, citing the examples of two *ulama*-led revolts in Iran in 1892 and 1906 (see below). On the issue of laws and law-making, he argued that the *sharia* would of necessity predominate, to be supplemented by a secondary body of law (*qanun*) dealing with issues associated with modernity which the *sharia* could not be expected to cover (Sardar 1985: 133–4).

The nature of the Islamic state has been addressed by both Sunni and Shia scholars. In a sense, however, such concerns are premature. Islam is usually an ideology and mobilizer of opposition, although as we shall see several governments *claim* to have established Islamic states. Only in Iran has a fully fledged Islamic state been established by revolution; in other examples an Islamic state has been announced from above rather than formed by agitation from below. Upheavals associated with modernization and social change, which Muslim societies became embroiled in after the Second World War, form the salient context for the formation of Islam as a politico-religion in the modern era (Green 1985: 318–20). At the same time we must be aware that modern political Islam is not merely a product of modernization *per se* nor even a symptom simply of the latter's inapplicability to 'traditional' societies. It is not just an ideology in which the political is of more importance than the religious. It *may* be strongly connected with sub-state nationalism or ethnicity (it is in the Sudan, but not in Pakistan). Islamic thinkers are not often concerned with class issues, although justice and equity are among major interests of socio-political analysis. Perhaps above all, we must not conceive of political Islam in the terms of either modernization theory or neo-Marxist analysis. Both see 'religion' as merely a vehicle for secular ends involving power accretion. For analytical purposes the religious verities of an undifferentiated Islam must be qualified by the divisions between societies, regions, history, geography and theology. It is unsatisfactory, therefore, to perceive Islamic ideologies and movements as uniformly

> extremist, anachronistic, and retrogressive, seeking to turn the already slow historical clock of their societies back to a medieval social order bereft of such quintessential achievements of modern civilization as secularism, rationality, science and technology, and respect for the right of the individual.
>
> (Banuazizi 1987: 300)

In this chapter, I examine how and why Islam became a focus of both rulers' hegemony and opposition groups' challenges in a number of Arab and non-Arab states. I shall investigate and analyse the process of the politicization of Islam. It will become evident that even in modern political settings Islam and politics are inseparable. This is not to imply that the modern Islamic revival is in some way a reversion – or a desire for a reversion – to an older, 'purer' type of governance. As the respected Muslim scholar Ziauddin Sardar argues,

> It is an undeniable fact that, perhaps apart from Iran, traditional leaders in almost every Muslim country, from Nigeria, Sudan, Egypt, Saudi Arabia, Pakistan, Bangladesh to Malaysia, are among the most narrow-minded, bigoted, antiquated, thoroughly chauvinist and opportunistic groups in society. For them, Islam is a personal property to be rented out and leased, hired and sold.
>
> (Sardar 1985: 148)

Sardar (1985) asserts that the 'average Muslim cringes with fear at the mention of "Islamic rule" '. It must be added that this is the view held by many non-Muslims, especially in the West. 'Islamic rule', conventional wisdom would have it, is the slogan of the dictator who grabs power in the belief that he has a divine mandate to impose Islam on the people. He introduces 'Islamic law', comprising 'Islamic punishment' for transgressors. Religious figures and Islamic political parties seek government jobs, while women are declared of reduced social, political and economic status. Yet none of this is essentially 'Islamic'. What will be demonstrated in this chapter is the diversity of perceptions, issues, programmes and goals that may be included in a conception of Islamic state or world view.

Islam and the state: political conceptions and roles

An understanding of Islam as anti-modern, anti-progress, anti-democracy is not novel: Islam has been in hegemonial contention with the West since before the Arabs retreated from Western Europe 500 years ago. One of the justifications for Western encroachment into Islam's realm was the claimed deficiency in Muslim (both Arab and Ottoman Turk) leaders' conceptions of rule and societal relations. From the late eighteenth century, Islam succumbed to direct or indirect infidel (i.e. Western) rule, control and subservience (Vatikiotis 1991: 59). This development was vigorously fought against in Egypt, Algeria, the Sudan, Turkey and elsewhere; in each case Islam was the vehicle of resistance through *jihad*, albeit without final success. By the late nineteenth century European control (or at least Europeanization of the military, education, bureaucracies and legal systems) was established. Close economic and diplomatic ties, with their inevitable consequence of acculturation, were the result.

By the beginning of the twentieth century, the West's dominance was clear: the Arab world seemed unable to respond to the onslaught, except in areas untouched by Europeanization, such as Arabia. Here in the late eighteenth century the Sunni, puritanical Wahhabis established a new, ascetic order based on the teachings of the Quran and the Sunnah of the Prophet. The house of Saud, in alliance with the Wahhabis, established a kingdom. Until the discovery and exploitation of oil deposits in the twentieth century and the accompanying introduction of Western influences, successive rulers managed to keep the infidels at bay both literally and figuratively.

Generally, however, in Muslim countries politics were dominated after the Second World War by trends towards Western-styled modernization: state-centric nationalism, the centralization of political and administrative mechanisms, and statism (sometimes, as in Algeria or Syria, labelled 'socialism'). The trend was stimulated by the destruction of the Ottoman Empire in 1918, and by the emergence of secular Turkey from 1924. Centralizing leaders (some of whom came from the military) exercised power, attempting to control religious leaders by co-optation. The ruled carried on much as before, leading their lives on the basis of religion-inspired social values under the guidance of religious teachers. Many of the new rulers ruled neither justly nor well, nor according to pre-existing Islamic norms.

Rather than representing a uniform position, Islam's political role ranges along a spectrum of authority and power. At one extreme it may be a device for regime legitimization and preservation of the status quo, while at the other it may be a vehicle of protest or even of revolution (Ayubi 1991: 61). What may be labelled *establishment* Islam seeks to buttress the political elite's legitimacy, as in Iran, Morocco, Saudi Arabia, Pakistan and Sudan. Governments in these countries seek to utilize Islam primarily to bolster their own positions and those of influential followers, as well as secondarily to provide society with an organizing set of precepts.

Islamic movements seeking to oppose entrenched rulers are examples of *popular* Islam. The first wave of twentieth-century Islamic opposition came in the 1930s. Rida's model of a modern Islamic state (see above) was adopted by various Islamic movements fighting to establish Islamic states. The

Muslim Brotherhood, active in Egypt, Sudan and elsewhere in North Africa and the Middle East, adopted the model with one important modification: the state of *sharia* law was to be established, by consensus if possible, by a militant and armed movement if not. From the 1930s to the 1950s, the Muslim Brotherhood became the largest mass Islamist movement. Its involvement in Egyptian and neighbouring states' politics posed a serious security threat until it was proscribed and (temporarily) dissolved by the regime of Nasser in the 1950s. One result was that for a period the Brotherhood lost political and social importance. Another, and from the state's perspective less welcome, sequel of its persecution was to give rise, twenty years after its proscription, to

> a new ideological and organizational development . . . that was far more radical and uncompromising in its characterization of present-day Islamic society, state and rule as un-Islamic and infidel (*jahiliyya*), to be fought relentlessly and destroyed, and to be replaced by a purely Islamic order.
>
> (Vatikiotis 1991: 62)

Offshoots of the Muslim Brotherhood rejected both the separation of Islamic society and the state, and the political quietism of conservative religious teachers. The militant groups' goal was a new Islamic dominion free of Western and other non-Islamic encumbrances. The polluted, corrupt society around them, perceived as un-Islamic, was rejected. These new radical Sunni Muslim organizations, to be found in Algeria, Indonesia, Egypt, Malaysia, Syria, Lebanon, Saudi Arabia, Pakistan, Tunisia and elsewhere in the Muslim world, led the drive for Islamic and societies and states (Rubin 1990a: 10–26). Islamic militants claim that there can be no genuine Islamic state 'unless and until its rulers implement rigorously the Word and Law of God [as outlined in the Quran] thus enabling the believers to live complete, integrated Muslim lives. No believer can or must accept any law or regulation that derives from non-Muslim sources' (Vatikiotis 1991: 11).

Islam may also provide a basis for solidarity for minorities, as in Burma, Thailand and the Philippines. In addition, Muslims wherever they reside may agitate for the ability to practise Islam within a juridicial system based on the *sharia*. The goal is not independence, but rather the recognition of the needs of Muslim minorities. Obviously this will have political connotations. Examples includes Muslims in India, Nigeria, Burma, Thailand and the Philippines. Needless to say, such groups and organizations are not by any means ideologically identical. There is also the important doctrinal division *between* sects within Islam, broadly the Sunni–Shia division. This rift helps to illuminate some of the causes of recent conflicts both *between* states (e.g. Iran and Iraq during 1980–8) and *within* states (e.g. aspects of the 1975–91 Lebanese civil war or the Shia revolt against the government of Saddam Hussein in Iraq following the 1990–1 Gulf War). Thus, for analytical purposes, it is unhelpful to treat 'Islam' as a uniform socio-political phenomenon encompassing undifferentiated manifestations and beliefs which transcend place and time.

It is appropriate to define categories or types of Muslim because political choices may or may not be expressed through an Islamic focus. Four categories may be identified: nominal, traditionalist, mainstream and radical. First, there is the nominal Muslim who is only so described because he or she was born to Muslim parents. Examples are Muslims born in Britain, France or elsewhere in the West who adopt all the trappings of Western society. For such people the state of being a Muslim is irrelevant to both political and social beliefs. Second, there is the observant Muslim, the follower of the five Pillars of Islam: the belief in one God whose Prophet was Muhammad, daily prayer, alms giving, fasting during Ramadan and pilgrimage to Mecca. He or she is unlikely to perceive politics through an Islamic focus and may be described as a traditionalist. Then there is the group which we may call 'Islamic reformers' or 'Islamic liberals'. They wish to retain the Islamic framework but to add to it by, for example, the creation of a modern infrastructure or banking system, which would involve compromise and contact with the West, in order to gain technological, financial and investment opportunities. In other words, Islam in this perspective is regarded as a belief system that is 'broad and flexible enough to be able to accommodate itself effectively to the changing requirements of time and place' (Ayubi 1991: 67). Neither of these categories of people perceives of Islam as a political belief system or ideology.

Continuing along the spectrum we come to those often labelled as 'fundamentalists', although I prefer to call them 'Islamists' – followers of a politico-religion – for reasons noted in Chapter 2. Ayubi (1991: 68) usefully identifies such people as followers of the three Ds: Islam as a *din* (religion), *dunya* (way of life) and *dawla* (an Islamic state). Islamists may or may not advocate or use violent tactics to attain their objectives. Some accept the desirability or at least necessity of *jihad*, i.e. a struggle, sometimes violent, to achieve Islam's hegemony, as the *de facto* 'sixth pillar' of Islam. Such groups include Egyptian organizations such as al-Jihad (responsible for the killing of President Sadat in 1981), Lebanon's Hizbullah (responsible for kidnapping and imprisoning Westerners in the late 1980s), Algeria's Islamic Salvation Front (FIS), the al-Shabiba al-islamiyya of Morocco, el-Nahad of Tunisia, and HAMAS, active in Algeria and Palestine (Voll and von der Mehden 1990: 113). It is not my intention here to describe such groups in detail, as a number of useful accounts already exist (see, for example, Sivan 1985; Rubin 1990a; Voll and von der Mehden 1990; Ayubi 1991). Fundamentally, within different national contexts, each wishes to see the creation of some form of 'Islamic state', one in which Islam is the dominant philosophy. Below we shall look at Islam in government; in Iran from 1979, Sudan from 1989 and Pakistan from 1990. We shall also examine radical Islamic groups whose aim is to establish an Islamic state, in Algeria, in Saudi Arabia and in Tunisia. Finally, in order to highlight the differing nature of Islam in different cultural settings, we are also concerned with Islam in Indonesia and Malaysia.

From the perspective of this book, with its focus on religion in politics within a number of Third World contexts, we need to analyse the background to the emergence of radical Islamic groups in the context of modernization and the dominance of the West. Contrary to the usual Western assumption that Islam was rampantly triumphant in recent times, the fourteenth century of the Islamic era (which ended on 19 November 1979) was regarded by many Muslims as one of the 'eclipse of Islam and the proliferation of the challenges to its call' (Sivan 1985: 1). Even though the Muslim century ended with the successes of the Iranian Revolution and the storming of the Grand Mosque in Mecca by Islamists, they came after a long run of defeats. The abolition of the caliphate (1924), the military victories of the (Jewish) Israelis over the (Muslim) Arabs (1948, 1956, 1967 and 1973) and the invasion of Lebanon (in 1982) were regarded as defeats for Islam by many Muslims. Other setbacks included the official marginalization of Islam in Turkey, the Soviet central Asian republics, Albania, South Yemen and Bangladesh. Muslim minorities were persecuted in the Philippines, Burma, Thailand, Ethiopia and elsewhere. In addition, as we have already noted, rulers became increasingly secularized, even if a separation between religion and state was rarely formally undertaken. Nationalism seemed to undermine religious solidarity, and sometimes to replace it. The Islamic establishment was regarded as often completely subservient to government, acting as its justificatory mouthpiece. Individualism and materialism appeared to have replaced Islamic solidarity, as Westernization – cultural, economic, social and political – took over.

The Islamic resurgence is a direct result of both the defeats and the West's apparent dominance. It is reflected in a number of characteristics. It comprises:

> an evident regeneration of *culture*, a profound renewal of *religiosity*, a political exploitation of the *Islamic vocabulary* by governments that use it to reinforce their legitimacy and to strengthen their power, and a *use of religion* by a political opposition that is often left with no other means of expression . . . along a scale going from conservative fundamentalism to extreme radicalism.
>
> (Vatin 1982: 246–7)

Thus the major concerns of the Islamic resurgence are 'a reaction to alienation and a quest for authenticity' (Ayubi 1991: 217). To those resisting foreign domination in Iran, Algeria and elsewhere, Islam provided a 'medium of cultural nationalism that is both defiant and self-assuring' (Ayubi 1991: 217). In other words a type of revolution – of ideas, of education, of popular culture, of the economy, of politics – in relation to perceived Western domination is spearheaded by the Islamists. Despite doctrinal differences between the Shias and Sunnis, the single most influential impetus for the Islamic resurgence was the Iranian Revolution of 1978–80. This was of quintessential importance because it demonstrated that Islam could be a force of such power as to unseat even the most apparently entrenched, pro-Western leaders and governments. Radical clerics and a militant Islamized popular movement combined to overthrow the bastion of Westernization in the Middle East, Shah Pahlavi and his regime. As a result of its international importance, we need to look first at Iran's revolution, as well as the resulting 'Islamic state', as together they symbolized the political re-emergence and rejuvenation of Islam as a world political force.

Shias, Sunnis and the Iranian revolution

Because of Islam's pivotal role, the overthrow of the Shah in 1979 was one of the most spectacular political upheavals of recent times (Cammack *et al.* 1989: 175). The Shah's regime was not a shaky monarchy but a powerful centralized autocratic state possessing a strong and feared security service (SAVAK) and an apparently loyal and cohesive officer corps. Unlike earlier revolutions in other Muslim countries, including Egypt, Iraq, Syria and Libya, it was not a secular, left-wing revolution from above but one which had massive popular participation. The outcome of the revolutionary process was a clerical, authoritarian regime. The forces which overthrew the Shah came from all urban social classes, the different nationalities and ideologically varying political parties and movements, but an Islamic Republic was eventually declared. Although Islam was a declared characteristic of Colonel Gadaffi's ideology after the 1969 revolution (especially in terms of stated foreign policy goals, as we shall see in Chapter 5), in Iran Islam was the supreme domestic mobilizer. It was the *ulama* organized in the Islamic Republican Party which came to power, established an Islamic constitution and dominated the post-revolutionary institutions.

Iran's revolution was internationally significant in a number of ways. It was the first in modern history (i.e. since the French Revolution of 1789) in which the 'dominant ideology, forms of organization, leading personnel, and proclaimed goal have all been religious in appearance and inspiration' (Halliday 1987: 32). The guide for the post-revolution Iranian state was the tenets of the Quran and the Sunnah, i.e. the traditions of the Prophet, comprising what Muhammad said, did and approved. Linked to this is the second point: while economic and political factors played a major part in the growth of the anti-Shah movement, the leadership of that movement (i.e. the clerics) saw the revolution's goals primarily in terms of building an Islamic state in which Western materialism and political ideas would be rejected. This was to be of major and growing importance in the context of Iran's poor international relations with the West generally. Yet the rejectionist tendency within Iran's ruling post-revolution elite was to lose much of the ground it had gained, following the death of Ayatollah Khomeini in June 1989, just months after the end of the bloody Iran–Iraq war in 1988. The result was the growing dominance of the pragmatic state president, Hashemi Rafsanjani, and his political allies as it became clear that Iran's government was in dire need of Western investment, technology and aid to help build its revolution in the context of growing societal discontent. The lesson of this was that even a successful Islamic revolution cannot succeed in splendid isolation. Iranians, like people everywhere, hoped for improving living standards and were not content with increased Islamization of state and society, which many perceived as little more than political and social repression behind a religious facade.

Third, the Islamic government in Iran was more concerned than the supposedly internationalist Soviet revolutionary regime after 1917 with spreading a universalist ideology. Iran was projected 'as the first part of an insurgent Muslim community to overthrow its oppressors' (Halliday 1987: 33), i.e. the 'Great Satan' (the USA), its allies and the 'godless' Soviet regime. Iran's Islamic government has paid much more than lip-service to the idea of *Dar al-Islam*, i.e. the nation of Islam. Yet, as we shall see in Chapter 5, Iran's religious goals coincide with more prosaic national security concerns. This suggests that the Western conception of the state as a discrete polity behind 'hard' frontiers remained as important to Iran's Islamic rulers as to secular leaders elsewhere.

Fourth, Iran is in a unique position in that it is the only Islamic country where the official religion and the religion of the overwhelming majority of the people is Imamite Shiism. This is of significance in assessing the impact of its revolution internationally. According to Shias, the rightful imam after Hussein was his son; then the imamate descended from father to son until the twelfth imam, who disappeared shortly after his birth in 874. The Imamites claim that the twelfth imam has not in fact died but rather gone into a state known as 'occultation' (*ghayba*: literally, absence); he is believed to be alive and at an appropriate moment will return to set things right in the world. The 'Hidden Imam' is also known as the 'guided one' or Mahdi, a kind of Messiah figure.

There is an important body of Imamite Shias in Iraq, amounting to about half of the population, living in the south and in the forefront of attempts, with Iranian help, to overthrow the regime of Saddam Hussein following the Gulf War in 1991. Smaller groups of Shias live in Lebanon, Saudi Arabia and Bahrain. Militant Shias had an integral impact both on the course of the 1975–91 civil war and on the Western hostages imbroglio of the mid-1980s to the early 1990s. Shia members of the Lebanese wing of Hizbullah, the captors of Terry Waite and other Western hostages, had close links with elements within Iran's governing circle. Attempts to resolve the Western hostages issue in 1991–2 were perceived to be closely linked with the desire of 'moderates' (led by President Rafsanjani) to re-forge Iran's links with the United States, Britain and others, despite the *fatwa* issued by Ayatollah Khomeini against the writer Salman Rushdie (Parry *et al.* 1991: 2–4).

Groups of Imamite Shias, with close ties to Iran and Iraq, live in Bahrain, where they were implicated in a December 1981 plot to overthrow the sheikh, and are scattered elsewhere throughout the Middle East (Lawson 1989: 18). Altogether, however, Shias constitute only about 8 per cent of all Muslims in contrast to nearly 90 per cent who are Sunnites. The other forms of Shiism, Zaydism and Ismailism, represented by the Imams of Sanaa in Yemen and by the Aga Khan's community respectively, form only 2–3 per cent of all Muslims, and do not regard themselves as akin to the Imamites. The impetus to political radicalism has been Iran, yet the very nature of Imamite Shiism contains within it the seeds of rebellion.

Imamite Shiism has an image of itself which differs from that of Sunnism in important ways (Montgomery Watt 1990: 127–8). It regards itself as alone the true Islam, since the Sunnis allegedly fell into error when they accepted Abu-Bakr and rejected Ali as the rightful successor to Muhammad in 632. A distinctive feature of the Imamites is that they are looking forward to the return of the Mahdi, and in the meantime it is a temporary measure that they follow the teaching of their imams as interpreted by the *ulama*. The Imamites think of themselves as distinguished by their loyalty to the house of the Prophet, commemorating the martyrdom of his grandson, Hussein, at Kerbela (where in an act of great religious symbolism for Shias, Saddam Hussein's armed forces massacred thousands of Kurds in 1988 by the use of poison gas). Thus at the heart of Iranian Shiism is the figure of Hussein, the pure and upright, struggling against the powers of evil represented by the armies of Yazid. Indeed, Iranian Shiism regards itself as the citadel of truth and light holding out against the error, darkness and evil of the Sunnis and the non-Muslims.

Although much of the Sunni world view and self-image is shared by the Imamite Shias, there are also differences. In the latter view there is less emphasis on unchangingness, since worldly conditions will be changed for the better when the Mahdi appears. There is the same idealization of Islamic life under Muhammad himself and under Ali, but there are criticisms of life under the first three caliphs. There is not the same emphasis as among Sunnis on Dar al-Islam (world of Islam), doubtless because of the restricted numbers and geographical distribution of the Shias. In short, Shias tend to be much more questioning of the status quo than do the Sunnis; it is this that forms the basis of their willingness to take radical political actions.

Shias have not always been in a pre-eminent political and religious position in Iran. For some six centuries the Imamite Shias were scattered throughout Islamic lands in small groups, and included Arabs as well as Persians. A great change was brought about in 1501 when a leader, Shah Ismail, conquered much of Iran and made Imamism the official religion. This led gradually to a concentration of Imamites in Iran, apart from the large body in Iraq where there were important Imamite shrines, and a few smaller groups in other localities; at the same time the Sunnis in Iran faded out. Iran also became a centre for Imamite scholarship. The dynasty founded by Shah Ismail, the Safavids, continued to rule Iran until 1722, and by that date Imamism was well established. Despite the periodic occupation of Iran by Afghan warlords during the eighteenth century, Imamism remained the dominant religion. The Qajar dynasty, which came to power towards the end of the eighteenth century and continued until 1924, before being replaced by the last Shah's father, Reza Khan Pahlavi, needed the support of the Imamite scholars and in return supported them (Montgomery Watt 1990: 127). His son attempted to modernize without sufficient concern with Islam and tradition; as a result he was overthrown.

There is wide agreement that the root cause of the Iranian Revolution was the social upheaval occasioned by the rapidity with which Reza Shah was able to pursue modernizing policies after the increase in oil revenues from 1973. Yet earlier moves towards the secularization of Iran's politics and society initiated by his father, Reza Khan, contributed substantially to the tensions which were finally to explode in the revolution of 1978–80. The Pahlavis, deeply impressed by Kemal Ataturk's political and social reforms, sought to emulate Turkey's modernization. Reza Khan's reform of Iranian law led to the replacement of the *sharia* by a non-religious legal code based on the French *Code Civil*. His educational reforms, designed to create a Westernized bureaucracy, also reduced the scope of Islamic influence by undermining institutions of traditional Muslim education, such as *maktabs* (mosque schools) and *madrassas* (seminaries) (Shaikh 1989a: 110).

The attempted modernization of Iranian society mirrored Turkish developments in two other important ways: women were legally required to abandon the veil, while a series of land reforms sought to modify proprietary relations between landlords and peasants; both incurred the wrath of conservatives. These modernizations – and the *ulama*'s reaction to them – should be understood against the tradition of political activism among the Iranian clergy. The Tobacco Revolt of 1892, for example, led thousands of Iranians to refrain from smoking tobacco as a result of a religious ruling issued by Iran's leading clerics, and the Constitutional Revolution of 1905–9 ensured that no laws repugnant to Islam were passed by an elected Assembly (Montgomery Watt 1990: 132).

In reflection on the causes and peculiarities of the Iranian Revolution, it is noteworthy that an apparently stable, Western-supported, modernizing regime, backed up by a large, well-equipped army and internal security force, could be brought down relatively easily by a mass protest movement, led and articulated by religious teachers. It is superficially plausible to argue that the Shah's fall represented a backlash by reactionary elements, notably the *ulama*, the bazaar merchants and the socially disoriented new urban migrants who had, in some way, missed out on the fruits of petrodollars-driven modernization. Such an assessment is only a partial explanation, however. To equate the opposition to the Shah with a general, defensive reaction against modernity misrepresents the nature of the opposition movement, and falls into the trap of seeing Islamists as reactionaries in religious garb.

The anti-Shah revolt was a result of the patchy nature of modernization rather than a reactionary response to the process *per se*. The key to understanding the overthrow of the Shah is to comprehend the class nature of the modernization programme. In other words, the incompleteness of Iran's capitalist-oriented development disproportionately favoured the Westernized, middle-class urban groups who were in a position to benefit, as well as the skilled and semi-skilled labour aristocracy in the modern industrial sector. This development unsurprisingly heightened the already growing polarization between the 'haves' and 'have-nots', which exacerbated pre-existing structural inequalities in the country. In addition, the perceived subservience of Iran to the United States, the Shah's apparent contempt for the traditional culture of Iran, the endemic corruption associated with modernization, and the increasingly autocratic and repressive nature of his rule, combined to energize and mobilize a protest movement which took to the streets in the only possible form of mass protest.

Under the circumstances it was the Iranian *ulama* that were able to unite and focus disparate opposition groups. Practically all the opposition groups in Iran except the small secular communist groups used Islam as an ideological referent, but this is not unexpected given the problems associated with both (Western, 'godless') capitalism and (Soviet, 'godless') communism. Given Islam's cultural position in Iran it was very likely that opponents of the Shah's regime would locate their criticisms within an Islamic world view; at the same time, part of the attraction of Islam, especially in its Shia context in Iran, is its perceived breadth and attraction to people of varying ideological adherence, including

> Its powerful symbolism of steadfastness, suffering and self-sacrifice in pursuit of truth and justice displayed in its various dramatic rituals; its remarkable capacity for redefining political conflicts in religious terms; its populist logic and vocabulary of pitting the 'disinherited' against the 'oppressors'; and its messianic promise of a just social order with the return of the 'Hidden Imam' make it an unusually powerful religion of protest.
>
> (Banuazizi 1987: 304)

Islam was sufficiently broad and imprecise, a catch-all repositry of hopes and ideals, for it to act – albeit briefly – rather like the Roman Catholic Church did in Poland and elsewhere in Eastern Europe in the late 1980s during the death throws of communism. Religious beliefs and religious leaders both symbolized and galvanized much wider constituencies, stimulating decisive political choices. As in Eastern Europe, however, it was not religion *per se* in Iran that remained the unchallenged hegemonic force in the post-revolutionary period, when practical economic, political and social issues had to be addressed. Even though Islamic world views dominated, they were by no means undifferentiated. Different versions of Islam appealed to particular social strata or groups that played a role in the revolutionary struggle. Nor was it a simple matter to keep together an ideologically disparate coalition which had been united only by hatred of the Shah, his kow-towing to Western interests, and his socio-political and economic systems. Both the *ulama*'s domination of the anti-Shah coalition movement and its later political hegemony should be seen as unexpected triumphs of the clerics' organizing and mobilizing skills in the context of a divided society.

The political role of the *ulama* in the post-Shah era had been prefigured in the early 1970s by ideas expressed by the eventual leader of the revolution. Whereas in the early 1960s Ayatollah Khomeini had championed a parliamentary form of government, a decade later he argued that the clergy had to rebel against despotic governments. He declared the monarchy an un-Islamic institution and called for a total reform of political society in which the *ulama* would take a direct and active role in the creation of an Islamic state. Although it was based on a long tradition of *ulama* opposition to the abuse of monarchical powers, this was an important innovation. Following the success of the revolution, Khomeini attempted to institutionalize the political power of the Islamic clerics in an Islamic republican system of government (Ferdows 1983: 254). This form of rule was based on an Islamic constitution, underpinned by all-encompassing Islamic laws. The new system was believed by Khomeini and his followers to be the panacea for all the socio-economic and political ills of Iran and, for that matter, the whole Islamic world. Khomeini claimed that the new society would be based on simplicity, Islamic morality, brotherly [*sic*] love, close and caring relations, and economic equity and social justice. It would be run by a divinely sanctified leadership, headed by Khomeini himself (Banuazizi 1987: 304).

The legitimacy and authority of the post-revolutionary state was rooted in consultative mechanisms, prefigured in Khomeini's ideal of an Islamic state described earlier. It was centred on the concept of Vilayat-e-Faqih, the Guardianship of the Jurisconsult, the supreme authority of the state (Sardar 1985: 142). This was initially Khomeini, until his death in June 1989. His successor was Ali Khamenei, although it would be legitimate for the office to be filled by a committee rather than an individual. In the absence of the still-awaited Twelfth Imam, the Vilayat-e-Faqih has wide-ranging, but not absolutist, powers. These include the ability to declare war and to appoint the armed forces' commanders, the Chief Justice, and the six jurists (*fuqaha*) of the Shura-e-Nigahban (Guardianship Council).

The Shura-e-Nigahban is the second most powerful political body. Half of the twelve members are lawyers, elected by the Majlis-e-Shura-Islami (the Parliament). Matters of Islamic principle are determined by a majority vote of the six jurists. The entire Council approves all the legislation passed by the Majlis. The third non-elective body is the Supreme Judicial Council, the head of the independent judiciary of the state. These unelected bodies are supplemented by three others, whose members are voted into power. These are the Majlis-e-Khubragan (the Assembly of Experts), who elect the Vilayat-e-Faqih; the Majlis-e-Shura-Islami, consisting of 270 elected deputies, the main legislative organ of the state; and, finally, the office of the President, elected by direct ballot and ratified by the Vilayat-e-Faqih.

The former nominates a prime minister who in turn chooses the Cabinet (Council of Ministers).

From this brief examination of Iran's structures of governance, it would appear to be a theocracy. Yet the Muslim belief that 'no man [sic], class . . . or sect has any special relationship with God' means that the Vilayat-e-Faqih does not have any particular spiritual powers and is not God's representative (Sardar 1985: 143). He does not rule like the Roman Catholic Pope, who issues decrees which have the status of religious law. The Vilayat-e-Faqih may be dismissed by the Guardianship Council if he acts, in their opinion, contrary to Islamic law. In fact, no single institution has absolute power; a system of checks and balances ensures that there are contributions from all sides in law-making. Bearing in mind the responsibility to enact laws which accord with the *sharia*, there has been a flow of legislation in Iran from Parliament to the Guardianship Council and back again. In this way, new legislation was introduced with the aim of building a modern Islamic society. Areas of concern included land reform, nationalization of certain sectors of the economy and Islamization of the banking system.

Ayatollah Rouhollah Khomeini and his clerical cohorts thus founded a potent revolutionary ideology, a practical programme for an Islamic state and a structure of governance to carry out the political programme. Khomeini was of such stature that he was able, for a time, to bring together the many disparate forces of opposition into a single revolutionary coalition. Opposition groups, spanning the secular ideological spectrum, yet underpinned by an Islamic religious and cultural reality, believed that they would be able to dominate the post-shah period politically, but underestimated the *ulama*'s political skills. In the post-revolutionary period, however, the skills that allowed the *ulama* to dominate opposing political groupings were found to be inadequate to the demands of running a state of 58 million people. The 1980–8 war with Iraq, costing hundreds of thousands of lives and hundreds of millions of dollars, masked for a time the inadequacies of the government in socio-economic development matters. Not long after the *fatwa* against the author Salman Rushdie, and the accompanying hardening of Western attitudes against the regime, Ayatollah Khomeini died in June 1989. From that time, the regime began to try to rebuild its relationship with the West as it became clear that it was desperate for foreign investment. The denationalization of economic enterprises, the coming to positions of influence of technocrats rather than Islamic hardliners, the un-Islamic introduction of a serious family planning programme and the in-fighting within the government between 'pragmatists' and 'hardliners' revealed that the pragmatists were in the ascendant. Such a view was reinforced by Iran's failure to support the Muslims of Iraq in their fight with the 'great Satan', the USA and its allies, in the 1990–1 Gulf War. All this points to the conclusion that the attempted introduction of an Islamic state was far more difficult than the founders envisaged, especially in the context of an economy severely dislocated by war and revolution.

The salience of Islam politically in Iran should be understood in relation to the particular historical, socio-economic, political and cultural conditions within which it took place. More specifically, relevant factors include the unpopularity of the Shah's regime; the social inequalities produced and exacerbated by the country's particular path towards economic development; the cultural dualism created by the overtly Western-oriented regime and elite; the curtailing of the *ulama*'s institutional prerogatives; the inherently oppositional character of Shia Islam *vis-à-vis* the state; and its extensive mobilizational resources across social strata. The revolution in Iran did not reflect the predominance of modern groups or ideologies, such as nationalism, secularism or the workers. Religious actors and their supporters did not seem to be hampered by their 'traditional' beliefs. The latter were most effective in articulating the demands of a movement for social change within the context of an authentic Islamic identity, and in inducing collective action of as radical a nature as any of their modern, secular counterparts. In addition, it was certainly not the case that only anomic and socially dislocated individuals found the Islamic movement politically attractive: in Iran support for the revolution was widespread, crossing social and class barriers. Finally, adherence to a 'traditionalist' religion-based ideology was no bar to the development of considerable political talents. The way in which, for a time, the *ulama* in Iran completely dominated the political scene would appear to suggest that the supposedly unworldly clerics were able to exercise an almost Bolshevik-like degree of political dominance in suitable conditions, with a corollary being a corresponding ability to eliminate political opponents.

None of this should be taken to imply that popular identification or subservience to, and acceptance of, a religiously oriented government can easily be duplicated elsewhere. As I have stressed, much depends on particular social and cultural characteristics which are not readily replicable elsewhere. Yet the new mode of revolution exemplified in Iran appealed to many Muslims in the Third World, given the widespread dissatisfaction with economic and political progress in recent times. This is the case even when the leadership of Shiism is not accepted.

Despite the exemplary impact of the Iranian political upheavals no further examples of popular Islamic revolution occurred in the 1980s and early 1990s. Yet, as was noted earlier, Islam was the banner of numerous opposition movements throughout the Middle East, North Africa and elsewhere where Muslims were substantive groups. The socio-political conditions that were necessary for the emergence of political Islam were by and large the same. They included the experience of one-party or dictatorial regimes which disallowed political opposition; the underpinning cultural effects of Islam; long-term, close ties with either the capitalist West or communist East; political and economic corruption of elites; attempts to develop religion as a tool of the state; and, finally, disenchantment with secular ideologies, including capitalism, socialism, communism and, on occasions, state-centric nationalism.

The characteristics of the Islamic revolution in Iran allow us to make certain tentative conclusions which have a more general relevance. First, and most obviously, the Iran experience indicates that the structural changes accompanying modernization do not necessarily bring about secularism, either at the level of political institutions and processes or in the attitudes and values of individuals who have been exposed to modernizing experiences. Second, Islamic movements have to be seen in relation to the specific processes of social change taking place in their societies, in particular to the issues of the changing position of classes and groups, political participation, identity crisis, the stability of regimes and distributive justice (Dessouki 1982: 8). We shall examine these issues further in other contexts below. To this end we next examine the rise of Islamists in Algeria. Elections in 1990 and 1991 confirmed Islam's position as the chief ideology of opposition, yet a military coup in early 1992 deprived the Islamists of electoral victory in a negation of democracy that ensured the continuation of Algeria's discredited socialist regime.

Algeria, Tunisia and the political challenge of Islam

Algeria represents one example of the typical form of Arab political organization since the Second World War, one of secularism, socialism and one-party power. Following a bloody civil war against the French colonizers the dominant anti-colonial group, the National Liberation Front (FLN), took power in 1962. When the FLN emerged triumphant from the war, organized Islam was seen by the new leaders as a subservient part of the state structure. It was seen as a means to mobilize support for the new state and to reinforce the national identity which had been forged during the nationalist struggle (Deeb 1989a: 6). Unlike in Saudi Arabia, although Islam was the state religion the *sharia* was not made an integral part of the state legal system nor were the *ulama* allowed to play an independent role in legislative matters at the national level. Instead, a Minister of Religious Affairs was appointed, ostensibly to safeguard and promote the interests of Islam. In reality his role was to co-opt Islamic leaders, to ensure Muslims' subservience to the secularized state.

By the mid-1970s, a state-led attempt to secularize and modernize Algerian life – in the name of a Cultural Revolution – had an unwanted consequence: the founding of Islamic revivalist movements (Roberts 1988: 567–75). Following the death of the powerful state president, Boumedienne, in 1978, and the triumph of the Islamic revolution in Iran a year later, an autonomous Islamic movement, Ahl al-Dawa, emerged as a leading opposition voice. Articulating the concerns of many Algerians at the failure of the state's development programmes and its inability to champion Islam, its goal was to introduce an Iranian-style regime. It campaigned for the introduction of *sharia* law, stricter dress codes for women, more religious broadcasts on television and radio, and the banning of alcohol consumption. Following a number of violent clashes in the early 1980s between

Islamic revivalists and those who did not adhere to their views, the government clamped down on Ahl al-Dawa's activities.

By the late 1980s, following the state's acceptance of the desirability of multi-party politics after 30 years of single-party rule, Islamic movements surfaced again to articulate and lead the anti-regime opposition. In the wake of falling world oil prices, the Algerian government, which depended on the monies accrued from the sale of petroleum products for the bulk of its revenue, decided in late 1988 to cut the state subsidies on a number of basic commodities. Serious riots broke out in the main cities and towns as a result. From March 1989, the government deemed it expedient to allow the formation of the first Algerian Islamic political party, the Islamic Salvation Front (FIS).

In the local elections of June 1990, the FIS won 55 per cent of the vote, making it the largest Islamic revivalist party in the Arab world. It gained control of every big city and 32 of Algeria's 48 provinces. FIS-run assemblies soon proceeded to put into practice their plans: in areas they controlled they enforced bans on the sale of alcohol and the wearing of shorts and swimming costumes in the streets, tried to prevent mixed-sex schooling, and stopped *rai* music (a fusion of traditional Algerian and Western rock music) festivals (*The Economist* 4 August 1990: 51). Because of the scale of the FIS victory the FLN government was forced to announce that elections for the National Assembly would be held a year early, in the first quarter of 1991. Later the date was amended to late 1991.

As with other North African and Middle Eastern governments, the FLN was surprised at the scale of support for Saddam Hussein in the 1990–1 Gulf War. Demonstrations in early 1991 organized by the FIS had two demands: that the FLN government express unequivocal support for Saddam Hussein and that it allow general elections immediately. General elections were announced for 27 June 1991, but were postponed following widespread political violence and a number of deaths, and the announcement of a 'state of siege' by President Chadli following the resignation of his cabinet in early June. The FIS's two main leaders, Abbasi Madani and Ali Belhadj, as well as 800 supporters, were arrested. The two were later charged with 'leading an armed conspiracy against the state'. In the ensuing violence more than 40 people were wounded, leading to the resignation of President Chadli as chairman of the FLN (Hooper 1991). These events symbolized the political, ideological and economic bankruptcy of the FLN after three decades of rule.

Following emphatic electoral victories in June 1990 and December 1991 it appeared as though nothing but a coup d'état could prevent the formation of North Africa's first Islamic government. In the event, however, the FIS was denied its expected victory following a coup. The prevention by the army of the FIS taking power was for Islamists the proof that even if Islamic parties gained political power by the ballot box there was no guarantee that they would be allowed to govern. Following widespread protests, 150 Algerians were killed, 700 wounded and 16,000 detained without due process of law by late February 1992 (*Friends for Democracy in Algeria Bulletin* 1 (March 1992): 1). In early March the FIS was banned. The stated justification for this was that the FIS was guilty of electoral malpractices, but the real reason was the determination of Algeria's rulers together with the army and Western governments to prevent an 'Islamic fundamentalist' government from achieving power, *even though this was by the ballot box.* Although there may have been some electoral fraud this was not of sufficient gravity to warrant the military's actions. Rather it showed that 'democracy' was not a desirable end *in itself* if this resulted in rulers unacceptable to governing elites and influential foreign governments: Neither of these wished to see 'another Iran'. The military justified their actions as necessary to protect democracy, arguing that if the FIS came to power it would proclaim an Islamic state and outlaw secular parties. Thus it was necessary to crush democracy to protect it!

The FIS was not the only Islamic party, but the one which had the best organization and strongest social links. Its mostly urban constituency was organized into two wings: a 'moderate' group called Djezara and a 'radical' section known as Salafiya. The former believed in exercising power through joint rule with the President; in effect, a pragmatic, measured process of Islamization. This group was dominant within the FIS at the time of its banning. The Salafiya group believed in a swift transition to an Islamic state by any means necessary, including insurrection or revolution. In a sense the debate about how to achieve an Islamic state mirrored the early twentieth-century argument between secular socialists in Russia: how to achieve the desirable political system, by the ballot box and reform or by revolution. The crushing of the FIS by the military-dominated government did not settle this question. There was no likelihood of the Islamists fading away. If support could no longer be expressed through the FIS then its rivals HAMAS (Islamic Society Movement) and An Nahda (Renaissance) would almost certainly be the recipients of the FIS's proscription. Both of these groups were transnational groups: HAMAS had links with the Egyptian Muslim Brotherhood and was active within the Palestinian resistance on the West Bank and the Gaza Strip. By the early 1990s it was challenging the secular Palestine Liberation Organization for political leadership. As in Algeria, in occupied Palestine the rise of radical Islam reflected years, if not decades, of cultural suppression, political repression and economic disappointment.

The second group, An Nahda, had its roots in Tunisia and was especially strong within Algeria's Constantine province, which borders that country. An Nahda was the lineal descendant of the banned MTI (Islamic Tendency Movement), which had been formed in the early 1970s. Initially encouraged by Tunisia's secular government as a counterweight to increasing left-wing agitation emanating from the campuses of the University of Tunis, by the end of the 1970s MTI members were being imprisoned and leaders sentenced to death accused of various political crimes (Deeb 1989b: 268). By the early 1980s MTI was effectively banned. Some of its more zealous members turned to terrorism, including bomb attacks in Tunis, which frightened both the government and foreign tourists, who stayed away from the country, greatly affecting its economic well-being. The state attempted to crack down hard on the Islamists. By late 1987 President Bourguiba, who is claimed to have been senile by this time, planned to extend the death penalty to all convicted members of MTI. The fear that such an action would lead to more violence and bloodshed was allegedly the chief reason for the overthrow of Bourguiba (Deeb 1989b: 269).

The new ruler, Zine el Abidine Ben Ali, set in motion a process which resulted in the 'Tunisian National Pact of 1988'. This conference of significant political and social groups – including the armed forces – was an attempt to articulate a consensual path for politics and society. It reflected both the undiminished strength of the Islamists and the government's pragmatic ability to understand that it could not defeat them by terror and brute force. The elections of 1989 saw the formation of 'son of MTI': An Nahda. The state did not allow An Nahda to use the word 'Islam' in its name. Despite this An Nahda received 15 per cent of the vote nationally and some 30 per cent in several urban areas, including Tunis (Anderson 1991). Nevertheless the ruling party, the Constitutional Democratic Rally, allegedly rigged the poll to take every seat in parliament (*The Economist* 18 May 1991: 75). By early 1991, conditions between radical Islamists and the government of President Ben Ali had deteriorated. Arrests of An Nahda members increased, with some 8000 incarcerated in 1991 according to Amnesty International (*The Guardian* 4 March 1992). Its newspaper was closed and its student group was proscribed. The Gulf War led to a split in An Nahda between a pro-Saudi wing and a pro-Iraq wing, broadly, as in the FIS in Algeria, into 'moderate' and 'radical' factions. The government was quick to exploit the split. Negotiations ensued between the 'moderates', led by Abdelfatteh Morou, for the legalization of a constitutional Islamist party.

The crackdown by the Algerian and Tunisian regimes against Islamic political parties was welcomed by the Egyptian and Moroccan governments, each of which was trying to control its own Islamic movements. Fear of Islamic rhetoric to 'fundamentalize' the states was sufficient excuse to clamp down on the Islamists. Such governments publicly espoused a plurality of political expression and parties, in line with world opinion, while at the same time effectively squashing Islamic groups. Opposition leaders and human rights campaigners argued that the repression which halted Tunisia's and Algeria's tentative steps away from one-party rule weakened the moral high ground that democratic elements could claim, while at the same time playing into the hands of those who wished to impose an Islamic state by force. Yet, as we have seen, Islam is not the reified, undifferentiated force it is often portrayed as. 'Militant' or 'radical' wings compete with more 'moderate' groups. The former, by no means necessarily dominant, wish to create Islamic states by any means possible. They are impatient, and dismissive of the ballot box as a Western imposition over divine rule. 'Moderates', on the other hand, would welcome power-sharing with secular regimes and would be content with a gradual, partial Islamization. The danger in crushing all Islamic-oriented dissent is that alienated individuals would turn to terrorism to accomplish their objectives. The problem was how to arrive at a viable *modus operandi* which would allow governments to begin to tackle the serious problems in a consensual manner. The Tunisian model of consensus was seen as appropriate only as long as Islamists remained quiescent. The divergence in political goals between secular and non-secular perceptions remained.

Islam in government: Sudan, Pakistan and Saudi Arabia

Generally the Islamic revolution in Iran exemplified wider developments which have manifested themselves in the rise of political Islam. Sometimes, Islam was proclaimed as the hegemonial ideology in a bid for both domestic support and international succour. In Sudan, for example, the military regime of Lt-Gen. Omar Hassan al-Bashir cynically called itself an Islamic government, and instituted *sharia* law for three reasons: to gain aid from the Muslim countries of the Middle East; to justify harsh treatment of those forced to steal to live in the absence of alternatives; and to unify the northern Sudan Arabs against the Christians and animists of the south in the long-running civil war, which cost $1 million a day in one of the world's poorest countries (Mallia 1991). The power behind the al-Bashir regime was the National Islamic Front, which introduced the amputation of limbs for theft. This bears no relation to the spirit of Quranic law, which stipulates that if someone is driven to steal by poverty, compassion should be shown. That the amputees in Sudan are predominantly black, non-Arab and poor highlights the crude racism of those in power. Iran was a major backer of Sudan's Islamic government, partly for ideological reasons and partly out of strategic concerns.

The establishment of an Islamic state in Iran was via revolution and in Sudan by military coup. In Algeria Islamists were denied political victory by the armed forces, while in Tunisia they were dealt with heavily by the state, briefly tolerated, then circumscribed again. In Pakistan, by way of contrast, Islamic rule came by the ballot box in October 1990, even though Pakistan was founded in 1947 specifically as a homeland for India's Muslims (Islam 1981: 55). The state was founded on the idea that the Muslims of India formed a secular *nation* and were entitled to a territorial homeland of their own, in much the same way that Jews (and especially Zionists) in the diaspora considered that they would only flourish within their own nation state (Lapidus 1988: 742). Yet Pakistan (initially in two halves: East and West, separated by over one thousand miles of hostile Indian territory) had practically no history of national unity (Shaikh 1986). Members of the Pakistani 'nation' did not speak a common language; they did not have a homogeneous culture; they did not even have a common geographical or economic unit. Thus Pakistan was emphatically not a nation in the traditional Western sense: a group of people living in a contiguous territory who believe they have the same ethnic origins, and share linguistic, religious and other cultural attributes. There were, then, remarkable ethnic, linguistic and geographical differences between the two parts of Pakistan. They proved to be insurmountable: following a civil war, in 1971 the independent state of Bangladesh (formerly East Pakistan) was created with India's help.

At the time of the state's establishment, the main problem for Pakistan's rulers was how to create a national identity to suit the reality of the new political boundaries and to create an acceptable and stable regime for a populace divided by sharp ethnic, cultural, regional, economic, linguistic, ideological and even religious differences. Initially, it was assumed that the larger umbrella of Muslim identity would take care of these differences. The political elite espoused an Islamic form of nationalism as a unifying symbol for the state of Pakistan. The appeal to their heterogeneous people's shared Muslim heritage was enough to overcome the immediate differences but not enough to suppress the contradictions of Muslim religious feeling, regional nationalisms and class antagonisms within the new state. As Lapidus (1988: 742) puts it: 'Pakistan was born as an Islamic state to differentiate it from the rest of the [Indian] subcontinent, but Muslim identity [did] not prove adequate to unite the country internally.'

Pakistan came into being in 1947 with at least two different concepts of what it meant to be an Islamic state. Over the next 45 years, political power in (West) Pakistan reflected this, oscillating between secular and Islamic politicians. On the one hand, the secularized political elite considered Islam a communal, political and national identity stripped of its religious content. On the other, a segment of the populace, led by the *ulama* and other religious leaders, expected a state whose constitution, institutions and routines of daily life would be governed by the *sharia* and Islamic norms. A struggle over both the role of Islam and the ethnic and regional rivalries between West and East Pakistan delayed a constitution until 1956. This declared Pakistan to be an 'Islamic state', and made all parliamentary legislation subject to review by an Islamic Research Institute. In 1958, following a military coup led by General Ayub Khan, the constitution was abolished and a Republic of Pakistan declared, the aim was to try to curb the power of the religious leaders (Shaikh 1989b: 205). Muslim orthodox opinion was fiercely critical of the regime's new reforms. The *ulama* mobilized public opinion and forced the National Assembly in 1963 to restore the Islamic provisions of the 1956 constitution.

In March 1969, popular pressure forced Ayub to step aside in favour of a transitional military government headed by General Yahya Khan. Pakistan's first general election was held in December 1970, with the main political issue being the rivalry between the Western and Eastern parts of the country. The results confirmed the *de facto* political division: Sheikh

Mujibar Rahman's Awami League gained an overwhelming majority in the East, while Zulfiqar Ali Bhutto's Pakistan People's Party was successful in the West (Shaikh 1989b). Fundamental disagreements concerning the modalities of power, not over the role of Islam, but in particular the right of Sheikh Mujib to form a government, led subsequently to the civil war which concluded with the founding of Bangladesh.

In January 1972, Bhutto was sworn in as Prime Minister of a truncated Pakistan. High on the agenda was the question of an Islamic state. Its significance was all the more poignant as it was clear that a distinct Islamic identity, which had ostensibly been the basis of Pakistan in 1947, had failed to guarantee the unity of the state. Even though Bhutto's preference was for an essentially secular constitution, in order to secure the political support of religious parties, such as the Jamiat-al Ulema-i-Islam, he found it expedient to describe the new political programme as one based on the notion of 'Islamic socialism', and to declare Islam as the state religion. This was not, however, enough to keep religious parties acquiescent in Bhutto's rule. The conduct of his personal life, his disregard for religious observances and his liking for alcohol allowed the religious opposition to fuel public sentiment against his government and to press for the introduction of an Islamic state. In July 1977, as opposition rose to a crescendo, heightened by economic failures, Bhutto was deposed by a military coup led by the recently appointed army chief of staff, General Zia ul-Haq (Islam 1981: 58–9).

While the justification for Zia's coup d'état was to restore the country's political stability, he was well aware of the need to gain the support of the country's powerful religion-based political parties. Early in 1979, Zia announced his government's intention to introduce an Islamic system. This was followed in June 1980 by the introduction of a legal code that was deemed to be consistent with the *sharia* (Shaikh 1989b: 207). However, far from uniting the country as Zia had planned, the new reforms led to widespread criticisms. On the one hand, women's groups and human rights organizations condemned Zia's proposed Islamization as a curtailment of freedoms; on the other, the programme met with resistance from Pakistan's Shia minority who were critical of the government's proposals to introduce *zakat* (alms tax). The Tehrik-i-Nifaz-i-Fiqah-i-Jafria (TNFJ; the Movement for the Implementation of the Shia Code) was formed in early 1979, later (in 1987) transforming itself from a religious pressure group into a political party. The TNFJ's main political goal was to enable Shias to resist the application of Hanafi laws, i.e. the main Sunni code, and to opt instead for laws based on a Shia code derived from the Jafria school of jurisprudence. Domestically support for the TNFJ was high in the Shia areas of Pakistan, i.e. in the North West Frontier Province and in parts of Baluchistan in the south. Internationally, strong links were forged with the Shias' co-religionists in Iran.

The issue of which religious code to follow in Pakistan was the cause of sectarian violence between Sunnis and Shias, which led to over 70 dead between 1984 and 1988. The violence was not stopped by the controlled (perhaps rigged) 'no-party' elections of 1985, won by Zia's protégé, Mohammad Khan Junejo. In August 1988, the leader of the TNFJ, Allama al-Hussaini, was assassinated at his home in Peshawar. Shia outrage at the murder fuelled speculation later in August that Shia militants were behind the plane crash which resulted in the deaths of Zia and top members of Pakistan's military establishment soon after (Shaikh 1989b: 208).

Just before his death, Zia presided over the introduction of the *sharia*, simultaneously repealing all existing secular civil laws. The new ordinance contained provisions for Islamic fiscal laws and the creation of religious courts, or Shariat Benches. The latter were to introduce Islamic personal law, especially in areas relating to women's rights, which had until then been regulated by the Family Laws Ordinance of 1962. The new ordinance also provided for two new commissions on the Islamization of the economy and the country's education system. Zia's death effectively postponed the introduction of the *sharia*, however, as a general election in November 1988 led to the re-election of the PPP, now led by Bhutto's daughter, Benazir. The failure of Zia's military regime to deal with sectarian violence and the apparent widespread dislike of the speed and lack of widespread consultation of the attempted Islamization of the country was the background for her electoral victory.

Benazir Bhutto found herself excoriated by Islamic figures because she was a woman in power (Thapar 1990). Violent protests in Pakistan's capital Islamabad, in early 1989, against Salman Rushdie's *The Satanic Verses* gave the dissatisfied the signal to attack. Riding on the wave of Islamic outrage against the book, a gathering of 2000 religious leaders declared that it was against Islamic principles to have a woman as head of an Islamic state (*New Internationalist* June 1989). The religious leaders who attacked Bhutto in 1989 were the same people, by and large, who had led protests against her father in 1977. On that occasion, the charge had been 'godless socialism'. The anti-Benazir Bhutto coalition, affiliated to a number of Islamized political parties, including Jamyat-i-Islami, Jamyat Ulema Islam and Jamyat Ulem Pakistan, won very few seats in November 1988's National Assembly elections.

Pakistan's second major political issue, that of ethnic and regional rivalries, combined with the Islam issue to bring down Bhutto's government in October 1990, less than two years after it took power. While the PPP commanded a clear majority in Sind, and could depend on working a coalition in the North West Frontier Province and Baluchistan, it was unable to form a government in the Punjab (Evans 1990). Here, a provincial government, the Islami Jamhoori Ittehad or Islamic Democratic Front, espoused both a desire for Islamization and the championing of Punjabi autonomy. The importance of religion in Pakistan's complex mosaic of interests was underlined when the PPP government made it plain that it was not out to antagonize the Islamic establishment. Bhutto made no real moves to dismantle the foundations of Zia's Islamic state, and was forced by male bigotry to 'Islamize' her own appearance: red lipstick and large, flamboyant earrings were out; headscarves, shawls and plain clothes were in.

Such gestures did not save her from crushing electoral defeat. The opposition Islamic Democratic Alliance (IDA) won 105 seats to the PPP's 45. Mian Nawaz Sharif, a youngish former minister of Punjab province, was guaranteed the support of tribal members, the IDA and independents. As a result, the IDA was guaranteed a solid majority in the 217-member National Assembly (Thapar 1990). Sharif's savouring of victory was short-lived, however. As with Middle Eastern Muslim states, the 1990–1 Gulf War threw the country's politics into a further period of turmoil. While the National Assembly voted to make the *sharia* code the country's supreme law, Islamic militants rioted in July 1991; nearly 200 were arrested following an anti-government rally in Karachi against the regime's support for the United States in its continuing 'phoney war' with Iraq. The irony here for the government was that the introduction of the *sharia* was now not enough, as it was tainted by its pro-West stance during the Iraq–UN confrontation. Yet Pakistan was never an 'Islamic state' in the same sense that Iran was. Religious allegiance was not enough to overcome serious divisions (even after the schism that resulted in the founding of Bangladesh), which centred on regional, ethnic and class issues. Saudi Arabia, after 250 years of religion-oriented government, was not riven by the same kinds of problems, yet its monarchical, authoritarian, puritanical state and government were under growing pressure from Islamic militants in the 1980s to Islamicize the country further. In order to assess fully the nature of Islam's interaction with politics, we need to look at the reasons why a pre-existing Islamic state was attacked for not being Islamic enough.

Saudi Arabia: Islamic government under attack

The present Saudi state has its origins in a politico-religious alliance entered into in the 1740s, when Muhammad ibn Saud, the ruler of an oasis close to the modern city of Riyadh, accepted the revivalist message of the reformer Muhammad ibn Abd al-Wahhab and made use of the latter's unitarian principles as a means of building a power base. By the beginning of the nineteenth century the Saud family and their followers were posing a serious threat to the Ottomans, sacking the Shia shrine of Karbala in 1801 and occupying the holy cities of Mecca and Medina in 1806. Following the weakening of the Ottoman empire in the early twentieth century, Abd al-Aziz ibn Abd al-Rahman al-Saud was able to establish the Saudi state within its present boundaries, with the ideology of Wahhabism. The kingdom of Saudi Arabia was established in its present boundaries in 1934.

Saudi Arabia is an Islamic state in the sense that there is no secular constitution and no secular laws apart from those concerned with the operation of commercial companies (Farouk-Sluglett and Sluglett 1989c:

232–3). The *sharia* forms the basis of the legal system, and the state is supposedly governed according to Islamic principles. In practice, however, the King and the royal family rule absolutely, without any democratic decision-making processes (Ayubi 1991: 99). The rulers have derived much of their domestic and international legitimacy from their guardianship of Islam's two most holy places: Mecca and Medina. Religion is used, as in Iran and Pakistan, as a tool for social control and political legitimization. This is achieved through three institutions: the religious (*shari*) courts; the Organization for the Enforcement of Good and Prevention of Evil, established in 1929; and the Orwellian-sounding 'Moral Police' (*mutawwi*), members of which on occasion literally whip people to hurry them to prayer (Piscatori 1980).

A manifestation of opposition to the regime and its leaders – spurred by the Iranian Revolution – was the armed takeover in November 1979 of the Most Sacred Mosque at Mecca, the very birthplace of the Islamic faith, by a militant Islamist group. The main issue was the alleged moral consequences of sudden great wealth, although a secondary concern was clearly the rule of the Saud family (Ochsenwald 1981: 271). A decade later further anti-government opposition surfaced, this time encouraged by the Saudi government's partnership with Western governments during the Gulf war. King Fahd came under strong pressure from the country's religious establishment to introduce major Islamic reforms of the country's institutions. In May and June 1991, members of the *mutawwi* served Fahd with a reminder of their power by arresting and beating individuals close to the royal family for their alleged transgression of Islamic laws, including the drinking of alcohol (Darwish 1991). This followed a demonstration involving members of the *ulama* and the *mutawwi* and thousands of their supporters who marched in protest at what they saw as an un-Islamic government. Such people saw the successes of Islamic revivalists in Iran, Sudan and Algeria, along with the Islamic challenges to the status quo in Tunisia, Jordan and elsewhere in the region and, coupled with the Saudi government's close ties with the United States, this gave them the encouragement and impetus to challenge Fahd's rule (Murphy 1991). They wanted an even more austere Islamic state in Saudi Arabia, with political power taken from the ruling family and put into the hands of the *ulama* and supporters, as in Iran.

The examples we have looked at in the context of the Islamic state have included both Islamist opposition and government. The Algerian case is an example of a widespread disaffection with failed political and economic programmes which afflicted most of North Africa and the Middle East in the 1980s and 1990s. In Algeria and Tunisia Islamists led societal protests against their governments. In each case governmental support (or at least, ambivalence with regard to Iraq) for the United States and its allies in the 1990–1 Gulf War was a key to understanding the articulation of anti-government sentiments, although these were already present in the atmosphere of political and economic failure. Yet it is by no means clear that all or even most of the individuals who took to the streets in protest at governments in Muslim countries actually wanted Islamic states along the lines of Iran. It is most likely that in an era in which both socialism and capitalism were looked upon disfavourably, a possible 'third way' – Islam – appealed principally by virtue of the fact that it had not been seen to fail in the way that both socialism (economically and spiritually) and capitalism (spiritually) were judged to have done. In Sudan, Pakistan and Saudi Arabia ruling elites used Islam as their ruling ideology, albeit for differing reasons. In Sudan the justification was straightforward: the northern Arab elite needed a unifying ideology against the southern non-Muslims. In Pakistan political instability, economic disappointment, anti-Westernism and the ineffectual nature of secular government combined to push Islam to the centre of the political stage. In Saudi Arabia an entrenched Islamic elite was attacked for its excesses. It is not clear, however, how widespread the Islamic opposition is in a state where any sign of discontent is quickly dealt with. Yet it was not the case that all countries with large Muslim populations experienced either Islamic governments or anti-government Islamic agitation. For the purpose of comparison we can turn finally to an examination of three non-Arab, but Muslim, countries to assess to what extent Islam acquired political salience out of the Muslim heartland of North Africa and the Middle East.

Islam as social cement: Indonesia, Malaysia and Brunei

Whereas in Algeria, Iran, Pakistan, Saudi Arabia, Sudan and other Muslim states of North Africa and the Middle East, the political salience of Islam had to be taken into account – sometimes to the point of setting the agenda – the case of Muslim East Asia is different. On the face of it, Indonesia, with a population of over 170 million of whom 87 per cent (155 million) profess to be Muslim (making Indonesia the largest Muslim state in the world), should be an example of a country in which Islam has immense political salience. Yet it has not become a crucial political issue, in the sense of calls for an Islamic state, although at times government has had to be wary of its influence. Indonesia provides us, instead, with an example of how the ruling system managed to deal with fissiparous tendencies in a state beset by centrifugal ethnic, regional and religious pressures, of which Islam is only one.

During the colonial period, when Indonesia was ruled successively by the Dutch (1914–42, 1945–9) and the Japanese (1942–5), Islam became the focus of resistance to foreign domination. This led to a degree of revival of Islam and a recovery of confidence in Muslim identity. The first mass nationalist party, Sarekat Islam, was Islam based. In this period most Christians (now approximately 9 per cent of the population) were more sympathetic to the colonial authorities, although a minority were proto-nationalist (von der Mehden 1989b: 107).

After the Dutch left in 1949 there was a decade of political instability derived from both ethnic and religious factors. In West Java, South Sulawesi and other parts of the country a radical Muslim movement, *Darul Islam*, fought (unsuccessfully) in a long conflict intended to establish a Muslim state. Meanwhile, in Ambon and elsewhere, Christian insurgents unsuccessfully fought the Indonesian armed forces in order to achieve autonomy or independence from the authorities in Java. By the 1960s these activities had generally been crushed. However, in 1967, following an abortive coup attempt in which the Communist Party was implicated, Muslim organizations cooperated with the military in a *jihad* against the atheist communists, and in the massacres which ensued over 300,000 people were killed (Smith 1970: 164).

Since 1945, the work of governing and administrating Indonesia has been largely in the hands of *abangan* (i.e. nominal Muslims) of rather secular outlook, with the result that at times Islam became a focus of opposition to President Suharto (Montgomery Watt 1990: 67). In this matter conservative practising Muslims have been more influential than liberals, especially through the organization of Nahdatul Ulama (the Awakening of the Ulama), founded in 1926 (von der Mehden 1989: 107). At the electoral level the most active opposition to the government came from the Islamic PPP (Partai Persatuan Pembangunan), as in the 1980s the Nahdatul Ulama withdrew from politics to concentrate upon religion and education. It organized schools that combined religious teaching with some non-religious subjects, while at the higher level State Institutes for Islam have been established.

Islam's political ambitions were partially checked, and Muslim cultural and political identity challenged, by nationalist secular ideologies and by the revival of traditional Javanese mysticism (Lapidus 1988: 773). Under the banner of secularism the Indonesian state began to encroach upon the areas reserved for Islamic law. The marriage reform bill of 1974 proposed secular inheritance and adoption laws in competition with *sharia*. In reaction Muslim courts resisted internal modernization and did not go through their own process of reform, as have Muslim courts in some Middle Eastern countries. In Indonesia, Muslims were more concerned with resisting state interference than with making legal reforms. In the absence of a strong internal push for reforms, Muslim judges tend to be poorly trained, lack authority and suffer from the competition of civil courts. In addition, the growth of Christian proselytizing and the emergence of Kebatinan, a Javan proto-nationalist movement with claims to be a new national religion, provided alternative religious vehicles to Islam (Lapidus 1988: 774). Thus, the exclusion of Islamic groups from political power helped to legitimize the drift away from Muslim identity.

At the same time, a feature of Islamic strength in Indonesia is the continuing importance of the rural *ulama*. In west Java and Sumatra, the religious teachers (*kiyayi*) exert substantial influence upon family, agricultural and other village affairs, apart from strictly religious matters. Through *ulama* and school networks, regional councils, national religious parties and the Ministry of Religion, the *kiyayi* exert a degree of influence on the government.

Apart from the essentially conservative rural *kiyayi* a further feature of Islam in Indonesia is the continuing vitality of the reformist and modernist movements. Muhammadiya remains an important force in providing a concept of community and a model of an ongoing Islamic society, offering clear and simple guides to personal conduct, espousing an ideal of rational, efficient and puritanical behaviour. The novelist V. S. Naipaul found a young enthusiast for Islam in Indonesia in whose opinion 'Islam was pure and perfect; the secular dying West was to be rejected.' This man was the president of an important youth organization attached to a mosque in a middle-class area (Naipaul 1982: 352). Muhammadiya and other Islamic movements have a combined membership of well over two million people, organized into over 2000 branches countrywide. Yet this basic strength was not sufficient, nor did it aim, to give the several Muslim movements control of the Indonesian polity.

Some Muslims in Indonesia responded to political and cultural pressures by accommodating to the secularization of state and society. Muslim politicians were apparently willing to put aside ideological objectives and to operate in a pluralistic political system as one group among many. For these people, many of whom had extensive business, regional and/or professional contacts, Islam was only one element of identity. For them, the Quran served theoretically to inspire and motivate behaviour, but did not provide precise rules for the organization of daily life, as it did for many Muslims in Islam's religious and cultural heartlands: the Middle East and North Africa.

Thus Islam in Indonesia was modified by: authoritarian secular government based on *pancasila* (the official ideology); an ethnic mixture comprising Indonesians and Chinese (usually Christian); and the inevitable fissiparity of a society split by living on hundreds of different islands. Despite these factors, however, political Islam became a growing threat to the political and economic elites. Many of the latter are Chinese; Islam became the vehicle of resentment of 'have-nots' who see in their frequent flaunting of wealth the satanic ways of worldly things. Periodic outbreaks of Islamic fervour in the past – including, in 1984, the shooting of hundreds of rioting Muslims in Tanjung Priok, Jakarta's port – testify to the periodic and continuing, although not predominant, salience of Islam in Indonesia's politics (*The Economist* 17 November 1990: 87).

Indonesia's neighbouring states, Malaysia and Brunei, are both states with numerical majorities of Muslims. Brunei is run as the personal fiefdom of the Sultan who, with a personal fortune estimated at £18.5 billion, is reckoned to be the richest person in the world. The Sultan's rule is encapsulated in the slogan: 'Muslim, Malay, Monarchy' (Vines 1991). Growing state Islamization appears to be little more than a desire to turn the screws on any pro-democracy movement which might surface. In Malaysia

– with half the population Muslim – Islam has had political salience that, as elsewhere, tends to increase or diminish in relation to perceived popular economic and social well-being. The dominant political division is ethnically derived, with half the population Malays, one-third Chinese, and the rest Indian. Thus Islam tends to interact with other cultural symbols (*The Economist* 13 October 1990: 78). As Malay society has become increasingly polarized – with the politically conservative Parti Islam Se Malaysia (PAS) picking up 40 per cent of votes cast in rural areas – the danger for the future is for Islam to be used as a vehicle of Malay hegemony over the ethnic minorities.

In assessing the disparate global manifestations of political Islam in the contemporary era, the first and most obvious conclusion to make is that there are evident differences between the political role of Islam in the Middle East–North African heartland as compared to the peripheral areas of South-East Asia. Yet there are also similarities. In both regions Islam assumed the status of mobilizer of political opposition in the wake of frequently authoritarian, economically unsuccessful and politically incompetent regimes. Second, the absence of realistic alternative ideologies not unsurprisingly focused opposition behind Islamists. Yet the very absence of useful role models (with the exception of Shiite Iran) meant that the practical problems of, for example, how to run an economy, institutionalize dissent or devise foreign policies could be regarded as something to be tackled once in power; the gaining of the latter was overwhelmingly *the raison d'être* of the Islamic groups. When, as in the case of the Islamic Salvation Front in Algeria, Islamists looked set to achieve political power by the ballot box then entrenched political and economic elites prevented popular will being expressed.

Third, Islamic movements have to be seen in relation to the specific processes of social change taking place in their societies, in particular to the issues of the changing position of classes and groups, ethnic jockeying, political participation, identity crises, the stability of regimes and distributive justice. In the case of the one Islamic state forged by revolution, Iran's experience confirms that structural changes accompanying modernization do not necessarily bring about secularism, either in political institutions and processes or in the attitudes and values of individuals who have been exposed to modernizing experiences.

We examined these issues in both the Tunisian and Algerian contexts. Electoral results confirmed Islam's position as the chief ideology of opposition, despite a generation or more of determined attempts at secularization and, in Algeria's case at least, socialism. The crackdown by the Algerian and Tunisian regimes against Islamic political parties was welcomed by neighbouring regimes, such as the Egyptian and Moroccan, themselves seeking to neutralize different Islamic challenges to the status quo. What this underlined was that 'Islam' should not be regarded as a reified, undifferentiated, 'fundamentalist' ideology. As with other contending political movements, militants and radicals compete with pragmatists and moderates both in the nature of their visions of the future and in the means judged appropriate for gaining power.

Fourth, once in power Islamic regimes used Islam as an ideology with differing foci and purposes. In Sudan the justification was straightforward: the northern Arab elite needed a unifying ideology against the southern non-Muslims. In this way racism and regionalism united as a potent justification for the ill-treatment of one segment of society by another. In Pakistan political instability, economic disappointment, anti-Westernism and the ineffectual nature of secular government combined to push Islam to the centre of the political stage and of the state's proclaimed goals. Yet the uniformity and solidarity forged by shared religious concerns was not enough to overcome serious divisions (even after the schism which resulted in the founding of Bangladesh), which centred on regional, ethnic and class issues. In Saudi Arabia, after 250 years of religious rule, the government was not riven by the same kinds of problems, yet its monarchial, authoritarian, puritanical government was apparently under growing pressure from Islamic militants to Islamicize the country. The entrenched Islamic elite was attacked for its excesses, although in a society unaccustomed to expressing political preferences it was difficult to assess the spread and depth of opposition, and to judge the status of potentially contending ideologies.

In this chapter, we have examined how and why Islam became a focus of both rulers' hegemony and opposition groups' challenges in a number of Arab and non-Arab states. We investigated and analysed the process of the politicization of Islam. It became evident that even (or, perhaps, especially) in modern political settings Islam and politics are inseparable. Yet this does not imply that the modern Islamic revival is an atavistic reversion – or desire for such a reversion – to an older, 'purer' type of governance. Above all, it is notable how wide is the diversity of perceptions, issues, programmes and goals that may be included in a conception of Islamic state or ideology. It is most likely that in an era in which both socialism and capitalism have been looked upon disfavourably, a possible, though not entirely thought through, 'third way' – Islam – has appealed principally by virtue of the fact that it has not been seen to fail in the way that both socialism (economically and spiritually) and capitalism (spiritually) are perceived by many to have done. Alone among the world religions, there has been no parallel agitation for some form of Christian polity. As we saw earlier this is partly because of the centuries-old separation of church and state in Christianity's heartland – Europe. Nevertheless, as with Islam, Christianity has become a vehicle for political movements of varying kinds in recent times. In the next chapter we shall examine and analyse differing manifestations of this trend in the Third World in recent times.

Third World Christianity and politics

Christianity, long regarded in the West as non-political or apolitical, became a vehicle for political ideas from the 1960s. There are an estimated 60 million fundamentalist or 'born-again' conservative Christians in the USA, i.e. more than a fifth of the population. They provided the core support for the arch-conservative 'televangelist' Pat Robertson's unsuccessful 1988 presidential campaign, and for Pat Buchanan's in 1992. The growth of fundamentalist Christianity was also clearly manifested in Latin America, where an estimated nine or ten thousand Catholics *each day* make the switch to conservative forms of Protestantism.

Growth in conservative Protestantism is not confined to the Americas. In the Philippines the Catholic Church, which claims to represent over 80 per cent of the population, is worried about the considerable increase in evangelical Protestant activity. The consciously 'apolitical' stance taken by the evangelicals has aided conversions by contrasting themselves with the more 'political' Catholic Church (von der Mehden 1989: 217). In Jamaica, the growth of Christian fundamentalist groups, principally pentecostals, has been swift since the early 1970s, affecting both Catholic and 'mainstream' Protestant churches. Over the past 15 years, there has been a tacit alliance between the conservative Jamaica Labour Party, and its leader Edward Seaga, and the rapidly expanding conservative evangelical community. A campaign by US evangelist Lowell Lundstrom was cancelled in June 1987 when the then opposition People's National Party uncovered promotional material claiming that the 'gospel invasion' would help to prevent communism in Jamaica (Wiebe 1989b: 141).

The areas where evangelical and pentecostal growth has been most swift are important foci of US geo-strategic concerns. The Catholic hierarchy in Central America calls it 'the invasion of the sects'. It places the blame squarely on the United States. The Honduran bishops accuse the United States Central Intelligence Agency (CIA) of covertly financing anti-communist evangelical growth; and the Guatemalan church hierarchy brands the evangelical movement an imperialist conspiracy to block revolutionary change and to maintain US political and economic dominance. As we shall see in Chapter 5, it is not difficult to find evidence linking the explosion of Protestant evangelical churches in Latin America – mostly the Assemblies of God Church and pentecostal sects – with Washington and right-wing groups right across the region. This is not to argue, however, that such groups are merely the stooges of the USA, but to note that they offer people – especially the poor and underprivileged – hopes of salvation and comfort. At the same time, certain US foreign policy goals – containment of communism, spreading of free markets, squashing of socially progressive movements – tend to be facilitated by the spread of conservative Protestantism, especially within the armed forces which traditionally hold considerable political clout in Latin America. In the 1980s, the USA, under the presidency of Ronald Reagan, aggressively sought to reduce or eliminate the threat of communist advances in its 'backyard' (Central America and the Caribbean) and in other important geo-strategic areas (e.g. the Philippines).

One dimension of the growth of Protestantism in Latin America is the influence of the USA. Yet rather than the growth of conservative Protestantism being seen as a sinister right-wing plot, the context of its spread in Latin America and elsewhere is also to be found in the historical global tussle for domination between Roman Catholicism and Protestantism. In Latin America, Christianity has been *the* province of the Catholic Church for 500 years. Rather like Islam in the Middle East and North Africa, Catholicism is (or has been until recently) more than 'just' a religion; it is the dominant culture, with deep roots throughout the hemisphere. To be Latin was to be Catholic. What happened to change things was that the traditional (Catholic) order began to collapse under the combined pressures of modernization, Americanization and urbanization in the context of two developments. The first was the declining ability of the Catholic Church spiritually to satisfy burgeoning populations enmeshed ever deeper in stultifying poverty and political inconsequence. The second was the degeneration of politics to a squalid struggle for power between the military and the political elites, on the one hand, and the guerrilla groups and trade unions, on the other. In this deadly battle many people were the targets of political violence *from both sides*. The response was to look for salvation (in the next world, if not in this one) in the burgeoning pentecostal and fundamentalist brands of Christianity being peddled.

Before we proceed it would be appropriate to define a few of the terms so far introduced. 'Fundamentalism' *can* simply mean a return to the basic principles and moral precepts of one's belief. In the context of the growth of Protestant fundamentalism, however, we are referring to an intolerant, intransigent set of beliefs that denies that Christians of a non-fundamentalist persuasion are Christians at all. Christian fundamentalists stress five main beliefs: the absolute authority of the Bible; Christ's virgin birth; that Christ died for people's sins; Christ's resurrection from the dead; and the second coming of Christ. Above all, fundamentalists believe that they alone will be saved on the Judgement Day, which will happen soon.

Pentecostalists share many of the fundamentalists' beliefs, but also differ from them in a number of respects. They put more emphasis on religious practice than on theology. The key characteristics of pentecostalists' religious practices are baptism in the Holy Spirit, healing by miracles and glossolalia ('speaking in tongues'). Pentecostalists put less stress on the inerrancy of the Bible than do the fundamentalists, but they share the latter's contempt for Christians who do not share their beliefs and, significantly, see communists as devil-inspired. Both groups are politically conservative and see their enemies in terms of a simple (or simplistic) divide between good and evil. Both fundamentalists and pentecostalists *may* be evangelical: this refers simply to the idea of proselytization of beliefs, and obviously pre-dates both fundamentalism and pentecostalism by centuries. In Latin America, *both* fundamentalists and pentecostalists (indeed, all Protestants) are known as *evangelicos* because they are the groups most active in proselytization.

Catholicism rarely attracts the label fundamentalist. This is probably because that label has are(a)dy been pre-empted by a particular kind of Protestantism. Yet it is possible to see certain groups within the Catholic Church, such as those represented by the late Archbishop Lefebvre and the Opus Dei organization, as forms of contemporary Roman Catholic conservatism that most approximates to 'fundamentalism'. Such groups are not active in the Third World, however, representing only tiny numbers of people organized in traditionalist Catholic splinter groups (Martin 1990a: 130). As a result we shall not be focusing on them, although Catholic charismatic groups are increasing in Brazil.

In this chapter we are concerned with Catholic liberation theology and Protestant fundamentalism and pentecostalism. While the first is associated with socially progressive ideas and the second with more conservative notions, they have in common: a dissaffection with the established, hierarchical, institutionalized Christian churches; a desire to find God through personal searching rather than through the mediation of hierarchical institutions; and a focus on the ability to make changes through 'people power'. In liberation theology terms, 'people's power' is the idea that individuals, when acting together, can change and confront existing social realities and unpopular rulers by direct action, as in Haiti, the Philippines, South Africa, Eastern Europe and elsewhere in the 1980s. In the conservative formulation 'people's power' does not have a political connotation *per se*, but refers to the idea of individuals getting together in religious contexts to pray and work for spiritual and material advance. To understand what happened – and why – we shall start by looking at the genesis and development of liberation theology, before examining the dramatic growth of Protestant churches and sects.

The rise, fall and rise again of liberation theology

First articulated in Brazil in the early 1960s, liberation theology became a widespread feature of socio-political division and struggle within the Third World. Liberation theology is an intensely political phenomenon, a response to the appalling social and political conditions of many poor people in (predominantly, but not exclusively) Roman Catholic Third World countries. Central to the concept of liberation theology is the notion of dependence and underdevelopment, the use of a class struggle perspective to explain social conflict and justify political action, and the exercise of a political role to achieve religious as well as secular goals.

Liberation theology concerns split the Catholic Church in Latin America and elsewhere, perhaps irrevocably. Contentions between the Vatican and Ernesto Cardenal (a prominent member of Nicaragua's Sandinista government until its electoral defeat in February 1990) and the Brazilian Leonardo Boff symbolized the rift between progressive theologians and the Pope. In addition, liberation theology was regarded by powerful conservatives, within governments and without, as something to fear. Prominent liberation theology activists were assassinated, including the Colombian Camilo Torres in 1965 and Archbishop Romero of El Salvador, who was gunned down in his own church in 1980. The murder of six Jesuit priests in 1989 in El Salvador by members of the military underlined the political and social divisions inherent in Latin American societies (Robertson 1988: 122; Keogh 1990). To understand why liberation theology developed in Latin America in the 1960s, we need first to examine the cultural legacy of Spain and Portugal.

Latin America was (and still is to a considerable extent) Catholic. This was a direct result of the first wave of European imperial expansion, which Spain and Portugal led from the fifteenth century in Latin America. In contrast, the Christian churches in both Africa and Asia derive mostly from the second wave of European expansion in the nineteenth century. This involved a greater degree of differentiation between imperialistic (political) and missionary (religious) penetration than was the case with the earlier imperialism. The important social and political result of this was that in Spanish and Portuguese (i.e. Roman Catholic) colonies religion created a world view that involved a certain, singular perspective on ordinary people. The later emphasis on *liberation* centred on the claim that it was first necessary to be 'humanized' (i.e. released from degradation and poverty) before becoming a religious Christian. Since such a process involved the comprehension of *the conditions* which historically created the phenomenon of 'the man who is not a man' (to use the phrase of the father of liberation theology, Gustavo Gutiérrez (1973)) that process could not be simply one of spiritualization, but had also to involve a socio-political 'conscientization'. Reflecting prevailing social conditions, liberation theology was a manifestation of new religious values and activities, which not surprisingly stimulated friction both within and between societies and the Church hierarchy (Eckstein 1989: 30).

Thus liberation theology was not only a spiritual development, but also one grounded in the complexities of material existence. It was no coincidence that it flowered alongside the widespread perception of a crisis of development which became acute in Latin America in the 1960s. It will be useful to provide at this point a brief account of both socio-economic and religious conditions in Latin America at the time.

During the Second World War and shortly after, the countries of Latin America enjoyed favourable terms of trade with the Western industrialized countries. During the war and the period of post-war recovery, the high demand for minerals and agricultural goods led to a high volume of trade on terms favourable to Latin America. This made it possible for some Latin American governments to initiate industrialization and for others to accelerate it. By the 1960s the favourable conditions had begun to deteriorate; as a result, a process of independent, self-sustaining economic development did not endure in the continent. At the time this was not clear to either professional economists or Catholic intellectuals. The Church shared the former's generally optimistic view that economic development would come sooner rather than later, based on a main premise of modernization theory: that the 'trickle down' effect of economic development would provoke individual well-being, social mobility and political maturity. In the modernization paradigm, as noted earlier (see Chapter 1), religion was viewed as increasingly atavistic, likely to disappear with modernization, epiphenomenal and an irrational alternative to politics. Reflecting the orthodox economic theories of the day, the Church tended to see ubiquitous Latin American socio-economic problems – such as the working conditions of the urban labourer, land tenure patterns, the economic plight of the peasant, high illiteracy rates and poor housing – as discrete problems unrelated to each other or to the subservient economic and political relationships between Latin American states and the industrialized countries of the West, and especially the USA. From such a perspective the Church could continue to pursue its traditional strategy of charity towards the poor while awaiting the alleviating effects of the development process. The ethos of an individualistic, competitive (i.e. capitalist) economy and society was not seriously questioned, probably because the only apparently viable alternative, the Soviet union, was an atheistic society and therefore not worthy of emulation in the Church's eyes.

President Kennedy's self-styled 'Alliance for Progress' with Latin America was forged in the early 1960s to stimulate socio-economic development through an international capitalist structure. At the same time, a number of Latin American intellectuals began to work within 'dependency' or neo-Marxist frameworks to challenge the evolutionary, cultural and individualistic assumptions on which modernization theory was based. They sought to analyse the nature of the asymmetry which Latin America's economies demonstrated in relation to the USA. They argued that Latin America's development must be understood in the context of global economic dynamics. As they witnessed their own countries' economies returning to a system based on the exchange of their raw materials for the manufactured goods of their industrial trading partners, the economic and technological development scenario forwarded by the modernization theorists began to look increasingly unlikely to be realized (Dodson 1979: 205).

The development predicament was paralleled by a near-crisis in Catholicism in Latin America, which helped to mould the church's response to it. A result of the reforms initiated by the Second Vatican Council (1962–5) was the perception that Latin America needed massive attention in the mission field. The largest Catholic continent in the world, Latin America displayed pastorally weak churches which had little appeal among the common people. Priestly vocations had fallen to acutely low levels. Protestant competition, directed from the USA, and secular political groups with radical-populist or revolutionary programmes, made serious inroads among the poor Catholics of Latin America. The Church's response to this was a commitment to seek to enlarge the number of clergy and to upgrade the quality of pastoral action. Foreign priests were urged to go to Latin America and to take up ministries among the poor, as many local priests seemed disinclined to do so. The former, already mostly politicized by 'dependency', socialist or militant Christian ideas, acceded to the call, and as a result the so-called 'worker-priest experiment' (founded in Argentina) was born. It was within the broad worker-priest sphere of action that the Church became intimately embroiled in the struggle to resolve the development crisis. In the process, the Catholic Church in Latin America split between social progressives and conservatives.

The theology of liberation grew out of militant priests' direct involvement with the working poor, both urban and rural. This involvement began quietly and modestly in the early 1960s with the promotion of the worker-priest concept in such countries as Argentina, Brazil, Chile and Uruguay. Aware that the Church seemed to be losing contact with the masses, particularly in the cities, bishops in many dioceses supported a plan for parish priests to take employment in factories and workshops in order to get closer to working people, understand their needs more intimately, and develop a ministry appropriate to them. For most worker-priests, direct involvement was a profoundly unsettling experience in consciousness-raising. Many realized that the Church was alienated from the poor, and saw it as primarily an agent of pacification and co-optation since it made little effort to change social conditions or draw attention to the structural causes underlying poverty. For clergy who wished to act on the basis of this new awareness, it became necessary to rethink the priestly vocation, the mission of the church, and even the very meaning of faith itself (Gutiérrez 1973: 203–8).

Clergy radicalized by direct involvement with the poor required tools for explaining the social relationships they encountered, and for justifying some form of political action to ameliorate those conditions. Liberation theory evolved as an amalgam of Marxist social analysis and a reinterpretation of the prophetic tradition in Christianity (Roelofs 1988: 550). The liberation theologians were essentially Christian radicals or militants; they approached Marxism from that foundation. They represented the renaissance of a profound biblical political radicalism. To many radical priests there was no contradiction between the political ideas and economic equality of Marxism and the types of reforms needed in their societies to liberate the poor. Later, once people were 'fully human', the spiritual side of religious belief could be stressed. Arguments of imperialist domination within the context of an all-pervasive global system of dependency informed the liberation theologists with a systematic, comprehensive, structural explanation for the occurrence of poverty in the modern world.

The birth of liberation theology took place within a small segment of the Catholic Church in Brazil. The Brazilian Church is of special significance not only in Latin America, but also within the wider Catholic Church itself. Brazil's 358-strong episcopate (i.e. order of bishops) is the world's largest and is responsible for the spiritual leadership of the world's biggest concentration of Roman Catholics. The country's population is over 140 million, the majority of whom (about 70 per cent) profess adherence to the Roman Catholic faith. As a result, Brazil's Catholic establishment exercises a special influence upon the Church elsewhere in Latin America (Medhurst 1989: 25).

Brazil's significance for the growth of liberation theology began to become clear in the 1960s. Socially progressive elements within the Brazilian episcopate emerged at that time as pacemakers within both the local and the wider Latin American Church. The effort in Brazil led to the coining of the (Portuguese) world *conscientizacion* (i.e. the development of awareness of one's identity and potential in a form of a politicization that goes beyond the manipulative mobilization of people by interested parties). The concept of *conscientizacion* was developed by a Brazilian Catholic intellectual, Paulo Freire, in connection with a programme of adult literacy training. His ideas spread far beyond Brazil, and informed political reform movements in Sub-Saharan Africa, the Philippines, Haiti and elsewhere. As Freire analysed the problem, the illiterate had an undifferentiated, magical perspective on reality. They saw their environment, both natural and socially derived, as the immutable given of life, to which attitudes of pessimism, resignation and fatalism were wholly appropriate. Their place at the bottom of the socio-economic pile was accepted. Existing methods of literacy, Freire argued, were paternalistic operations in which middle-class instructors from another world attempted to hand down smatterings of their culture to the masses, with the object of making them fit into the existing structures of society better (Freire 1970).

Freire's approach was to use the vocabulary of the illiterates themselves and by dialogue to encourage the development of a critical view of their environment, a consciousness of what things could in fact be changed. Freire regarded the skills of literacy as but a part of a general process of conscientization, a process which would allow the oppressed to move towards full human existence as people. This would only happen, Freire believed, when they cut the umbilical cord with nature and with a sacralized social order, in order to discover themselves as participants in a concrete historical process open to the future. Such politicization, although demanded in the name of Christian humanism, required a significantly secularized view of the world. It was this which led Freire's ideas to be regarded with horror by Brazil's ruling elites, who saw them, not surprisingly, as virtually revolutionary, as manifestations of communism and all that portended for the lifestyles – even the existence – of the very rich.

At the time Freire was developing his model of literacy training (between about 1960 and 1963), the Brazilian government, in cooperation with the national Bishops' Conference, started a countrywide campaign called the Basic Education Movement (MEB). Reflecting an acceptance of Freire's ideas, the MEB was run by a group of independent laypeople who saw their educational task in terms of conscientization. They used the media of books and radio to disseminate their message of liberation and social change. But the leadership itself was divided between the reformists who sought the integration of the depressed groups in society so that a major upheaval could be averted and the militants whose object was nothing less than a revolutionary transformation of society. Such a division reflected the increasingly dichotomized perceptions of the way the Catholic Church in Brazil should deal with growing demands from the have-nots for an improved position in the society.

The consciousness-raising period of the early 1960s associated with the dissemination of Freire's ideas coincided with, and was at least in part a result of, a period of democratic government in Brazil. This was ended by a military coup in 1964, which ushered in a 21-year period of army rule until 1985, when the officers handed power back to the civilians in the wake of serious economic setbacks. Despite its unconstitutional nature, the 1964 military coup was generally welcomed by the Brazilian upper and middle classes, who were fearful that conscientization, sponsored in part by radical Catholic elements, would soon give the masses a voice commensurate with their numbers and, more importantly, an ability to take politics into their own hands.

Despite the changed political climate in Brazil from the mid-1960s, the impact of the Brazilian conscientization movement was demonstrated at the Second Conference of Latin American Bishops held in Medellín (Colombia) in 1968. This conference was a watershed in Latin American Church history, as from it came the command that throughout Latin America (and by implication elsewhere in the Roman Catholic Third World) the Church should henceforward work for a reform of inherited socioeconomic and political structures. Thus the progressive elements within the Brazilian episcopate can be credited with helping to create the ecclesiastical climate that subsequently facilitated the emergence of liberation theology, the spread of basic Christian communities throughout Central and Latin America and beyond (see below), and the development of a so-called 'popular Church' which depended substantially on lay leadership.

Despite the suspension of reformist policies and programmes in Brazil following the 1964 military coup, they did nevertheless provide the Church with important precedents when it subsequently emerged as a major source of opposition during the 21 years of military, authoritarian rule. Partly because of the military government's single-minded pursuit for economic growth and partly because of its innate political conservatism, social reform programmes were not on its political agenda. Rather, the military government demonstrated its ideological approach of authoritarian control with widespread, and flagrant, abuses of human rights and an accompanying serious impoverishment of Brazil's poor (Medhurst 1989: 25). As a result, sections of the Church's leadership expressed support for outspoken radical colleagues. Socially progressive Catholics were thus again able to set the agenda of Brazil's national Church. At the episcopal level the policies of the regime were strongly criticized. At the local level pastoral programmes were mounted in defence of the urban and rural poor and of threatened indigenous populations.

If Brazil was the country where liberation theology first became of philosophical salience, it was Chile where such ideas became part of the ideology of political groupings, because it was here that free elections were fought at a time of military rule in Brazil (Pendle 1976: 240). By the time of Chile's presidential elections in September 1970, the plight of the urban poor – many of whom were living in vast slums outside the major cities, including Santiago – led a number of priests to back publicly the radical social policy of Salvador Allende (*The Times* 3 September 1970). They argued that it was in accordance with the Christian conscience. As it transpired, Allende's radical coalition defeated the Christian Democratic Party which was backed by the Catholic Church establishment. Allende became the Western hemisphere's first constitutionally elected Marxist president. Allende's pragmatic plans, social democratic in thrust rather than Marxist, included such measures as adequate housing, education and health services for Chile's poor, the abolition of minority class privileges, and state ownership of the banks and the country's important copper mines. Chile's civilian and military elites were alarmed, forecasting that the country would become 'another Marxist, anti-American Cuba'; US government officials in addition feared the establishment of a 'southern base for international Communism' (Pendle 1976: 240). Allende's experiment in what he called 'democratic decency' was short-lived: on 11 September 1973 his government was overthrown, and he was killed, in a military coup organized and financed by an alliance of Chilean and US conservatives, including the Central Intelligence Agency (CIA).

Communidades Eclesiales de Base and the politics of liberation

It was an essentially biblical radicalism which stimulated many Catholic priests to champion the concerns of the poor in Latin America in the 1960s and later. It was the same biblical radicalism which underpinned the formation of the grassroots basic Christian communities (Spanish 'Communidades Eclesiales de Base'; CEBs), a concrete manifestation of liberation theology's philosophy of personal liberation. CEBs proliferated in South America, Haiti, the Philippines and (with some differences) elsewhere.

Outside Third World Roman Catholic countries, in, for example, Kenya, Ghana, Burkina Faso, Nigeria, India and Indonesia, local self-help groups formed from the 1970s (Durling 1989). Although these latter countries did not have Catholic cultures they did have central governments unable to satisfy popular (and rapidly growing, demographically driven) developmental needs. In effect, it was not so much Catholicism *per se* that formed the socio-political context of the CEBs; rather it was the inability of central and local governments – often not driven by the need for re-election in a period of non-constitutional rule – to provide sufficient development goods in the circumstance of a Roman Catholic culture that formed their basis.

The origins of the CEBs in Catholic cultural contexts are to be found in the moves towards popular community leadership from the 1960s, a development especially encouraged by radicalized clergy at the grass roots. Such priests organized their followers for self-help and spiritual purposes, guided by a vision of the Christian promise of redemption which directly linked the temporal sphere with the spiritual. Linked to Freire's literacy campaigns, social change in the present was seen as integral to people's long-range spiritual redemption. Concretely, this meant the full participation of ordinary people in the shaping of their own lives. Profound dependence and passivity had to be replaced by full participation and self-determination in the economic and political spheres. To achieve these goals, radical priests became spokesmen for a broad political programme with two main aims: participatory democracy and development of electricity, schools, health posts, clean water, roads and latrines.

By the late 1980s there were a reported 100,000 CEBs in Brazil, with some three million members (Durling 1989). Impressive though these figures are, it should be remembered that Brazil's population is some 140 million. Thus although CEBs were important, they were by no means the only form of socio-political mobilization and organization in the country. Nevertheless, the CEBs were highly influential, especially in the 1970s and early 1980s. They produced leaders for mass movements, such as trade unions and the Brazilian Labour Party, which were important in the process of popular mobilization that ultimately helped to undermine the credibility and viability of the military dictatorship, forcing it to hand over power to elected civilians in 1985 (Medhurst 1989: 25).

CEBs are often idealized by liberation theologists (see, for example, Barreiro 1982; Torres and Eagleson 1981). Roelofs (1988: 565) asserts that the CEBs 'show extraordinary uniformities for a movement so widespread, uncoordinated, and spontaneous'. We should note, however, that there is considerable diversity in style, size and purpose to be found among the CEBs, with socially progressive groups side-by-side with the pentecostal type, whose outlooks are sharply conservative and otherworldly. Hewitt (1987a: 165) argues that in São Paulo some CEBs became vehicles for middle-class political activity, especially before the return to democracy in Brazil in 1985.

What this points to is that CEBs cannot easily be understood as homogeneous socio-political vehicles. The contribution that they made to the democratic transition in South America has been the subject of considerable debate (Hewitt 1987b). Different perspectives may be summed up as follows. First, those on the secular left wing, perhaps exhibiting a doctrinal unwillingness to believe that anything progressive can result from religiously inspired initiatives, tend to dismiss the groups as largely ineffectual agents of social change. A second analytical focus sees the CEBs as having a primarily secular impact in the electoral sphere, as nuclei of support for progressive political parties. Third, for those attracted to the theology of liberation, the CEBs represent the seeds of a new, more just and fraternal society, helping to transform societies from the bottom up through a variety of liberating practices. A final interpretation sees their role in more complex and abstract terms: the groups' primary contribution to democratization should be seen in their ability to forge a spirit of Tocquevillian enlightened self-interest among participants, forging a citizenry aware of political rights and duties (Roelofs 1988: 559).

Typically, CEBs are small, face-to-face groups of 15 to 20 families (20 to 40 people), frequently bonded by physical proximity and poverty. They often meet regularly, perhaps once a fortnight. Roelofs (1988: 558) notes that 'because of an extreme shortage of [Catholic] religious professionals in Latin America, [the priests'] efforts have been focused on getting the base communities to operate on their own.' This has meant in practice that CEBs demonstrate a wider diversity in both religious beliefs and roles and practices than many accounts suggest. Even so, three functions of the CEBs are common. First, *Bible study* is what brings the communities into existence and keeps them going. The Bible may of course be interpreted from either a fundamentalist perspective or from a reformist viewpoint. In other words, the Bible can be used as a justification either to attack the status quo or to support it; Bible study *per se* is ideologically free. Sessions may last an hour or so and involve the reading of selected passages and the unrehearsed discussion of them based on personal experience and reflection. These discussions are often combined with equally unrehearsed prayer and some liturgical experimentation, perhaps a communal meal. Second, *communal action* is ubiquitous, often comprising group projects with educational or health purposes, to improve the local environment. A third common aim of the CEBs, as we have already noted, is to *change people's self-consciousness*.

Typically, then, CEBs in Latin America share three basic orientations: Bible study, communal action and a desire to change people's self-consciousness. Yet their political orientation and the types of people who join them tend to be linked to the ideological nature of the regime under which they operate. In Chile, an increasingly politically repressive and economically stringent series of measures (whose net effect was seriously to disadvantage the poor) led to a radicalization of the local CEBs. Many CEBs became vehicles for those who wished to change society to empower the poor, those who were unrepresented – or at least seriously under-represented – in the power hierarchy. During the authoritarian rule of General Augustus Pinochet's junta (1973–90), members of local CEBs angered elements in the government and its supporters. Verbal attacks began to appear in the government-controlled media by 1977, charging that the Chilean CEBs' umbrella group, the Vicariate of Solidarity, harboured communist sympathizers and received foreign money to support political dissidents in Chile. As a result, local CEB members were harassed. Foreign priests were frequently perceived as politically undesirable by Pinochet's regime. Between 1973 and 1979 nearly 400 foreign priests were expelled from Chile, precipitating a net decline of over 10 per cent in the total clergy (Smith 1982: 343).

Typically, as in Chile, the most dynamic period in many CEBs' existence was during the long periods of military rule in Latin America in the 1970s and early 1980s. According to Rodolfo Cardenal (1990: 245) in his assessment of CEBs in El Salvador:

> The primary factor in the base Christian communities was the characteristic awareness of having overcome the alienating aspects of traditional popular religiosity. They rejected not what was popular, but rather the separation of religious values from the real and distressing problems of life which, furthermore, they discovered opposed popular Christian religiosity.

In other words, in El Salvador during military rule, CEBs became vehicles of liberation theology in the absence of alternative means of mobilization. In conservative Colombia, Catholic bishops vigorously attacked democratization within the churches, reserving special fire for liberation theology, the 'popular Church' and autonomous CEBs (Levine 1990: 26). On the other hand, socialist-oriented Nicaragua during the 1980s was the home of numerous CEBs, most of which were wedded to a radical vision of a Christian-socialist future. A few others were politically opposed to the regime. Nevertheless, the Sandinistas saw the CEBs as political allies and, as a result, encouraged them (Serra 1985; Cruise O'Brien 1990: 146–7).

A primary benefit of the CEBs should be seen in the contribution they make to the establishment of a sense of citizenship, primarily among lower-class participants, rather than in their impact upon the national political scene *per se* (Hewitt 1990: 142). At the same time, CEBs are almost invariably vehicles for conscientization: the poor, long enveloped in the patron–client mentality that has traditionally defined class relations in Catholic societies, are, for the first time, cooperating to create a world of their own making. In working together with pastoral agents to press local officials for infrastructural improvements such as sewers, streetlights and land reform, they are learning that sometimes the best way to achieve their goals is not by appealing as individuals to powerful figures and bureaucratic authorities, but by working together for the community as a whole. Hewitt (1990), in an analysis focusing on 22 CEBs located in Brazil's large and dynamic Archdiocese of São Paulo, shows them to be maintaining an effective presence on the Brazilian political scene. Nevertheless, his data suggest that the role of the groups is changing in such a way that CEBs *per se* may fade as *bona fide* agents of social and political transformation. Such a change is attributable to a multitude of factors, not the least of which are qualitative alterations in official Church support for CEB activation in the current democratic climate.

Outside mainland Latin America, liberation theology galvanized other Catholic communities long after it had become less influential in the region of its birth. In both Haiti and the Philippines, CEB-style grass roots organizations mushroomed in the context of repressive dictatorships. In the Philippines they are known as Basic Christian Communities (BCCs). Many were founded in the 1970s. They carry out a wide range of local community action programmes, reflecting many local priests' conviction that a principal role for the Catholic church is to aid the community in both religious and secular matters. The Haitian church-linked grass roots groups reminiscent of Brazil's CEBs or the Philippines' BCCs carried out the same kind of programmes, helping poor, rural Haitians to improve their living conditions and promote small-scale development projects. Beyond the control of local conservative Catholic bishops, as in Latin America, they were organized and supported by the more militant local priests (Gelber 1989; McBeth 1989: 30–1). In both cases 'people power' – sometimes led and coordinated by priests – resulted in the overthrow of both of those entrenched despots in 1986.

In both the Philippines and Haiti periods of dictatorship marked burgeoning struggles within the Christian community. In the Philippines the centre-left regime of Corazon Aquino helped to set a political agenda where the Catholic Church was forced towards a more socially progressive position because of a growing social awareness among Protestant groups, which make up 3 per cent of the population (von der Mehden 1989a). This rebounded on the government by mid-1989 when the Aquino government's foot-dragging on social issues – including government corruption, the failure of a land-reform programme, the control of the civilian militia and a number of human rights issues – led the formerly supportive Catholic Church, with its policy of 'critical solidarity', to criticize the government. Some radical clergy – numbering between 2000 and 4000, or some 15 per cent of the entire priesthood in the Philippines – are either members or sympathizers of Christians for National Liberation (founded in 1972), whose ideology is a mixture of liberation theology and secular Maoism (McBeth 1989). It is estimated that over 20 priests have actually taken up arms against the government during the past two decades, fighting within the ranks of the communist New People's Army (NPA). At the other end of the ideological spectrum, a politically right-wing religious cult, Sagrado

Corazon Senor, with a claimed 150,000 members throughout the Philippines and based in Mindanao, engages in vigilante activities against suspected communists. Devotees of the cult wear special amulets which, if their faith in God is strong enough, are claimed to allow bullets to bounce off their bodies rather than penetrate them. Communists, some of whom have fought the state in the NPA since the early 1970s, are judged to be the Devil's soldiers (Fineman 1987).

Haiti is the poorest country in the Western hemisphere, with a mere 0.9 per cent of GDP or US$3.44 per capita spent on public health in 1985 and with one secondary school teacher for every 189 members of the security forces. Catholicism is the official religion. Some 80 per cent of the population of seven million are adherents. Despite gaining freedom from France in 1804, independent Haiti experienced little except economic, political and environmental disaster. In 1957 the infamous dictatorship of François 'Papa Doc' Duvalier was established until his death in 1971. He was replaced by his son, Jean-Claude 'Baby Doc' Duvalier, who fled the country in 1986. Following several years of military-dominated rule, elections in February 1991 resulted in the coming to power, with 67 per cent of the votes cast, of a 38-year-old radical priest, Father Jean-Bertrand Aristide, who until then had run an orphanage in Haiti's capital, Port-au-Prince. Aristide led a political party, Lavalas (Avalanche), whose slogan 'Justice, Participation, Openness' reflected its desire to take Haiti out of its sordid poverty through the mechanism of popular participation. Seven months later, a military coup, led by General Raoul Cedras, resulted in Aristide's overthrow, with the loss of more than 1000 lives in the next few months (Chamberlain 1991). Aristide fled Haiti, and the Organization of American States, led by the United States, called for his return to power, a demand backed up by economic sanctions. Deadlock followed with supporters and opponents of Aristide dangerously polarized in confrontation. The impasse was finally broken in mid-1993 when it appeared that a US-brokered deal would allow Aristide to return to Haiti as President.

Aristide's radical aims, with his political programme couched in the tenets of liberation theology as a practical means to push through fundamental changes in Haiti's grotesquely divided society, reflected the growing schism which had split the Catholic Church in Latin America since the 1960s. Education programmes in Haiti reminiscent of Freire's in Brazil helped to produce radical local leaders and critics of the Duvalier dictatorship, many of whom became stalwarts of Father Aristide's political movement. For a period in the 1980s the Catholic radio station, Radio Soleil, also became a main channel for criticism of the government. Later, however, radicals within the station were replaced by conservative senior figures in the Church hierarchy, reflecting the disquiet which Aristide's revolutionary messages caused among them. Ironically, it was the American government, no longer frightened of revolutionary socialism with the demise of the Cold War, and in early 1992 contemplating invading Haiti to force Aristide's return to power, which did most to try to force Aristide's re-instatement (Tisdall 1991). Within Haiti, however, there were significant numbers of politically conservative Christian fundamentalists who feared the return of Aristide and his revolutionary policies. Some 20 per cent of Haitians are followers of Protestant churches (Gelber 1989: 92). The existence of such people and the groups they belong to, not only in Haiti but elsewhere in the Christian Third World, forms a second significant development in contemporary Christianity in the developing countries.

The history of CEB-type organizations in Latin America and elsewhere over the past three decades closely paralleled the fortunes of liberation theology itself. A decade of growth was followed by widespread military rule and repression in the 1970s and early 1980s. The return to democracy in Latin America saw a shifting of political focus from local level CEBs (as manifestations of socially progressive orientations) towards more conventional forms of political mobilization, such as political parties. By the 1990s CEBs had endured, but their initial inspiration – liberation theology – was linked in many people's perceptions to the depredations of guerrillas, such as Sendero Luminoso in Peru. As examined below, a popular response was to move towards the pentecostalist and other conservative forms of Protestantism in which individual salvation was the goal, rather than community progress.

Christian fundamentalism and syncretism in Africa and Latin America

Christian fundamentalist world views are tied historically, and by definition, to certain dogmatic fundamentals of Christianity, especially the supposed inerrancy of the Bible. This, along with a moral conservatism, usually strongly linked to a political position that aims to preserve conservative standards and values, establishes their socio-political position. However, 'the political consequences of fundamentalism will vary according to the extent to which [it] . . . makes claims over society or sets up norms which all citizens are expected to obey' (Martin 1990a: 129). One way of evaluating the political consequences of such groups is to seek to assess the degree to which they attempt to involve themselves, at the least, in the process by which public resources are allocated and, at the most, in attempts to forge a state in which religious laws are paramount. We noted earlier that 'fundamentalism' is a misleading term because it tends to conflate conservative versions of various religions into one unwarranted whole. Nevertheless, we use the adjective 'fundamentalist' to describe certain types of Christians, not least because this is the way they refer to themselves, especially in parts of Africa.

Unlike many Islamists, very few Christian fundamentalists wish to see (or perhaps, more accurately, find it possible to envisage) a theocratic state. Muslims of varying political beliefs may contemplate a future Islamic state based upon the current models offered by, for example, Saudi Arabia or Iran. Christian fundamentalists do not have a model to base a vision on. Moreover, in the United States at least, such people's religious roots are often in the Baptist Church, with its tradition of separation of church and state. Given that many of the pentecostalist and fundamentalist churches active in the Third World have their roots in the United States, it is not surprising that such groups wish to eschew 'politics'. As we shall see, this has political consequences in areas where these churches are active.

Fundamentalist and pentecostalist groups have been active in Sub-Saharan Africa for more than 50 years. Pentecostalist sects, such as the Seventh Day Baptists, the Brethren Church and the Open Bible Standard Church Group, were active in West, Central and East Africa as long ago as the 1930s and 1940s. The Seventh Day Adventists were estimated to have as many as 2000 missionaries in the field by the 1950s, while the American Assemblies of God had about 750. By the early 1960s, these two sects in particular had gained considerable numbers of followers (Wilson 1985: 309).

From the early 1970s a new wave of pentecostal churches made further inroads among Christians in Ghana, Nigeria, South Africa and elsewhere. A significant reason is that such churches offered comfort at a time of rapid social change, frequent economic hardship and sometimes serious ethnic rivalries. Existing alongside the official and independent churches, the pentecostalist churches became of socio-political importance. They targeted their message to the university campuses, where mass conversions took place. Such sects have a number of characteristics in common with independent African churches (see Chapter 2), which facilitated their consolidation within African society. Indeed, the demarcation lines between foreign and indigenous churches in this respect are not necessarily about differing religious practices so much as a reflection of the educational level of respective church leaders. To many educated Africans independent churches are embarrassing because they conduct services in vernacular languages rather than European ones. Yet they do offer comfort and hope to many people. As Martin (1990b: 160) puts it:

> On the one hand they ameliorate some of the problems of their respective societies by breaking down barriers and providing secure orientations which assuage anomie. On the other they easily assimilate to the norms of consumer capitalism and defuse fundamental attacks on the social order.

Members of pentecostalist sects will sometimes be in conflict with the established (and establishment) Christian churches, and may incur the displeasure of government. In Ghana, the Rawlings regime banned a number of sects in the mid-1980s, following campaigns by the mainstream Christian churches which highlighted their unconventional religious styles and practices (Haynes 1989: 86–7). In Nigeria, pentecostalists and other Christian conservatives find themselves in a triply conflictual situation. First, they are in opposition to those Christians they accuse of apostasy: Catholics, Methodists, Presbyterians and Anglicans, all of whom are 'bent on not conforming to the teachings of Christ' (Ibrahim 1991: 121), i.e. God is already the ruler of his kingdom, and to set oneself up as a political leader on earth is a challenge to his rule. A second conflict is with those Nigerians who are adherents to traditional religious practices, and a third is with Islamists (Haynes 1992).

The political significance of the fundamentalist and pentecostal Christian churches in Sub-Saharan Africa is three-fold. First, they are against socialism and atheistic Marxism; this attribute tends to make them averse to any socially progressive movement. Second, adherents believe that people's redemption is in their own hands (or rather in God's and the individual's hands), and that expectations that government could or should supply all people's needs is misplaced. Third, followers of these churches do 'not seek to form political parties or create political solidarity' (Abasiattai 1988: 500), believing that political rulers should rule, and religion and religious figures should stick to spiritual matters. What this implies is that followers of fundamentalist and penetecostal Christianity in Africa 'keep out of politics', believing that what happens on earth is all part of the continuing battle between the Devil and God for dominance. As a result secular rulers are not really thought to be to blame for what goes wrong. Such a belief in the tele-guidance of policy by God lets secular rulers off the hook:

> We must understand that quite a lot of the problems we face in the country today with relation to the politics, agriculture, weather, etc. may be due in part to the fact that certain things have been programmed by the forces of darkness through interference in the heavenly bodies. . . . The political, economic and social situations will be the result of what goes on in the spiritual realm. . . . Learn to DAILY pray and intercede for at least a prayer item concerning Nigeria.
> (Christian Students' Social Movement of Nigeria 1983)

Nevertheless, in December 1983 a group of austere senior military personnel gained power by ousting the corrupt Shagari regime in Nigeria following a coup d'état; Christian fundamentalists welcomed the event as 'God's intervention par excellence'.

In South Africa, types of extant Christianity reflect the polarized nature of that society. For example, 'prophetic Christianity, in relating biblical values to the analysis of society and the search for justice, has divided Christian communities, by confronting the established churches as well as the state' (Walshe 1991: 27). Because of the socio-political situation in South Africa, with still incomplete moves towards the dismantling of the apartheid system of separate development of black, white and 'coloured' people, many, especially non-white, Christians were stimulated by the tenets of Latin American style liberation theology. Many white people, on the other hand, especially Afrikaners, maintained beliefs characterized by much more spiritually and politically conservative ideals and ideas (Martin 1990b: 157).

It would not be correct to assert that Christian fundamentalists have had a major impact upon national level politics in Sub-Saharan Africa if we judge political influence solely by involvement in party politics. Given the novelty of such political competition in the region in recent times, however, it is difficult to ascribe precise political consequence to any form of religious mobilization, including Islam. The conservative world view of Christian fundamentalists has an impact upon politics that is difficult to quantify precisely without further research. The well-studied situation in South Africa (see Walshe 1991), where contending versions of politicized Christianity (liberation theology *versus* conservatism) have had a demonstrable effect on political competition, suggests that comparable research elsewhere in Africa would significantly enhance our understanding of political processes in the region.

Forms of Christianity often interact with other, often pre-Christian, beliefs to create syncretic religions in Sub-Saharan Africa. In Nigeria, sects like the Oberi Okaime Christian Mission (OOCM) of Calabar (which developed its own language) were founded in the colonial period in reaction to the European dominated Christian missions which were the vehicle of both religion and European cultural norms. This was not, however, only caused by resentment at European domination but was also a reflection of the rather staid (to many Africans) nature of the services. Adherents of OOCM not only sought out adherents of traditional religions and persecuted them (a practice which brought them into conflict with both chiefs and colonial officials) but also 'encouraged deep spiritual and emotional experiences. . . . Converts became "possessed" by "the spirit": their bodies shook violently, they "spoke in tongues" or prophesied; and they sang, shouted and clapped "wildly" "like mad people", stared with their eyes and shook' (Abasiattai 1988: 500). Thus traditional religious norms were juxtaposed with certain beliefs characteristic of the pentecostalist churches. In addition, there was the more straightforwardly, less syncretic pentecostalist Apostolic Church, introduced into Nigeria in the 1920s, which grew in tandem with the indigenous Aladura church; each offered more 'African' forms of worship.

Some anti-colonialist religio-ethnic movements used both Christian and traditional religious beliefs to forge a syncretistic ideology of anti-Europeanization. One of the most important was the Lumpa (Visible Salvation) Church of Alice Lenshina Mulenga, founded in 1954 in Northern Rhodesia (Zambia). African attitudes of rejection and attempted withdrawal from European influence are illustrated by the history of the Lumpa Church.

Whereas the Lumpa Church was an overt response to European colonization, it is clear that the rationale for its creation was not annulled by the withdrawal of the colonizers' control. Following independence in 1964, the Lumpa Church was banned after clashes with government troops that cost 700 lives. Alice Lenshina Mulenga was arrested and was still incarcerated when she died in 1978 (Gifford 1989: 330–1). Interpretations differ as to the wider socio-political significance of the Lumpa phenomenon. Van Binsbergen (1981) sees the Lumpa Church as reflecting the growth of a movement which sought to renovate peasant production and to defend rural communities against the impact of the threatening capitalist mode of production. This is more satisfactory than seeing Lumpa as simply the personal vehicle of a putative prophet, but van Binsbergen goes too far in seeing the Lumpa Church as a vehicle of class development. It is best to see it as an attack cult, as the political vehicle of rural people under threat of displacement by outside (i.e. state) powers seemingly bent on the communities' destruction.

More recently, in Uganda in the late 1980s, another anti-government spiritual movement emerged, headed by an Acholi woman, Alice Lakwena. She claimed to have been ordered by God to overthrow the Ugandan leader, Yoweri Museveni. Most of Lakwena's 'troops', lightly armed but apparently believing in their indestructibility as a result of Lakwena's blessing, were from the Acholi, who felt humiliated by their rough treatment at the hands of Museveni's National Resistance Army (Ingham 1990: 36). After some months of fighting the rebellion came to an end: Lakwena fled to Kenya, while many of her former fighters joined anti-government guerrilla groups.

The power and influence exerted over local people by both Alice Lenshina and Alice Lakwena were in part modern resonances of the widespread religio-political status which women enjoyed in many parts of pre-colonial Africa. A close historical parallel is Donna Beatrice, who established her own version of Christianity in Kongo (Angola) at the beginning of the eighteenth century. Donna Beatrice claimed to be St Antony, to speak to God, and that the Day of Judgement was at hand. Such was her persuasiveness that 'Almost the entire kingdom was disaffected and adhered to the Antonian sect' (Andersson 1984: 306). She led a rebellion against the pro-Portuguese Kongo leadership for which she was executed. In addition, Parpart (1988: 210) notes the role of Nehenda, a Shona religious figure, who was executed for her role in the 1896 uprising in Southern Rhodesia. Clearly, then, women were of significance in leading religio-political resistance to attempts by external forces to dominate local communities in pre-colonial, colonial and independence periods.

What the above examples suggest is that in rural areas of Africa threatened by crisis and the problem of deep social instability, provided there is a sufficient degree of community solidarity, religion-inspired resistance, utilizing both pre-modern and European-introduced beliefs in a complex interaction, may grow. One of the most recent examples of this phenomenon was the *naparamas* of the Zambezia and Nampula provinces in Mozambique. These were two areas most seriously affected by the Renamo rebel incursions against the Frelimo government. The latter was completely unable to provide protection for local people against Renamo attack. As a result, the *naparamas*, a virtually unarmed spiritual movement, grew to prominence between 1990 and 1992. The movement was led by Manual Antonio, a young man who believed he was Jesus Christ. Following 'vaccination' against Renamo bullets by ash from a sacred bush, his 20,000 spear-armed followers drove Renamo out of large areas of the north of Mozambique. In a bid to thwart the *naparama*'s success, Renamo soldiers were in turn 'vaccinated' against their spears. In contrast to Lakwena's and Lenshina's churches the *naparamas* were warmly welcomed by the government, which regarded them as a 'return to traditional sources of peasant strength, abandoned in the years of the attempted rush to modernisation' (Brittain 1991). Despite the slaying of Manual Antonio in early 1992, which had an understandably disastrous effect on the *naparamas'* morale and a correspondingly uplifting one on Renamo's 25,000 troops, the lasting significance of the movement was to force the Frelimo government to recognize the political power of traditional culture and religion. In a parallel move the Frelimo government also sought to cultivate better relations with both Protestant and Catholic Churches – as well as the country's Muslims – in a further demonstration of a distancing from the formerly official Marxist-Leninist ideology.

Non-Muslim Sub-Saharan Africa presents a picture of religious complexity with multiple forms of Christianity often juxtaposed and interacting with pre-modern religious beliefs reflective of the region's rich social, political and ethnic history. It would not be appropriate to assert that religion overtly plays a large part in politics at national level, yet within the context of local-level politics especially, religio-cultural beliefs form the bedrock of people's world views. The fact that Africans do not necessarily associate religion with 'politics' (a term with often different connotations than in the West, and implying what rulers and other 'big men' do *to* each other and the people under their control, without the latter's ability to affect that process) should not disguise the potential, and at times actual, impact which religion has had on politics, as the examples above have shown. Nevertheless, we need to differentiate between African syncretic hybrids and pentecostalist and fundamentalist churches, and the Protestant sects encouraged by US 'televangelists' and spreading quickly in Latin America. The growth of such sects has significant implications for sociopolitical realities there.

Some argue that Latin America is rapidly 'de-Catholicizing'. *Every hour 400 Latin Americans convert to the pentecostal or other Protestant evangelical churches* (Lernoux 1988). Overall, one-eighth of the region's 500 million people (i.e. some 65 million) belong to pentecostal or fundamentalist Protestant churches. It is estimated that, on current trends, half the population of Latin America will switch to Protestantism by the end of the century. This means that annually some 3.5 million Latin Americans convert from Catholicism to conservative, usually pentecostal Protestant sects. Nearly 30 per cent of Brazil's population of 140 million belong to over 4000 different Protestant churches and evangelical sects (Rocha 1991). Thirty-five per cent of Guatemalans are *evangelicos*, as are 20 per cent of Chileans. In El Salvador, Honduras and Nicaragua, the figure is 10–15 per cent, with numbers of *evangelicos* growing three times as quickly as the populations as a whole (Stoll 1990: 335). To many people in these countries, racked in recent times by civil war and commotion, and stratified along racial lines, the new sects provided a safe haven. Many ordinary people perceive Protestant worship (especially through the burgeoning pentecostal evangelical sects) as a way of getting nearer to God, unmediated by a hierarchy as in the Catholic Church. Three categories of people were especially attracted to the Protestant sects: the politically weak and marginalized, the growing middle class, and Indians and those of mixed race. To the last the sects offered a semi-autonomous base in which some elements of indigenous language and culture could be preserved. At the same time, the Protestant churches bring with them a crusading anti-communist, millennialist and health-and-wealth theology which dovetails with military counter-insurgency efforts. Officials of the Roman Catholic Church in Latin America see the spread of Protestantism as a new form of 'Yankee imperialism'. This serves a dual purpose: It allows them to castigate the Protestant competition, while at the same time placing the blame for Protestant growth not on the local population, but on the alleged source of all world evil, the United States.[1]

Protestantism in Latin America and other Iberian Third World areas has a long history of being the minor player in an unequal relationship with the much stronger Catholic Church. From the early 1970s there developed, in addition, a division between different wings of Protestantism: one was the Protestant ecumenical movement; the other, of more significance politically, was the fundamentalist or born-again evangelicals (Alvarez 1981: 103–6). During the 1960s and early 1970s developments in Protestantism had paralleled those in Catholicism in Latin America. Among Protestants, there was a general concern with the position of the poor within the context of the growth in numbers of those afflicted by poverty. By the late 1970s, however, the explosive growth of the 'born-again' churches in the USA had spread to Latin America. The result was serious net losses in mainstream Protestant denominations (Wuthnow 1986: 17; D'Antonio 1990). Modern media and communications networks beamed the message of the so-called televangelists (such as Oral Roberts, Pat Robertson, Jerry Falwell and the since discredited Jimmy Swaggart and Jim and Tammy Bakker), and that of their religious organizations (such as the Church of God and the Southern Baptist Convention), into the homes of millions.

Even though the growth of Protestantism was most swift from the 1970s, its advance had begun in the 1930s (Bruce 1990: 161). Most people who converted changed to the pentecostalist churches. Wilson (1985: 299), writing in the 1960s, argued that their reaction

> towards the outside world is to suggest that the latter is corrupted because man [sic] is corrupted. If men [sic] can be changed then the world will be changed. This type of sect takes no interest in programmes of social reform or in the political solution of social problems and may even be actively hostile towards them.

Yet, since Wilson wrote some 25 years ago, the conversionist pentecostal sects in Latin America have become politicized. They reject all causal explanations that refer to the possible influence of environmental factors, e.g. poverty or landlessness, on people's behaviour, or indeed any other deterministic explanation.

It is possible to argue that this wholesale switching of religious allegiance is just the most recent phase in the centuries-old battle between Anglo-Saxon Protestantism and Iberian Catholicism, in which leadership of the Protestant side has passed from Britain to the USA. But it would be wrong to see the growth of pentecostalism in Latin America as a sinister right-wing plot, directed from the USA. There are parallels between the social and psychological roles performed by this new religion in Latin America and the appeals of Methodism in urban England in the second half of the eighteenth century. There is also a second precedent: the conversion of the Scottish highlands to evangelical Calvinism in the early nineteenth century, following the destruction of the clan system after 1745 and the displacement of an unwanted peasantry to make way for sheep and deer. Thus, as in eighteenth-century urban England and the Scottish highlands, in present-day Latin America, Bruce (1990: 162) argues,

> the market for a new religion has been created by the destruction of the social system which supported the old one. Millions of people are being displaced from the interiors by agri-business. The old hacienda system is decaying. Native tribes, once isolated on the fringes, are now being over-run and dragged into the modern world. Newly located and dislocated in the mega-cities, these people are in the market for a new vision to make sense of their present and future.

Pentecostalism offers a new character to people who are outside the downward thrust of elite power and free from the lateral ties of the organic community. New arrivals to the towns and cities (some fleeing from the deprivations of guerrilla–state warfare) may see in pentecostalism a means of self-help and admittance to a community. The networks of church fellowship frequently provide the social support of a cooperative individualism and thus prepare people for the new world while sheltering them from its most destructive effects. There is no one obvious political consequence to the spread of pentecostalism, other than the development of a certain political quietism which may colour one's politics a shade of conservatism. Pentecostals are said to be 'politically disinterested in Chile' (where they represent 80–90 per cent of all Protestants); with 'very weak socio-political engagement' among South American Indian pentecostals; to 'increased engagement in society by the Central American Pentecostals' (Marishane 1990: 9). Such quietude is not because such individuals are necessarily politically conservative in a left–right dichotomous way, but rather because the political world is deemed of little importance when compared to one's own spiritual development and the certainty of attaining heaven. Although some right-wing Americans may see the growth of conservative evangelical Protestantism and pentecostalism as de facto triumphs for American capitalist and 'family' values, there is no clear evidence that supports the view that Latin American countries with large pentecostal populations will be more actively pro-American than others.

Because of the location of the conservative Protestant sects' bases in the USA it is unsurprising that they should have directed their attentions to the geographically close countries of Central America. Although the Christian right considered itself the head of a domestic political crusade, its leaders also had a vision that went beyond North America to include a large but little-known international wing of the movement: 'born-again' Christian missionaries. Even though many Britons and other Europeans are vaguely aware of fundamentalist sects' activities (having perhaps encountered them on their doorsteps), this Christian foreign legion, including Mormons and Jehovah's Witnesses, grew especially swiftly in Central and Latin America, and in the Pacific Rim countries of South Korea and the Philippines from the 1970s. American televangelists (now loaded with dollars as gullible US citizens tried to save their souls in the only way they knew how) looked for ways to extend their influence. Thousands of born-again foreign crusaders promoted both US-style religion and right-wing, pro-USA politics in a number of Third World countries. It would not be going too far to say that the conservative Protestant movement represented a new, partially invisible strand of US foreign policy under the guise of religious dissemination. Vociferously anti-communist, its representatives worked to convert Third World masses to conservative faith and to promote US national interests, as they saw them.

Tensions were severe in Central America, where the religious war coincided with a shooting one. On the one hand, there were US and Central American Catholics who opposed Washington's policies in the region; on the other, conservative Protestants supported them. The competition for souls had strong political overtones, with the most serious clashes in Central America. Here US foreign policy aims in the 1980s were headed by the necessity of 'rolling back' the perceived tide of 'communism'. The latter was exemplified, until the electoral defeat in April 1990, by the Sandinista regime in Nicaragua and, until a peace treaty in early 1992, by the left-wing guerrilla incursions in El Salvador.

American Protestant conservatives were heavily involved in the Nicaraguan Contra war, which lasted into the early 1990s. The campaign to overturn the Sandinistas – at various times including three or four radical Catholic priests in government – attracted a stream of US evangelicals to the Contra camps on the Honduran border. As a result, Honduras was on the front line of both anti-communism and born-again evangelism. It was home base not only for the American-backed, anti-Sandinista Contras, but also for the hundreds of conservative American missionaries who had come to fight the Devil's work, i.e. communism. Allen Danforth, the US Director of World Gospel Outreach, a $2 million a year operation supplying medicine and food to hundreds of families across Honduras, regarded 'food hand-outs . . . as a bait to attract poor families to church services.' More importantly, 'evangelicalism can be a powerful tool to head communism off at the pass, in the name of Jesus Christ . . . Honduras is the front line between communism and Texas' (D'Antonio 1990: 149).

Such sentiments were not confined to ordinary missionaries. A 1988 US presidential candidate, Pat Robertson, and his organization Christian Broadcasting Network (CBN) were among the biggest contributors to the anti-Sandinista, pro-Contra campaign, raising millions of dollars for food, medicine, clothing, vehicles and other aid for Nicaraguan refugees in Honduras, many of whom were estimated to be anti-Sandinista fighters. While Robertson tried to claim at first that CBN contributions were not meant for the Contras, his organization did not deny that the supplies were being shipped through intermediary groups with close ties to the then Reagan administration or that they were being sent to the war-torn Nicaraguan border (Lernoux 1988: 53). On one occasion Robertson visited a Contra training camp in Honduras to preach his conservative Protestant gospel and to distribute good cheer. He compared the Contra aggression to the American Revolution and claimed: 'I think God is in favour of liberty and justice and He is against oppression. . . . If we can do something to help these men fight for freedom, I think it is perfectly in God's plan' (Lernoux 1988: 53). Robertson's claims did not go down too well with Bishop Walter Sullivan, a Catholic opponent of US aid to the Contras, who publicly criticized Robertson, saying: 'I cannot imagine Jesus reviewing troops.' In response, Robertson replied angrily that he had not been reviewing troops and that Sullivan should watch his words or he might find himself arraigned for 'libel and slander' (Lernoux 1988: 53). This incident illustrated the gulf between the conservative Protestants and the more open-minded, liberal Catholics in the USA over the Contra issue, reflecting the disputes on the ground in Latin America.

Latin American Catholic bishops sought to ascribe the inroads of the Protestant fundamentalists to the activities of the CIA (Cruise O'Brien 1990: 168). Brazilian bishops claimed that the American missionaries of the pentecostal and fundamentalist churches were more interested in right-wing politics than in matters of the soul (D'Antonio 1990: 148–9). Yet, just as the older Protestant churches were encouraged in the nineteenth century by Latin American liberal nationalist governments keen to break the bond between monarchy and Catholic Church, so right-wing military dictatorships have deliberately encouraged Protestant fundamentalist and pentecostal missionaries. Under the evangelical Protestant president, General Rios Montt (who stepped down for a civilian evangelical Protestant, Jorge Serrano, in January 1991), the Guatemalan government persecuted the Catholic Church and encouraged US-based fundamentalist churches (Bruce 1990: 162). Serrano's success underlined the growing political importance of fundamentalist Protestantism in traditionally Catholic Latin America. Evangelicals also played an important role in the election of Alberto Fujimori as Peru's president in June 1990 (Reid 1990). In Chile fundamentalists and pentecostalists were called 'Reagan cults' (after the right-wing US president Ronald Reagan, in office 1980–8) because of their supposed promotion of right-wing American values and interests. But while pentecostalism certainly acquires some additional social (and perhaps political) clout from its association with a very successful and powerful country, neither the political interests of the USA nor the more local interests of various governments explain why so many Guatemalans or Brazilians ·or Chileans or San Salvadoreans or Nicaraguans actually become pentecostalists.

The answer lies in the idea that pentecostalism holds an emotional appeal, particularly for poor Latin Americans, through its emphasis on ecstatic personal experience, such as speaking in tongues and receiving the 'gifts' of healing and prophecy. In other words Latin Americans (especially the poor and disadvantaged) appear to want 'more' religion, not less. Studies show that one reason for the evangelicals' success is the lack of sufficient Catholic priests to serve the burgeoning Latin American population. In parishes in Brazil and elsewhere in Latin America there is sometimes only one priest to serve up to 50,000 faithful. In the absence of the hoped-for benefits deriving from the reintroduction of democracy in 1985, after 21 years of military rule, poor people are unsurprisingly impressed by the evangelicals' emphasis on strict morality, and the way conversion can transform some-one hitherto identified as a 'neighbourhood bum' into an upright community leader. 'Once a man surrenders his life to Jesus', proclaims the Argentinian evangelist Luis Palau, 'he finds he can stop drinking and chasing women' (Lernoux 1988: 51). In other words, becoming an evangelical Protestant offers people a chance of enhanced self-esteem which continued adherence to Catholicism does not necessarily do.

Of equal importance in explaining and understanding the evangelical surge are the deteriorating social and economic conditions in much of Latin America, which political democratization in the 1980s has not ameliorated. Since the 1950s, millions of peasants have left their villages to seek a better life in the cities, changing the balance of Latin America's population from rural to urban. Uprooted from families and religious traditions, living in slums and at the mercy of criminals and frequently governmental predators, the urban poor are a fertile seedbed for evangelical proselytism. Pro Mundi Vita, a Belgium-based Catholic research body, put it this way: 'Many peasants and slum inhabitants need religion as a refuge in a society in permanent and progressive disintegration in order to deal with fear, threats, repression, hunger and death.' Too often, Pro Mundi Vita claimed, the Catholic Church has ignored such needs because it lacked clergy, money and imagination (Lernoux 1988: 52). In addition, the division between those in the Catholic Church adhering to the ideas and values of 'liberation the-ology', on the one hand, and those conservative Catholic Church figures who have fought against the development of radicalism and church mili-tancy, on the other, have presented an unattractive face to would-be adher-ents. The result has been that the conservative Protestant sects have stepped into the vacuum.

The Vatican came to a similar conclusion in a 1986 study (Sects or new religious movements: pastoral challenges). While the authors agreed with the Latin American Catholic bishops that the 'new' churches were created and maintained by powerful ideological forces as well as economic and political interests in the United States, they did acknowledge that the conservative Protestant churches were fulfilling

> needs and inspirations which are seemingly not being met in the mainline churches. The [Catholic] church is often seen simply as an institution, perhaps because it gives too much importance to structures and not enough to drawing people to God in Christ.
>
> (Lernoux 1988: 52)

The 500-year anniversary in 1992 of the 'discovery' of the Americas by Christopher Columbus focused human rights groups and local Indians' anger and resentment at the duplicity of the Roman Catholic Church, which had come to Latin America with a cross in one hand and a sword in the other. Indian leaders in Ecuador, Mexico, Peru and elsewhere saw the Catholic Church as part of the ideological domination of the Europeans, in the forefront of a cultural racism which had lasted until the current time. Such people, often at the bottom of the socio-economic structure, found in the pentecostal sects, with their cures and exorcism sessions, a welcome response to the poor population's desperate desire for welfare and medical treatment. At the same time, however, the Protestant fundamentalist sects led by North American missionaries in the field in Latin America were also regarded by the same Indian leaders as representative of the European invasion of their lands (Rocha 1991).

There was a sometimes uneasy ambivalence in local people's response to the 'invasion' of the Protestant fundamentalists, especially when their representatives became embroiled in domestic political issues. Many Latin Americans certainly found spiritual comfort in the immediacy, closeness and apparent concern demonstrated by the conservative Protestant churches. Yet many Chileans, for example, took exception to what they perceived as political statements made by the since discredited US televangelist Jimmy Swaggart during his visit to the country's capital, Santiago, in early 1987. On that occasion Swaggart defended the right-wing military regime of General Augusto Pinochet (1973–90), congratulating him for having expelled the 'devil' – meaning the political left – in the 1973 coup which overthrew the democratically elected socialist government of Dr Salvador Allende.

The conservative Protestants who had converted some 10 per cent of Chileans by the end of the 1980s, including 15,000 members of the armed forces, were clearly 'politicized', if by that one understands their general ideological position ('anti-communism') as going hand-in-hand with their spiritual certainties. Conservative American preachers including Swaggart, Pat Robertson, Jerry Falwell and Allen Danforth made frequent trips to Chile, hobnobbing with members of the Pinochet regime. It would be hard to deny that such people did not clearly associate God with right-wing authoritarianism and the political left with the Devil. The conservative Protestants were popular with the Pinochet government precisely *because* of their political conservatism and emphasis on passive acceptance of authority

– in contrast to more socially activist Catholic groups, some of which were inspired by liberation theology.

This chapter has demonstrated how Christianity forms a cultural – and hence political – background to society's aspirations in South America and other areas. Thirty years ago, the ideas of socially progressive liberation theology made a major impact in South America. More recently its ideas have found a constituency in Haiti, the Philippines and South Africa. The rise, fall and partial rise again of liberation theology was one side of the political equation. The other was the spread of fundamentalist and pentecostalist Protestantism to many parts of the Third World, including Sub-Saharan Africa, which not only reflected the impact of conservative politico-religious ideas, generally from the USA, but also often constituted an alternative choice for those disillusioned with Catholicism's spiritual lassitude. Many people in South America turned away from Roman Catholicism, partly because of a paucity of religious professionals and partly because of the attraction of pentecostalist and fundamentalist ideas which promised individual salvation rather than community redemption. I have tried not to give the idea that conservative politico-religious ideas were a from of 'Yankee imperialism' but this is how it was seen by the Roman Catholic Church and, to an extent, by the practitioners of the ideas themselves. Clearly we need to investigate this further. In the next chapter we shall examine the issue of religious goals in foreign policy within the context of both Islam and Christianity.

Note

1 I am indebted to Professor W. E. Hewitt of the University of Western Ontario, Canada, for this point.

Links between religion and foreign policy in the Third World

What may be called religion-oriented or religion-associated foreign policy goals have been pursued in the context of both relations within the Third World and relations of developed countries with the developing (Rubin 1990b: 51). These are in addition to, yet closely linked with and in some ways inseparable from, secular foreign policy objectives. The latter include the various facets of national security, such as territorial integrity and economic prosperity, the spreading of a state's 'values' and, sometimes, ideology, and the maintenance and, if possible, increase of diplomatic recognition. All states pursue such goals regardless of size, population geographical location and economic status. Foreign policy, following Holsti, is here defined as 'the actions of a state towards the external environment and the conditions under which these actions are formulated' (Holsti 1972: 21). We are, then, concerned fundamentally with state–state relations, and shall not be concerned with non-state actors, such as the Catholic Church, which may have a *de facto* foreign policy, but are outside the scope of this chapter.

We are concerned with the nature of, and weight to be given to, religion in foreign policy in Third World contexts. Generally, it is a most difficult task to separate ideological and non-ideological motivations of foreign policy actions. In this context I am using the term 'ideology' not in a Marxian sense, but to suggest a body of politico-economic ideas which forms the basis or rationale of a state's strategy, in this case its foreign policy. In this sense, ideology may be used to 'explain events and policies, outline the final objective of those policies, justify the choice of friend and foe, and legitimize . . . domestic and regional authority (Deeb 1991: 5). Thus if a state purports to be guided by a set of ideas, such as Islam, then foreign policy, as well as domestic issues, will be justified by reference to it. In other words, among states which profess an Islamic affinity, one would expect that 'Islam would constitute a significant influence on [foreign] policy' (Dawisha 1983: 2).

That being stated, Western foreign policy-makers and analysts have tended to misjudge or belittle the influence not only of Islam, but also of religious factors more generally, in Third World regional and international politics. The starting point of this problem is one we have already referred to: the understanding and transference of European historical concerns and developments that Western political leaders, policy-makers and intellectuals apply to Third World realities in an inappropriate manner. The articulation of modernization theory was in the context, as well as the offspring, of the notion of the idea of the modern nation state, the intellectual legacy of Machiavelli and Bodin. *Realpolitik*, and its understanding of the relations between states based on power expression and wielding, remains the commonest ideological underpinning of foreign policy formation and analysis.

National interest concerns may dictate either a similar or a different analysis to an assessment undertaken with ideological considerations foremost. The USSR, for so long the dominant power in Eastern Europe, had both ideological considerations (the spreading of Communism) and national interest concerns (to maintain a ring of buffer states against Western attack) to justify its foreign policy there. Yet more often than not, foreign policy-makers undertake courses of action for their states *as a response to developments in a political arena that is beyond their control*. Whereas governments purport to, and indeed often do, control reasonably well their domestic sphere, this is frequently not the case outside the state's boundaries. This is so regardless of the state's status, size or power attributes. For example, the USA, since the demise of the Soviet Union, the only superpower, was unable to control Saddam Hussein, a leader with whom it previously had close, if somewhat covert, relations, in his audacious attempt to integrate Kuwait into Iraq other than by a massive use of force *after the event*. Saddam, for his part, made an appeal to Muslims worldwide to condemn the USA's action on the grounds that the 'infidels' were attacking Islam by the aggression against Iraq. This was despite the fact that the Iraqi government had spent the 20 previous years energetically attempting to snuff out any domestic manifestations of Islam as a political challenge to Saddam's regime (Farouk-Sluglett and Sluglett 1989b: 116–19). It would be fair to assert that Saddam's concern with Islam in this context was more to do with his regime's survival than a reflection of his religious fervour.

Sometimes, however, the ideological proclivities of the state's policy-makers may be a clear guide to its foreign policy orientations. For example, Ethiopia's foreign policy, before the fall of Mengistu Haile Mariam's revolutionary socialist government in mid-1991, was based on a simplistic division of the world into two mutually antagonistic groups: socialist states and imperialist countries (Tekle 1989: 495). In a sense it is irrelevant whether foreign policy-makers in Ethiopia *believed* that such a division was a reasonable reflection of the real world. Ethiopia was highly dependent on Soviet military, technical and other forms of aid. In the context of the Cold War it was clear that continuing support of the USSR for Mengistu's regime was a foreign policy goal for the latter which transcended all others.

As a result it made sense to adopt the ideological perspective of the Soviet Union internationally in order to ensure the continuance of preferential treatment. This was of especial concern in the context of accelerating domestic conflicts, which finally brought the regime's demise.

Such a perspective was useful for another purpose: it helped to provide simple answers to any questions. The 'communist' Soviet Union would be prepared to offer 'socialist' Ethiopia unlimited military, economic and diplomatic assistance by virtue of a shared ideology. The 'capitalist' United States (or its regional allies, such as Somalia) could serve as a scapegoat to explain any past, present or anticipated future difficulties. Slavish solidarity with the USSR compelled Ethiopia to back the Moscow line on each and every issue. Yet such an ideologically derived foreign policy more often than not contradicted Ethiopian national interests as Ethiopia came to be viewed in the rest of Africa as a Soviet stooge. This was especially unfortunate for Mengistu, as he was convinced that destiny called him to lead 'progressive' African forces that would pursue the goals of socialism, end imperialism, neo-colonialism and apartheid, and, in the process, promote world peace. To this laudable end, Ethiopia was committed to undertakings unwarranted by its resources, including the arming and training of a number of southern African liberation movements.

It would appear that religious objectives, in the case of Marxist-Leninist Ethiopia, were by no means an important determinant of foreign policy goals. (Unless, of course, we think of communism as a 'secular religion'.) Two other professed revolutionary states, Libya and Iran, both proclaimed that Islamic goals were a fundamental constituent of their foreign policies (Deeb 1978). At the other end of the revolutionary scale, conservative, pro-Western Saudi Arabia also utilized Islam as an ideological referent. Each of the states used Islam in the same way that Ethiopia used communism, i.e. to divide the world neatly into good and bad, black and white. Unlike Ethiopia, however, Libya, Iran and Saudi Arabia were not in the least subservient to, or even dependent on, other states for economic and diplomatic support. Saudi Arabia relied heavily on US military protection, however. Above all, oil revenues ensured that each of the states received sufficient funds to pursue independent foreign policies.

Nevertheless, we need to bear in mind that *all* states pursue a number of common foreign policy goals, regardless of professed ideology, level of economic development or geographical position. There is no corresponding uniformity when it comes to understanding specific foreign policy actions: several of culturally Christian Ethiopia's predominantly Muslim neighbours, especially Saudi Arabia, gave aid and succour to a number of Ethiopia's regional or ethnic anti-centre guerrilla groups, including the Eritreans, whose leadership passed from Muslims to Marxist-Leninists. This did not, however, cut off the supply of Muslim aid (Clapham 1989: 73). The reason is that Islamic Saudi Arabia had anti-communist national security goals which necessitated the undermining of Marxist-Leninist Ethiopia. In other words, the Saudi Arabian rulers were more concerned with preventing the propagation of class conflict in their polity – via Ethiopia – than they were with the perpetuation of Islam in Eritrea. In this case, national interest goals clearly dominated over ideological concerns.

Generally, three factors need to be borne in mind when we examine the influence of religion on Third World foreign policies. The first involves the domestic religio-cultural context. In Marxist-Leninist Ethiopia, as much as in Islamic Iran, religion should be seen as a central political pillar for any ruler. A commission established in 1986 in Ethiopia to draw up a new socialist constitution included the leaders of all the country's religious groups; a prohibition on polygamy, included in an early draft, was finally excluded due to Muslim leaders' insistence (Clapham 1989). Mengistu clearly understood that the quiescence (or better yet, acquiescence) of important religious constituencies was a key issue in promoting Ethiopia's stability. Even in officially secular, socialist or socially progressive Third World states, religion plays its role as the defining characteristic of politically contending constituencies. This is obviously at odds with the prevailing Western assumption that religion-oriented debates are politically trivial, abstracted from real considerations of power. In the absence of a heated and open theological argument, religion as a major communal identity is all but totally neglected in such perspectives.

Second, Western foreign policy-makers tended until recently to assume invariably that religion's power and influence would inevitably decline in the secularizing modernization process. Noting that process in most of the West and other industrialized countries such as Japan, many Western thinkers assumed that the rest of the world – as it developed – would follow broadly the same pattern. A modern worldview made up of scientific, technological and secularist concerns would prevail over the idea of religious concepts of the universe that dominated pre-modern societies. Yet, it was frequently forgotten that many non-Western societies had been 'force fed' with such concepts, which did not, however, everywhere or easily take root (Pipes 1983–4: 4–7).

Third, it was assumed by many in the modernized world – both capitalist and communist branches – that following Marx, religion was to be regarded primarily as a popular, mind-fuddling drug, an 'opiate' which worked to restrict people's worldviews. Once religion's dangerous misapprehensions were removed the masses would see the world as it really is. The problem with such a view, however, is that many people have been less attracted to Western (or for that matter socialist or communist) secular ideologies than they are with enduring religious beliefs. Thus even when an atheistic ideology apparently dominates – as in communist or other modernizing regimes such as the Shah's – it was not the case that people were willing to give up their religious beliefs. The resurgence of, for example, Catholicism in Cuba and Poland, of Shiite Islam in Iran and of Sunni Islam in Tajikistan provide sufficient testimony to the continuing power of religion to win people's allegiances even after long periods of official secularism and secularization (Rubin 1990b: 52).

Such is religion's continuing stature that the only interest group in most Third World states which may be of comparable strength and (sometimes) independence to the military is the religious establishment. It is, of course, very likely that when the military has a predominant influence on a state's foreign policy then the latter's goals reflect this. The state, spending huge amounts of precious foreign exchange on military hardware, seeks to justify such spending by the creation or amplification of real or would-be foreign enemies. Part of the military's role – at least from a self-interest perspective – is to ensure that an array of enemies beyond the state's boundaries are deemed to be sufficiently threatening.

Religious establishments, for their part, influence foreign policy-making in different ways, and not only in the Third World. First, they claim to champion norms of behaviour to which society as a whole, including the decision-makers themselves, are expected to adhere. For example, the USA, a *de facto* Christian country, is, at least nominally, bound by the notion that it is wrong to kill. If the USA is to use armed force as an instrument of policy, it must do so in a way sanctioned as an exception to this general rule, if it wishes to maintain the backing of Christian religious leaders. In the 1980s the religious establishment included increasing numbers of born-again Christians, represented by such televangelists as the 1992 presidential candidate, Pat Buchanan, who preached that it was justified to fight Satan (i.e. communism) with armed force. This gave a veneer of religious respectability to otherwise morally indefensible US foreign policy activities in Central America (such as, in Nicaragua, arming Contra terrorists and mining harbours). There was no serious debate, however, as to what constituted 'communism'; increasingly it appeared to be defined by any policies that sought, however timidly, to establish a measure of social justice in dangerously socially and politically polarized countries in Latin America and the Caribbean, including Brazil, Guatemala, Nicaragua and Jamaica.

Religious conservatives in the USA established links with like-minded individuals and groups in Central America and elsewhere. Such links were also of significance in the Muslim world. Islamists in one country tend to cultivate links with similar groups in other countries, a process facilitated by both history and culture. Examples include the attempted liberation of the Shiites of Iraq from the bloodthirsty rule of Saddam Hussein by co-religionists from Shiite Iran, and the close ties between elements of the Afghan mojahiden and the Algerian Islamic Salvation Front. Such links may or may not be sanctioned by the state's political leaders. Generally, however, many Muslim states' foreign policy goals include religious goals, established at the urging of the religious establishment. In other words, a community of believers, beyond the state's boundaries, may constitute a special field of interest for the foreign policy-makers of a particular country. This is not to argue that such goals are pursued solely for religious reasons, but rather that religious and national interest objectives may conveniently dovetail to provide dual justification and rationalization.

A number of governments have developed religious foreign policy goals which complement rather than replace other goals. Most of the examples that will be presented in this chapter derive from those states pursuing what might be broadly called Islamic goals, such as Libya, Iran and Pakistan. There are no parallel examples of Christian regimes overtly pursuing religious goals *per se*. Part of the reason for this is that, as we have already noted, Christianity is not an all-encompassing socio-political system as is Islam: the nature and characteristics of a putative Christian state in this sense are unclear. Indeed, the very notion has been off the political agenda for some 350 years, i.e. since the separation of church and state in Western Europe following the Thirty Years War and the Treaty of Westphalia of 1648.

It *is* the case that the USA's foreign policy in parts of Central America in the 1980s under President Reagan gave succour to some particularly unsavoury right-wing regimes. This was, in part, defended in the idea that they were Christian, anti-communist regimes, and thereby worthy of support. This understanding was generally shared by the often politically right-wing evangelical missionaries who flocked to the region, and were a factor in its growing protestantization. The goals they shared were: containment of communism and the gaining of power of so-called 'strong' (i.e. perhaps military, certainly authoritarian), free-market oriented governments. As with an earlier era, when it was believed that 'what was good for General Motors (and by extension other transnational corporations) was good for America', in the 1980s and 1990s what was good for right-wing Protestantism was, apparently, equally salutary for the USA's foreign policy goals. The thrust of the analysis should not be overstressed, however. The decidedly socially progressive Haitian leader, Fr Jean-Bertrand Aristide, was overthrown in a military coup in September 1991. The USA was in the forefront of the demand for his reinstatement because he had won elections in early 1991 by a landslide – 68 per cent of the vote. Thus despite the fact that the USA may have preferred for ideological reasons a political conservative in Haiti, its liberal, constitutional tradition resulted in a foreign policy which sought to ensure that democracy and the popular will took precedence. In any case, the alternative to Aristide – the continuation of the rapacious, gangster-type regimes which had endured for more than 30 years – was not able or willing to introduce and sustain the socio-political stability which the US saw as vital to its interests in the Caribbean.

There is, of course, a state – the Vatican City – whose *raison d'être* is *overwhelmingly* the dissemination and promotion of Christian values, especially in that still largely Roman Catholic area, Latin America (Hehir 1990: 26). Yet even in this unique case, foreign policy aims and aspirations beyond the theocratic may be identified. The joining of religious and non-religious concerns was exemplified by the meeting in December 1989 between Pope John Paul II and the former Soviet president, Mikhail Gorbachev. The meeting was not simply a manifestation of Gorbachev's understandable desire for publicity for his domestic reform efforts; rather it should be understood in the light of the interplay between religion and politics in both the Soviet Union and strongly Roman Catholic influenced areas, such as Latin America and the Philippines. For Gorbachev the meeting was an opportunity to reassert moral and religious values derided by his predecessors; for John Paul II it was partly a manifestation of his conviction that religion has a significant social (and therefore political) role in *every* culture and social system. It was also symptomatic of the way the Vatican had moved from a generally pro-Western international position to a position of political non-alignment, equally critical of both West and East. Moreover, it was the first time in many years that the Vatican had assumed an overtly political role in international relations, as distinct from a religious one. Indeed, not since the Middle Ages can a comparably broad conception of papal activity be found. Because of the significance of the evolving papal foreign policy initiative for a number of Third World states, we need to look at its background and origins.

John Paul II, who came to the papacy in 1978, took his position at a time when liberation theology had firmly put the Catholic Church in a position where inactivity and lack of comment on development and social justice questions could no longer be justified; at the same time he insisted that the Church's efforts should not be politicized. This was an attempt not to antagonize either foreign governments, jealous of their sovereignty, or the conservative hierarchy of the Catholic Church. Yet he was apparently convinced that the Church should address major global policy issues and maintain regular contact with as many governments and international institutions as possible (Mews 1989b: 319). Thus there was the paradox that the Pope was a world figure and leader, yet denied that what he said should be interpreted politically. He wanted a socially significant Church but not one identified with any political movement. As a result, the Vatican dealt uneasily with Catholic politician-priests – such as those in the Sandinista government – whom it saw as transgressing the boundaries of religious acceptability.

The Pope argued that underdeveloped countries must be helped to develop by the richer. He called for the industrial states to respond with resources and new global political institutions to help meet the Third World's needs, echoing the unsuccessful demands for a new international economic order which many Third World governments had been making collectively since the early 1960s. Yet the Vatican did not accept that *all* the Third World's economic problems were caused by external factors. The Pope backed the position of South American Church figures, such as Cardinal Paulo Evaristo Arns and Archbishop Helder Camara in Brazil, as well as Archbishop Arturo Rivera y Damas in El Salvador, who – following the tenets of liberation theology – called for land and human rights reforms, including the economic and cultural rights of workers, peasants and the indigenous inhabitants. John Paul II juxtaposed calls for reforms with an equally vociferous commitment to non-violence: no use of force to effect social change (Hehir 1990: 46). At the same time, he managed to encourage the socially activist church in Latin America even while he criticized aspects of the liberation theology that sustained much of its activity on behalf of the poor.

It should be remembered that even though the Vatican *acts* like a state, that is not *all* that it is. Its diplomatic reputation and its humanitarian instincts, for example, allowed it to provide 'temporary asylum' to the former Panamanian dictator, General Manuel Antonio Noriega, following his deposition by US marines in December 1989. By this act the fighting was quelled, saving both American and Panamanian lives. In one sense the Vatican's foreign policy is about extending certain moral values, such as 'justice' and 'humanitarianism', internationally; yet it can only do this by diplomatic pressure. The Vatican's foreign policy is uniquely based on Christian values, yet the broad Christian church itself – including both Catholic and Protestant branches – is divided between political conservatives and radicals, a factor that was a moulding force behind both domestic and international politics in a number of countries and regions in recent times. The Vatican is denied the use of force to get its objectives, 'normal' state authorities rarely (if ever) rule out an ultimate recourse to force, should all else fail. This is the case even when religious goals – such as the geographical spread of Islam – are high on the list of a state's foreign policy goals. In the next section we shall examine the foreign policies of three Muslim countries – Libya, Iran and Pakistan – whose religious goals are closely linked with, if not inseparable from, strategic aspirations.

Libya: an Islamic foreign policy?

As noted earlier, Islam is by no means a homogeneous body of ideas, and encompasses both radical and conservative interpretations, as well as sectarian divisions between Sunni and Shiite branches. Any assessment of Islam in foreign policy must be informed by the tendency towards such diversity of understanding among the world Muslim community. For example, Libya's policy of Islamic reformism is rooted in the ideas of Jamal-al-Din al-Afghani (1839–97) and Muhammad Abduh (1849–1905). Following the accession to power of Colonel Muammar Gadaffi after a military coup in 1969, the ideas of al-Afghani and Abduh were built upon to provide a vision of Islam as 'permanent revolution', suited for all societies (Deeb 1978: 13). One of Gadaffi's chief revolutionary aims was a thoroughgoing Islamic cultural revolution which aimed to transform not only the government but the entire life of the people of Libya. In addition to a radicalization and Islamization of domestic society, Libya embarked on a pan-Islamic crusade in contiguous geographic areas, especially West and Central Africa and the Middle East. Gadaffi's foreign policy was religious–strategic in orientation, involving the encouragement of both governments and, if necessary, opposition movements to be Islamic, revolutionary and anti-imperialist (the Irish Republican Army (IRA), one of the Libyan government's recipients of aid, may not have been Islamic but it was seen as having the last two characteristics), attributes which described Libya itself.

During the 1970s and until the mid-1980s, when oil revenues were buoyant, Gadaffi had at his disposal abundant petro-dollars for the prosecution of his foreign policy aims and objectives. Apart from establishing Islamic centres in a number of African cities, including Niamey (Niger) and Accra (Ghana), Gadaffi helped to finance the formation of Islamic fundamentalist parties in a number of African states, including Senegal (Imobighe 1981). Here, he encouraged the formation of a political party, Hizboulahi (Party of God), which aimed to turn Senegal into an Islamic state. Thus, Libya's foreign aid to such organizations was tied up with an understanding to spread Islam. In the 1970s, the aim of Islamic proselytizing led Gadaffi's government to support such brutal rulers as Jean-Bedel Bokassa (Central African Republic) and Idi Amin (Uganda), who also happened to be Muslims. It seemed that as far as Gadaffi was concerned at this time, a willingness to profess Islam was sufficient qualification to gain a portion of Libya's foreign aid. According to Gadaffi, Bokassa's 1976 conversion to Islam marked 'the beginning of the cultural revolution in the [African] continent'; the end-result envisaged was to be a pan-Islamic radical belt stretching from Chad to Port Sudan (Imobighe 1981).

The pursuit of religious goals in Libya's African foreign policy dovetailed neatly both with Gadaffi's strategic designs and with searches for sources of essential raw materials. Clearly, the installation of friendly governments in Sudan, Chad, Senegal, Niger, Ghana, Nigeria and so on would go a long way towards the creation of a group of pro-Libya regimes that would tolerate neither French 'imperialist' troops nor bases for anti-Gadaffi guerrillas. In addition, in the case of Chad, Libya had a long-standing interest in gaining control of the uranium to be found in the northern Aouzou strip (Deeb 1991: 125). To this end, Libya annexed the area in 1989 following its occupation since 1973. The Libyan leader made no secret of his intention to establish a 'science centre' for the purpose of bringing Arab/Islamic scientists together to develop a nuclear capacity to be used, if necessary, in developing a so-called 'Islamic bomb' to confront Western imperialism on its own terms. Thus Gadaffi's championing of Islam, and his aggressive foreign policies in Africa, should be seen as concrete signs of his determination to establish some kind of pan-Islamic super-state that would be a match for the imperialists. A second (although not necessarily secondary) aim would be to increase both Gadaffi's personal influence and power in particular, and Libya's more generally. Such dual aims become clear when the case of Chad is examined.

Chad is one of those African countries (such as Nigeria and Sudan) with a socio-political division between mutually suspicious Islamic and Christian constituencies. About one-sixteenth of the population of some six million is Christian, a half is Muslim and the remainder are overwhelmingly followers of traditional, indigenous religions, usually animist in nature. Despite the numerical superiority of the Muslims, many of the country's economic and political elite are Christian.

At independence in 1960, Chad had two main political parties, the Chadian

Progress Party, which drew its support almost exclusively from the Christian and animist south, and the National African Party, whose adherents hailed from the Muslim north. This division was partly the result of colonial experiences. French policy in Chad (as elsewhere in Africa) was one of cultural assimilation: Chadians should, as far as possible, become replicas of French people. The policy fared well in the south of the country, where the socio-economic elite generally adopted one of the main characteristics of the French colonialists: Christianity. In the north, however, Islam was already entrenched: many people were Muslims as a result of earlier conversion by Arabs. As a result of the *de facto* north–south split, it was members of the Christianized southern elite to whom power devolved at the time of independence (Deeb 1991: 43). Following Gadaffi's gaining of power in Libya, he sought to utilize his northern Chad co-religionists' resentment at perceived southern Christian dominance to extend the northerners' power and Libya's influence. Until Libya's crushing defeat by the Chadian army in 1989 (which ironically occurred because the previously fragmented Chadian religious factions united to expel the Libyan aggressor), it would not be incorrect to understand Libya's policies in Chad as a kind of dualistic crusade involving both religious and anti-Western motivations: Islam against Christianity, Libya against France. At the same time, the suspicion was clearly extant in Chad itself that French neo-colonialism would be replaced by a Libyan hegemony that would not necessarily be more favourable to Chadian national aspirations of independence from foreign hegemony.

The fear of Libyan adventurism was heightened by subversive tactics in other neighbouring African states. During the 1970s and the 1980s, Gadaffi attempted to exploit internal dissension in a number of African states which had both Christian and Muslim constituencies. Libya financed and trained anti-government subversives in The Gambia; Ghana's military ruler, Jerry Rawlings, was helped to power in a coup d'état in late 1981 with the aid of Libyan funds and training for his co-conspirators, as was Thomas Sankara in neighbouring Burkina Faso in 1983; military and financial aid was supplied to Malian dissidents based in Libya's capital, Tripoli; and in Senegal, as previously noted, Libya encouraged the formation of Hizboulahi and allegedly trained Islamic guerrillas. The aim here was to build Senegal (more than 90 per cent Muslim, although secular in political orientation) into a radical, Islamic state and, perhaps more importantly in the context of Libya's foreign policy aims, to give the latter a strategic foothold in West Africa.

Libya also turned its attentions to the West African giant, Nigeria, with Muslims making up approximately one-third of its population of an estimated 120 million. Nigeria has a long history of Muslim–Christian rivalry and antipathy, with a population fairly equally split between the two creeds, along the lines of Chad, roughly on a north–south basis. During the Chadian civil war, Nigeria was one of the main recruiting areas (along with Ghana and Mali) for Gadaffi's so-called 'Islamic Legion', which purported to be a volunteer army dedicated to fighting for Islam (*The Concord* (Lagos) 17 April 1986), but was in fact used to support one of the factions in the Chadian civil war.

Whereas Libya's ability to influence neighbours' domestic politics declined along with oil revenues in the 1980s, there were (real or imagined) further attempts at meddling in Nigeria into the 1990s. An editorial in *The Nigerian Herald* in May 1986 asserted that Libya had 'been attacking Nigeria for a long time because of her peace moves in the Chadian conflict in 1978', when Nigeria was a sponsor of a short-lived peace arrangement. The same paper had earlier alleged Libyan involvement in the serious religious disturbances in the northern Nigerian city of Kano in 1980 (partial transcript of 'Press Review', Lagos domestic radio, 20 May 1986). On this occasion, during three days of rioting, more than 4000 people (mostly Christians) died, and the local jail was stormed and 2000 (mostly Muslim) prisoners were released (O'Connell 1989: 201; *Sunday Concord* (Lagos) 11 August 1985). There were further serious religious disturbances, once again in northern Nigeria, in Maiduguri, in 1982 and 1984, and in Yola in 1984 when about 1000 people died. In addition riots in Kaduna, also in 1984, claimed 20 lives (Ibrahim 1991). There is no clear evidence that such outbreaks of politico-religious violence were at the behest of, or stimulated by, Libya; rather they reflected the growing three-way division in Nigerian society, between Islamists and fundamentalist Christians, and between Muslim radicals and the state.

At the same time, Libya would obviously exploit where possible internally derived schisms for its own foreign policy goals. It seems clear that Libya's secular and religious foreign policy goals in West and Central Africa from the early 1970s were juxtaposed. In effect, the Libyan encouraged spread of Islam to previously non-Islamic areas and countries would go hand-in-hand with the spread of Libyan influence for strategic purposes. This is not necessarily to imply that Gadaffi tried to use religious means in the pursuit of strictly secular goals, but merely to reinforce the oft-repeated idea that in Islam there is no clear, explicit division between religious and secular ideas and ideals. In effect, Gadaffi's espousal of an Islamized revolutionary ideology gave him the means to conduct a two-pronged foreign policy offensive. Yet such an attack was dependent on the continued flow of abundant oil revenues: since the mid-1980s, as such revenues have shrunk, so have Libyan delusions.

Iran and the export of an Islamic ideology

A similar approach to the gaining of foreign policy goals was evident in the case of post-revolutionary Iran. As we noted earlier, the late Ayatollah Khomeini's Iran is a radical Islamic republic committed to both strict application of *sharia* laws and a confrontationist stance against Western international domination. From the time of the revolution in 1978–80, the country was linked with the political struggles of Shiite groups in Lebanon, Bahrain and elsewhere, with the attempts of co-religionists in Iraq to unseat Saddam Hussein, and with the attempted Islamization of parts of Sub-Saharan Africa. Once again Nigeria was a special target of attentions. During 1985, for example, Iran's embassy representatives were accused of distributing pro-Khomeini posters and literature which the Chief Imam of Lagos Central Mosque, Ibrahim Liadi, criticized as perilous to the religious peace in the country (*The Guardian* (Lagos) 17 August 1985). For its part, the Nigerian government condemned the alleged role of some Iranians and Lebanese who, it claimed, tried to introduce what it called 'fundamentalist and revolutionary doctrines' to corrupt Nigerian Islamic culture and forms of worship (*The Standard* (Lagos) 23 April 1985).

The Iranian attempt to 'export' its favoured type of revolutionary Islam was one of the clearest examples of religious goals pursued through foreign policies. The Iranian government wished to create religious theologies designed to accommodate and direct an increase in domestic religious political activity internationally for reasons of perceived national interest. In other words, leaders of the Islamic Republic of Iran made it clear that it would 'export' its revolution to other parts of the world 'until Islam reigns supreme the world over' (*The Triumph* (Lagos) 19 February 1986). Further justification for subversive attempts to destabilize other states' (sometimes legitimate) governments was provided by Iran's spiritual leader, Sayyid Ali Khamenei, who stated in February 1986, on the occasion of the seventh anniversary of the Iranian Islamic Revolution, that: 'We will survive, defend and protect our revolution and help others in the same cause of Islam to establish the rule of God wherever they are in the world' (*Sunday Triumph* (Lagos) 23 February 1986).

Iran's foreign policy thus included a specifically religious aim: the establishment of Islamic polities in countries which had adequate numbers of Muslims. This was not only for the fundamental state goal of seeking good relations with as many governments as possible in order to facilitate the prosecution of foreign policy aims, but also for expressly religious and internationalist reasons. In this respect, Iran's recent history is the best example of the centrality of religion as a factor in international relations. The post-revolutionary government's ideology and actions were manifested through religious vocabulary and institutions. Thus, while the Iranian revolution was undoubtedly a result of a number of specifically Iranian factors, some of these equally clearly had serious implications for other countries and their governments.

Following the triumph of the Islamic Revolution in February 1979, it was perhaps unsurprising that Iran's clerics, already highly respected because of their part in the anti-Shah movement, should seek to amplify their own version of revolutionary Islam. It was not the case, however, that international solidarity and help for foreign Shiites was contemporaneous with the 1978–80 revolution, although from this time it received state backing, becoming a foreign policy goal.

The contemporary movement for the political emancipation of Shiites began in the early 1960s when the Iranian-born Shia cleric, Musa al Sadr, moved to Lebanon and helped to mobilize the Shiites of Lebanon in the hope of enhancing their social, economic and political power (Newman 1991: 468–9). Al Sadr and his co-religionist, Ali Shariati, had led the way in using Shia symbolism in the struggle to oust the Shah. The religious and political legacy was manifested in the cleric-led anti-Shah front which seized power. The use of religious myth, so important in justifying clerics' rule, paved the way for the resuscitation of religious political activity, initially in the Shia world, before spreading to the wider Islamic constituency where the Iranian clerics' militant rhetorical and ideological appeals often found a receptive audience. More recently, however, Iran's desire to lose its pariah status with the West led it in late 1991 to utilize its considerable financial, diplomatic and religious influence to persuade radical Lebanese Shia groups to release their Western hostages. This was the *quid pro quo* demanded by the USA for Iran's re-entry into the international community (Evans 1991). This is not to argue that Iran lost its desire to spread and perpetuate Islam and its values in the post-Khomeini era, but rather to affirm that as the domestic economic situation deteriorated it was essential to bring in Western financial aid, investment, technology and business interests. As a result, in the short term, the spreading of Islamized revolution would take a more covert, if not subservient, position within the parameters of Iran's foreign policy.

Pakistan: Islamic foreign policy and *realpolitik*

Libya and Iran are examples of states that utilize reformist or revolutionary Islamic values and imagery in pursuance of foreign policy aims and objectives, Pakistan, like Saudi Arabia, on the other hand, uses a more conservative interpretation of Islam in its foreign policy, which is in clear contrast to, and in competition with, the Islamic understanding of Iran. Part of the reason for the different Islamic interpretation is that the majority of Pakistanis are Sunnis of the Hanafi school of jurisprudence, while most Iranians are Shiites. As a result, there is not present to the same degree the *revolutionary* perception of Islam. This is not to say that Pakistan's foreign policy did not incorporate Islamic expansionary ideas and ideals. This was particularly the case from the late 1970s, as Pakistan became increasingly Islamized. The process culminated in the decision to introduce a legal code in 1980 that was deemed consistent with the *sharia*. In June 1988, a presidential decree formally introduced the *sharia* and simultaneously repealed all existing secular civil laws (Shaikh, 1989b: 208). The Islamic trend was reinforced after 1990 and the ousting of the social democratic Pakistan People's Party government of Benazir Bhutto, with the accession to power of Nawaz Sharif at the head of an elected Islamist coalition government.

One of Pakistan's most abiding foreign policy aims during the period of communist government in neighbouring Afghanistan (1978–92) was that regime's overthrow. As with Libyan and Iranian policies in Sub-Saharan Africa, Pakistan's policy towards Afghanistan involved a combination of both religious and strategic elements. The accession to government of the revolutionary regime in Iran in early 1979 supplied a further dimension to the conflict in Afghanistan. The superpowers' use of Afghanistan as a battleground for a *de facto* proxy war involved each side's protégés. Yet the struggle for power was not simply one of a unified mojahiden fighting to replace 'godless communist' government with a more appropriate regime. It became, in addition to the superpower context, an internationalized contest involving Tehran's and Islamabad's different religio-strategic aims. Tehran backed a coalition of eight Shia Islamic resistance groups (the 'Iran Eight') in their struggle against the Soviet Union-backed communist government in Kabul. The Pakistan government aided and armed rival groups of Sunni guerrillas, based in Peshawar and abetted by military and political support from the American CIA (Shaikh 1989c: 3–4). The bitter fruit of the divide and rule tactics was manifested following the Soviet withdrawal of its troops from Afghanistan in early 1989. The disunited mojahiden factions were unable to defeat militarily the communist government's troops. This was the case even though the latter were now fighting with much diminished external support, and the regime was at best tolerated by Afghans, rather than overtly popular. It took three more years of civil war, and the implosion of the Najibullah regime, for the mojahiden to gain control.

The Afghanistan imbroglio, and the lack of success at establishing political and social stability in that country, clearly reflect the interlinking of local interests' and foreign powers' religious, strategic and ideological goals. Pakistan's religious aim – helping to defeat Afghanistan's aggressively secular regime to establish a government which shared its religious orientation – was supplemented by a strategic aim: to prevent the consolidation of unwelcome Iranian influence in Afghanistan, which might be used as a bridgehead for subversion in Pakistan. The situation was made more difficult to resolve by the eruption of the new Cold War between the superpowers from the late 1970s, and things became no easier after it finished a decade later. Even following the emergence of a much more pragmatic, if still Marxist-oriented, regime under the leadership of Dr Najibullah in November 1987, whose constitution specifically referred to Afghanistan as an 'Islamic nation', the Afghan Islamic guerrillas were unable to join forces. Even though they were ideologically united over the broad issue of an Islamic state of *some kind*, both religiously and politically they remained deeply divided. The formation of an interim (guerrilla-dominated) government based principally in Pakistan did very little to resolve differences between the Pakistan-backed Sunni 'moderates' and the Iranian-backed Shiite 'radicals', or to get the latter to join the government-in-exile. Militarily, until spring 1992 it appeared that the mojahiden were as far as ever from overthrowing the government, or even establishing control of the larger cities. It was the dramatic collapse of the Najibullah regime in the wake of the withdrawal of all support by the former Soviet Union which allowed the divided guerrilla factions to claim undisputed power. In the short term, however, dreams of an Islamic Afghanistan – or more prosaically a return to their homes and an almost forgotten normality – continue to elude many of the more than three million Afghan refugees resident in Pakistan and Iran.

The struggle involving the USA and the USSR, as well as Iran and Pakistan, over Afghanistan's future was not the only regional foreign policy issue in the early 1990s that had both religious and strategic dimensions. The demise of the Soviet Union allowed religious and ethnic considerations to come to the fore not only in the European areas of the former superpower but also in Soviet Central Asia. Tajikistan, linked culturally with its neighbour Afghanistan and linguistically with Iran, was the site of a struggle between religious and secular forces, with the Muslims dominant in mid-1992. Turkey was not only concerned with the possibility of another Islamic state close to its borders (in addition to Iran and Afghanistan), but was also concerned to dilute Iran's influence for strategic reasons. In addition, Turkey was anxious to become the dominant influence for both commercial and cultural purposes (Palmer 1992). Turkey, wishing to become the pre-eminent role model in the region, appealed to the EC and NATO for economic and military support to deal with the Iranian threat, while seeking to confirm itself as the secular, democratic alternative to the Central Asian former Soviet republics' putative Islamization.

Foreign policy and religious heterogeneity

Each of the foreign policy issues discussed so far involved state attempts to further national interest and security aims through the use of religion. Commonly states will use foreign policies to deflect criticism from domestic failures: the Argentinian *junta's* use of this tactic in the Falklands/Malvinas conflict of 1982 is clear, as is the Israeli government's sanctioning of periodic military forays into Lebanon. Our examples of religious foreign policies are not of the same type: while Libya was seeking to Islamize as much of Africa as possible it was embroiled in war in Chad; Iran fought a war with Iraq throughout much of the 1980s, a period which corresponded with its attempts to spread its version of Islam; Pakistan already had an established international *bête noire* (i.e. the status of Kashmir in relation to India's claims on the area) to help deflect internal criticism should it be required for domestic political purposes. At the same time, these states' comparative religious homogeneity dovetailed well with Islam's position as the ideology of state hegemony (Halliday 1987: 33). This was in contrast to other Muslim societies, where political Islam served as an expression of opposition, as in Iran before the Revolution of 1979, in Turkey, Egypt, Syria and, following the ending of the Gulf War in early 1991, among the minority Shias in Iraq.

Heterogeneous religious populations often affect the stability and foreign policy of Middle Eastern countries, including non-Islamic states, such as Israel. Conservative, orthodox Jewish political parties and radical Islamic groups from the underdog Arab Palestinian population pose threats to the continued stability of the polity. That the conservative Shamir government was aware of the need for restraint in this regard was well illustrated by its decidedly muted response to the Iraqi Scud missile attacks on Tel Aviv and other population centres in Israel in late 1990 and early 1991. The government was probably concerned about possible domestic political repercussions from radicalized Muslims when it chose not to enter into the war against Saddam Hussein. It should be borne in mind in this context that a much lower level of provocation (i.e. small-scale Palestinian guerrilla attacks) was used to justify repeated incursions into Lebanon in the 1980s, albeit at times of lower levels of religiously oriented politicization of the disaffected Palestinian youth.

Another example of the impact of heterogeneous religious populations on Middle Eastern states' foreign policies is to be found in the case of Syria. The majority of Syrians are Sunni Muslims, but the ruling establishment is overwhelmingly Alawite from the north-west of the country. The Alawites are a small sect whose status in Islam is by no means clear. This has been the case since 1970 when the current ruler, Hafiz al-Assad, seized power. Al-Assad is also leader of the secularist political party, the Ba'th. In the 1970s the Ba'th government had close ties with the Soviet Union, and pursued state-centric economic and progressive social policies, which aimed to break the power of the old elites (Farouk-Sluglett and Sluglett 1989a: 263). Such policies incurred the wrath of the Sunni religious establishment, which hitherto had enjoyed a measure of economic dominance. The Ba'thists were accused of 'atheism'. Such critics also disapproved of Syria's close links with the Soviet Union. A combination of grievances aided the formation of opposition groups of Islamists in the late 1970s, whose influence was detected behind a wave of assassinations of prominent Alawites associated with al-Assad's regime. The latter responded with large-scale killings following urban risings in Aleppo, Hama (where up to 10,000 were killed in early 1982), Jisr al-Shughur and Day al-Zur between 1979 and 1982. After 1982 there was no overt manifestation of religion-based hostility towards the regime, which, for its part, continued its former practice of emphasizing its Islamic credentials and generally endeavoured to avoid offending the religious sensibilities of the more conservative elements in the population (Farouk-Sluglett and Sluglett 1989a).

One way in which the regime underlined both its revolutionary and its Islamic credentials was in the form of an expansionist foreign policy vis-à-vis Lebanon, which resulted in the carving out of a pax Syriana in 1991. This followed 16 years of civil war, and was opposed both by Syria's regional rival, Iran, and by the latter's Shia protégés, the guerrillas of Hizbollah. The antagonism between groups such as Hizbollah and the Ba'th underpinned Syria's foreign policy in Lebanon (Rubin 1990b: 58). In order to help forge domestic unity and prove themselves good Arabs and Muslims, the Alawites tried to be steadfast in fighting Israel and US 'imperialism'. At the same time, however, al-Assad's desire for peace and security on his borders gradually began to outweigh the desire to appease Muslims at home. With the end of the Cold War, and the concomitant ability to play one side off against the other, Syria wished to appear as a regional stabilizer, anxious to help forge a lasting Middle East peace settlement.

During the broad period of Cold War (i.e. later 1940s to late 1980s), the superpowers' view of Third World religio-political issues was limited by their salience to the USA's and the USSR's strategic aims. Even though they attempted to use religious groups for their own ends, they found – as with the mojahedin in Afghanistan or the liberation theologists among the Sandinistas in Nicaragua – that they were beyond their control, even if supplied with both weapons and financial support. What the superpowers failed to take fully into account was that the rise of reformist or revolutionary Islamist and Christian movements reflected specific combinations of political, social, economic – and sometimes ethnic – factors unique to each country which experienced such movements. Yet everywhere they generally reflected rapid urbanization and socio-economic change, which in itself was contradictory and, at times, bewildering. That is to say, 'Islamic fundamentalism' – often mistakenly adjudged a uniform, reactionary response to over-rapid modernization – challenged the domestic (and by extension international) stability of a number of states of concern to both the superpowers, such as Bahrain, Israel, Jordan, Kuwait and Saudi Arabia, as well as former or current client states such as Iran in the case of the USA, and Syria and North and South Yemen in the case of the USSR. Moreover, both the superpowers saw Islamist movements in terms of the strategic and regional benefits or threats that they presented. The USA favoured the Islamic oppositions in Syria and Afghanistan, even though the latter worked counter to the US goal of achieving a negotiated settlement (Halliday 1987: 34). For the USSR the situation was also contradictory, and Soviet policy in such states as Afghanistan and South Yemen encouraged the regimes to use Islam as a socio-political cement for state-stabilization purposes. In the US government's perception, one formed and perpetuated by a Cold War mentality, it was *always* better to undermine the Soviet Union than to be overly concerned with the settlement of regional disputes. There was, however, less consensus in the case of Iran, where US foreign policy experts were divided over the best means to deal with the Islamic republic. On the one hand, some US officials feared 'Islamic fundamentalism' nearly as much as communism, and advocated the containment of Iran; on the other, a second group viewed 'Islamic fundamentalism' as a potentially powerful ideological tool that could be used against the Soviet Union, and should, as a result, be tolerated or even covertly supported (Hooglund 1989). The result of the internal wranglings, unsurprisingly, was a foreign policy that was at times contradictory.

United States foreign policy and Christianity

The American government's Cold War oriented view led it to perceive attempts by Latin American states to introduce domestic policies of social fairness as virtually *always* teleguided by Moscow. The view is well expressed in the following:

> Neither the security of the United States and other free societies in the Americas nor the protection of human rights is threatened by the type of liberation theology that seeks genuine justice, peace, freedom, and prosperity. However, many if not most liberation theologians reject democracy and just-market economies in favor of Soviet-style communism . . . insofar as they approximate communist ideology they will likely result in less, rather than more, true liberation for people, whether they are poor, middle class, or rich.
>
> (Cooper 1988: 288)

The above quote captures well US governments' ambivalence when trying to confront the complexities and paradoxes associated with the Christian religion in Latin America. On the one hand, so-called 'genuine' justice, peace, freedom and prosperity are unequivocally welcomed; on the other, where liberation theology was perceived as the ideological foundation for communist revolution or subversion in Latin America, it constituted a threat to United States security and human rights, and was, therefore, to be opposed.

The twin *bêtes noires* of the USA in this regard were Cuba and Nicaragua. The key factors framing Cuba's role in the world were, and continue to be at the time of writing (mid-1992), revolutionary messianism, an anti-US and anti-imperialist stance, a legacy of defiance and Marxist-Leninist ideology (Del Aguila 1990: 449). US foreign policy-makers found it convenient to see Nicaragua under the Sandinistas as an imitator of Cuba, likely to foment communist revolution in other Central American countries. The US government – in a Latin American version of its (in)famous Vietnam-inspired South-East Asian 'domino theory' – considered that Guatemala, Honduras, El Salvador, Mexico and so on would come under increasing pressure to radicalize politics and to placate or align with the Soviet bloc. The United States would then face serious regional opposition to its interests (Cooper 1988: 301). Such a fear of 'sovietization' was not new. The US government, since the beginning of the Cold War, had been concerned with the threat of communist revolution in Latin America, and sought to prevent the installation of pro-Soviet governments in the region by any means deemed necessary. In this battle for hearts and minds the concerns of liberation theory – personal liberation of the poor and politically insignificant, political assertiveness, community organization, the challenging of established interests – were seen as the manifestations of a dangerous mixture of Marxism-Leninism and radical Christianity, with the emphasis on the former. Significantly, US foreign policy-makers saw little or no difference between the liberation theologists of the Sandinistas and the Marxist-Leninists of Cuba. Both served other masters: the Soviet Union.

We noted earlier that a conservative form of Christianity began to dominate in the United States from the 1970s. The understanding of the Christian message was heavily influenced by the images of the Cold War, which dominated US perceptions of the international system. US foreign policy concerns, rooted in fear of the threat of communism in the geographically contiguous Central American region, were both echoed and reinforced by the goals of the burgeoning numbers of Christian fundamentalist missionaries who were convinced that communism and the Devil were synonymous. Before examining the issue of the impact of American conservative Christianity on US foreign policy in Central America, we need to get an idea of the geographical spread of its influence.

Such USA-rooted sects appear, for example, in Nigeria where they are not of political salience in foreign policy terms, even though 'The charismatic movements . . . took their origin from the worldwide spread of the pentecostal and charismatic movements from North America and Britain in the 1960s' (Ojo 1988: 175). Yet here, as elsewhere in Sub-Saharan Africa, the growth of pentecostal and charismatic movements would seem to have few, if any, direct links with US foreign policy aims. The reason is that Sub-Saharan Africa, in contrast to some other Third World regions, is not deemed either of special importance to US strategic concerns or of great interest to American Christian-conservative missionaries. Rather, these forms of Christianity seemed to respond primarily to the 'existential needs of a people within their specific cultural and historical *milieu*' (Imasogie 1983: 19–20).

In considerable contrast to Latin America, the Christian churches in both Africa and Asia derive mainly from a later stage of European expansion, i.e. during the nineteenth and twentieth centuries. This process involved a greater degree of differentiation between imperialistic penetration and missionary endeavour than was the case with the sixteenth-century Iberian moves into Latin America. Moreover, some of the initial missionary effort in Africa and Asia was directed from within the United States, which at the time was not extensively engaged in expansionist activity outside the Western hemisphere (Robertson 1988: 123). Probably the most important contrast between the African and Asian circumstances and that of Latin America is that, with the important exception of the Philippines, Christianity did not clearly triumph numerically or socio-culturally over indigenous religions.

The island chain of the Philippines was annexed by the United States in 1898, after which the American principle of separation was imposed, i.e. the severing of church and state, in contrast to the earlier Spanish-Catholic model. That the vast majority of the population of the Philippines can be classified as Christian (with a quite militant Islamic minority) is due not to the US takeover but almost entirely to the earlier Iberian phase of imperialism. Thus in a special sense the Philippines is as much a Latin American as an Asian society. The only other case of an Asian country where

Christianity is strong both numerically and institutionally is Korea. North Korea was originally the most Christian, but since the communist takeover in 1949 the South has proportionately far more practising Christians. The introduction of Christianity was largely the result of Korea's encounters with more powerful nations such as Russia, Britain and France, and of the influence of American missionaries in the nineteenth century. Both the Philippines and South Korea are, of course, of great contemporary interest since they have recently taken steps in democratic directions, with religious leaders and groups playing a significant part in those developments.

Christianity entered Korea as a kind of liberation theology, nationalistic and radical, in response to the breakdown of Korean society occasioned by Japanese colonialism. Because of Korean militancy, involving violence and demonstrations, US missionaries concentrated on fundamentalist aspects of Christianity as an alternative to political involvement. 'They emphasized peace and reconciliation and also went so far in dissociating the church from political agitation that they were accused of adopting the role of quislings' (Martin 1990b: 149–50). There were two main reasons for such an approach. The first was a reflection of the Christian church's apolitical and pietist tradition in the USA; the second was that the missionaries were influenced by American geo-political calculations which in the 1920s and 1930s favoured cooperation with Japan at the expense of the Korean nationalists.

The Catholic Church in Korea, following a period in the early 1940s when it was at the forefront of anti-Japanese agitation, split in the early 1970s along ideological lines reminiscent of the schism in the Catholic Church in Latin America in the same period. From that time elements in the Catholic Church led Korean opposition to the government's author-itarian and, at times, repressive tactics when dealing with manifestations of dissent (Digan 1984). Such activists were not only in contention with their own government but also viewed the United States as an imperialistic power aiming to usurp Korea's independence and sovereignty.

The US presence in South Korea was firmly established following the latter's liberation from Japanese domination after the Second World War. The civil war of 1950–3, which resulted in the *de facto* partition of the country, and the coming to power of a Christian president, Syngman Rhee, combined to bolster both a pro-USA position and an emphatic anti-communist one. During the modernization of the economy from the 1950s many Koreans became alienated as a result of the immense changes in their lives, with 'hundreds of thousands (seeking) refuge in sectarian groups, particularly the Pentecostals. There they sought a definition for the self and a network of communal support' (Martin 1990b: 150). By the 1990s, more than 300 kinds of new religions, including foreign religions, were being propagated. Syn-Duk Choi (1986: 114–16) suggests a number of reasons for the rapid growth of new religions, which include the changing (and, for many, precarious) politico-social and economic conditions, growing religious freedoms, rapid social change and mobility, and, finally, the failures of existing religious groups. Two of the most prominent, the Holy Spirit Association for the Unification of World Christianity ('Unification Church') and the Full Gospel Central Church, were led by charismatic leaders, Reverends Cho and Moon respectively. Both adhered to the pattern of Christian fundamentalist religious movements in the USA: they are politically very conservative, stress the importance of the stability of the family and its role in society, are strongly anti-abortion, believe in glossolalia and have unshakable faith in the literal truth of every word in the Bible (Robertson 1988: 132; Martin 1990b: 160).

The Unification Church's conservatism is not, of course, the same thing as a CIA plot to spread and underpin conservative religious movements in Korea for the purposes of US foreign policy. Yet, at the same time, the frozen civil war and accompanying communist threat from the north ensures that South Korea will be a loyal ally of the United States. According to Martin, the South Korean evangelical explosion seems 'explicable without invoking the omnipresence and omnipotence of American intelligence' (Martin 1989: 31). At the same time, as Martin admits elsewhere, the development of evangelical and pentecostal Christianity in South Korea was facilitated by US politico-religious involvement, partially 'expressed through a close working relationship between the US and Korean Central Intelligence Agencies' (Martin 1990b: 149). There does seem a very fuzzy dividing line between the involvement of non-state and state actors from the USA in South Korea's domestic politics. What is clearer is that as long as North Korea remains a communist state it will feature highly on the USA's 'problem states' list and be a focus of foreign policy.

This is equally the case in the Philippines, where the US government supports socio-political stability, whether it be à la Aquino, Marcos or anyone else. As in the case of South Korea, however, there is no incontrovertible evidence that the USA utilizes politically conservative Christians to further its foreign policy aims. The same could not be said of Latin America, where support for the conservative Protestant sects is strong among political and economic elites and within the top echelons of the military. In this case, there is a clear link between anti-communism, conservative evangelical Protestantism and US foreign policy. This relationship is strengthened by the activities of certain American missionaries. In El Salvador, for example, American foreign policy-makers have encouraged US-based evangelical groups for 'obviously political reasons' (Medhurst 1991: 212).

The accession to power of the Sandinistas in Nicaragua in 1979 – in tandem with a renewed cooling of relations between the USA and the USSR in the wake of the Afghan revolution – helped to give the Christian-conservative religious movement in the United States further impetus. Its leading figures shared the US government's view that the Soviet-backed Cuban and Nicaraguan regimes were trying to export their revolutions to the countries of Central America in order to threaten the USA and its proclaimed values: justice, peace, freedom and prosperity (Norton Moore

1985: 78; D'Antonio 1990). This *de facto* geographical extension of the Cold War to Central America warranted the Christian-conservatives' fulsome support for the so-called 'counter-revolutionaries' or 'Contras' who fought against the Sandinista government during the 1980s (Kornbluh 1989). Contra supporters perceived the survival of the 'authoritarian, communist' Sandinista regime as decidedly unwelcome, while many American adherents to a progressive, socio-political version of Christianity considered the regime to be worthy of both religious legitimation and defence. Thus, the political problem of Latin American liberation theology both reflected and exacerbated a pre-existing ideological conflict within the United States grounded in different interpretations of Christianity.

The important question in the context of this chapter is: to what extent should we perceive the US conservative religious movements in Central America – known locally, like other Protestants, as *los evangelicos* – as an arm of US foreign policy? A number of Christian-conservative missionary groups have been active in Central America over the past two decades or more, sponsored by such groups as the Smithtown Gospel Tabernacle, World Gospel Outreach and Jimmy Swaggart's Assemblies of God (D'Antonio 1990: 159). Swaggart, whose television shows were regularly shown in Central America until his downfall following a sex scandal, preached 'that the world is divided into two camps, Christianity and communism. One representative of Christ, the other representative of the evil one, Satan' (D'Antonio 1990: 159). According to Randall Bardwell, Honduran co-ordinator of Swaggart's Assemblies of God:

> The number-one goal for us is to evangelize and save people from communism. . . . A person who is healthy, well fed, and saved won't listen to leftist agitators. . . . First you soften them up, get their attention really, with a medical van, for example. Then you introduce them to the Lord.
>
> (D'Antonio 1990: 159)

This is not to suggest that there are necessarily close links between US Christian-conservative religious groups and the Central Intelligence Agency (CIA), whether in Latin America, South Korea, the Philippines or elsewhere. Yet there are clear links between conservative religious movements in the USA and those in Central America based on the nature of shared goals: anti-communism and American values. There are also potentially very significant forms of modern linkage across other state boundaries; for example, involving some of the American Christian-conservatives and Zionist politico-religious militants in Israel (Robertson and Chirico 1985: 222).

This chapter has attempted to show how religious factors have become intertwined with strategic and national interest concerns in certain states' foreign policies. In addition, within both the Islamic and Christian worlds below the state level, there may be ascertained the circumstances of shared, religiously expressed movements on a number of continents. Yet the subject of the chapter is an elusive one, and has raised three major questions. The first is: to what extent does Islam provide a direction and content for foreign policy for states of which the inhabitants are mostly Muslims? Libya and Iran sought to use Islam as a revolutionary doctrine which would perpetuate and strengthen their own secular and religious goals. Iran, especially, saw itself as the first Islamic state, and as such had a duty to show others the way. In this respect, post-revolutionary Iran resembled the Soviet Union after 1917, but as with the USSR three-quarters of a century ago a purely ideological foreign policy was soon replaced by a much more conventional one based on the abiding concerns of *realpolitik*. Both Libya and Iran were forced in the wake of the twin pressures of falling oil prices and the end of the Cold War to tailor their foreign policies to the new international realities. Pakistan's governments, on the other hand, adherents to a more conservative Islamic formulation, sought to use religious influence to prevent revolutionary expansionism, and also to gain strategic benefits in Afghanistan. Nowhere, however, did Islamic goals outweigh strategic and national interest objectives.

Second, how far do 'Christian' states pursue 'Christian' foreign policies? The quote marks are necessary because, with the exception of the Vatican City, no state professes adherence to Christian values in an ideological sense. The USA, for example, does not claim to be guided by Christian values alone: the concerns of *realpolitik* clearly predominate. Yet as a militant form of anti-communist, politically conservative Christianity gained predominance in America, then there was a clear interaction of Christian (ideological) and foreign policy (national security) goals, especially in Central America and other strategically vital areas.

Finally, how far do foreign policy-makers justify foreign policies in religious terms? Clearly there are potential issues which could be amenable to such a treatment, whether it be Iran's policy against Iraq (Shiite versus Sunni), or the USA against the Sandinistas (Christian values versus communism). Nevertheless, both superpowers consistently overlooked religious goals as a partial motivation for some foreign policy actions. Syria, for example, used an expansionary, religion-oriented foreign policy to affirm its own Islamic and revolutionary credentials, in the wake of domestic opposition. Both the USA and the USSR, however, preferred to view *all* states as players (or pawns) in the Cold War. The outcome of the Cold War was, in a sense, unwelcome for both sides: whereas both the USA and the USSR could once count on their supporters, the post-Cold War era denied both the same leverage, with major ramifications for international order. In other words, self-driven foreign policies were of considerable international salience, and sometimes religious motivations were discernible.

6

Politics and religion in the Third World: continuity and change

Unquestionably the position of religion in politics globally has been of much greater salience, variety, and longevity than originally thought 30 or even 20 years ago. Confidence that the growth and spread of urbanization, education, economic development, scientific rationality and social mobility would combine to diminish significantly the socio-political position of religion in the Third World in particular has not been well founded. In this book we have focused primarily upon the two global religions, Islam and Christianity, in the related contexts of state power, authority and legitimacy, as well as in those of democracy and foreign policy. Based upon the arguments presented, four general conclusions are offered. First, and most obviously, religion in Third World societies often serves as a vehicle of political opposition. This is especially the case when rulers are unwilling to open up the political debate to those outside their circle, much less to give up political power through competitive elections. Religion as a vehicle of political opposition has grown in importance over the past 20 years. This has been because of two factors: the failure of state-promoted development plans and programmes and the inability of secular ideologies generally to serve as galvanizers or repositories of popular aspirations. Second, religion in certain contexts interacts with ethnicity and nationalism to produce a volatile and powerful ideological hybrid. Third, far from being anti-modern and traditionalistic, contemporary interactions of religion and politics emphasize Third World societies' dynamism and propensity to change over time. Contemporary religious resurgence with political ramifications is emphatically not the same thing as a quietistic retreat to traditional values and perspectives which were often judged to be a block on the modernization of Third World societies. Fourth, the impact of religion-based ideology upon certain states' foreign policies is clear: some Muslim states pursue a type of self-conscious 'Islamic foreign policy'; as a foil to this, Western and non-Islamist governments seek to prevent the spread of revolutionary Islam. In addition, the United States government, in tandem with private religious interests, has a kind of religious foreign policy in Latin America that is indistinguishable from its long-standing aim of combatting 'communism'. In this context the political thrust of the proponents of conservative religious dogma is aimed at socially progressive individuals and movements associated with the tenets of liberation theology.

In recent times, however, there has undeniably been a quantitative decline in the numbers of leaders and governments professing to rule by religious mandate. Yet there are still examples of individuals combining both secular and religious leadership: King Birendra of Nepal is regarded as an incarnation of the Hindu god Vishnu by conservative members of the society; King Hassan of Morocco claims descent from the Prophet Muhammad, as does King Hussein of Jordan. Tibet's former leader, the Dalai Lama, was the highest officer of both religious and secular administrative organizations until he was forced into exile in 1959. As we noted in Chapter 4, in pre-modern cultures religion and politics were not analytically separable areas of endeavour. Modernization, with its often closely associated process of secularization, led to their separation in most polities. At the local level, however, in societies more or less untouched by modernization, politics and religion remain close, sometimes overlapping. The process by which secular and religious authority separated, with the former dominant politically, began in Western Europe in the sixteenth century. The French Revolution of 1789 and the great increase in nationalist aspirations in the nineteenth century both confirmed and strengthened the division. By the middle of the twentieth century not only Western Europe, but also other areas, including North America, were deemed to be modernized and, therefore, secularized. Since about 1945 the separation of religious and political power in much of the Third World has followed the pattern laid down by the West. There, secularization, implying the loss of the political power of religion and the refocusing of societies away from concerns with the sacred and the divine, was claimed to have reformed the relationship between politics and religion (Moyser 1991: 14).

Of the four models in Medhurst's (1981) schema of the relationship of religion to secular power only one, the 'integrated religio-political system', features rulers with both temporal and religious powers. Within this category he cites Saudi Arabia alone as an example, with Iran as a second (at the time) potential addition. Since then a small number of Islamic states have been added to the category of 'integrated religio-political system'. Thus at one level there has indeed been a continuing secularization of Third World polities. Yet in the context of falling government legitimacy and authority and the associated decline in political salience of secular ideologies, religious ideals have often become either motors of popular mobilization or a reason to keep away from or opt out of 'politics'.

Thus, religion has declined in political salience at the level of state leadership in the Third World as formerly pre-modern polities have emerged as a result of decolonization into the international system, with its socializing rights and obligations. Increasingly, the notion of Third World (a political term originally implying a third way between the capitalist West or First World and the communist East or Second World) has become synonymous with the idea of 'developing country', an essentially economic term. In the process rulers have become increasingly secularized in terms of ideology, agenda setting, institution building, policy formation and constitutional thrust.

Religion as a vehicle of political opposition

The post-colonial state in the Third World is essentially a construct, attempting to oversee the formation or sustenance of national identity. Its function is primarily to boost or bolster up the cohort of ruling elites for four interrelated goals: regime continuity; public order maintenance; institutionalization of authority; and promotion of citizenship. The role of religion in politics in such polities is influenced 'by the specific kind of state and society relation that obtains in a given historical conjuncture' (Mitra 1991: 757). That combination of circumstances helps to explain the growth of a particular form of religio-political opposition at any given time. State preferences for economic modernization and secularization are, however, contextualized by the overriding aim of regime continuity.

The interlinked crises of social identity and regime legitimacy in many Third World countries are partly responsible for the resurgence of political religions. However, it might be useful to reiterate that the contemporary resurgence of religio-politics is not a unique development in recent times. Periodically over the past 100 years or so religious revivals have occurred that inevitably had their impacts upon politics. As Donald Eugene Smith (1990: 34) puts it, 'Religious resurgence is a cyclical phenomenon.' For example, Islamic revivalist movements emerged in the 1880s and 1890s in West Africa, and in the 1920s and the 1930s in the Middle East. The aim in both periods was the same: to oppose Western colonialism and its values, which were perceived to be undermining existing cultural and social norms. Protestant conservative groups grew in the late nineteenth and early twentieth centuries in the United States as a reaction to the changing social mores of a swiftly modernizing society. Socially progressive liberation theology galvanized Third World Christianity in the 1960s and 1970s, a reaction to modernization which in this context increasingly seemed to mean the growth and spread of poverty, misery and helplessness to burgeoning numbers of financially poor, politically marginalized people.

Certain events over the past 30 years have coalesced and interacted in such a way as to produce a contemporary religio-political situation which is qualitatively and quantitatively different from earlier manifestations. Three significant developments are: the emergence of a culturally disparate Third World, which is, however, closely linked by widespread poverty, environmental degradation and swift population growth; the common (although not ubiquitous) failures of state-directed economic and political modernization efforts in the Third World; and the 'shrinking' of the world as a result of the communications revolution and the associated globalization of ideas. This is contrary to the spirit of Smith's (1990: 33) assertion that 'Liberation theologians and revolutionary ayatollahs may be aware of each other's existence but have not influenced each other very much.' In an important way religion-based political ideologies of opposition have an impact upon other *not necessarily spiritually, culturally or geographically* linked movements. One reason for the contemporary explosion of religio-political ideas and movements is that ideologues and activists read in newspapers, magazines and journals, see on television screens and video-cassettes, and hear from radios and audio-cassettes the proclamations and stated aspirations, as well as the practical successes and failures, of politicized religious groups and movements around the world. This is most clearly the case in the context of Islamism, but is also true in relation to conservative and socially progressive Christians.

As a result of the globalization of ideas religion is a natural rallying point for opposition. This is especially true in the context of the widespread failures of economic and political modernization. Third World states that *have* seen prolonged improvements in both per capita incomes and 'quality of life' indicators have not experienced religio-political movements in recent times. Taiwan, Hong Kong, Mauritius, Singapore, Botswana and South Korea have been among the most economically successful of Third World states over the past 20 years. Crucially, the fruits of growth have been spread around *relatively* equitably within these societies. This is not to assert that religion *per se* is on the decline in these states, but to argue that religion has not been a platform for opposition political movements. On the other hand, states that have experienced severe economic decline and/or serious inequality in distributing available resources have experienced the growth of religio-political opposition movements, which are frequently influenced by external ideas and developments. Examples in this respect include Haiti and the Philippines, where the ideas of Latin American originated liberation theology found a ready audience. Others include Nigeria, Algeria, Malaysia, Indonesia and Trinidad, where the Iranian revolution helped to galvanize Islamists to action. Also of importance in the question of the salience of religio-political ideas upon and within a society are: the government's legitimacy and ability to deal with threats to rule; the unity of religio-political opponents; the popularity of contending ideological messages; the geographical proximity of the society to the religious ideas; and, finally, the residual strength and status of religion within a society. Overall, however, it matters little whether societies are Christian or Muslim in relation to the impact of a religious ideology in a context of serious economic decline or inequality and declining faith in secular ideological routes towards socio-political progression.

Also of importance is the relative independence or co-optation of the religious establishment. Sometimes it split under the destabilizing influence of economic decline and/or political authoritarianism. In Latin America the Catholic Church divided between liberation theology oriented and status quo oriented wings in the 1960s and 1970s. Yet individual Catholics left the Church in their tens of thousands from this time in the region because of its remoteness from their own lives. Pentecostal and conservative Protestant groups helped to fill the religious vacuum forming communities within the wider society. Thus it would not be correct to conclude that *all* religious ideologies were politically reformist or revolutionary. The withdrawal of the pentecostals and conservative Protestants from the political realm served to forestall a political challenge to incumbent governments to adopt policies to force improvements in popular living standards. The absence of a direct challenge to the established order tended clearly to have politically conservative consequences. Such groups denied any practical validity to political striving in this world, preferring to confine themselves to some general acceptance of established authority in the context of submitting themselves entirely to God's will.

Elsewhere, religion became the banner for radical reform and even revolution. Contemporary Islamism is not, as some suggest, merely a reaction to 'overly-secularized western values' (Moyser 1991: 16). Popular Islamism in the modern era always contains an element of challenge to ruling elites, who may be led by monarchs, secular leaders or military absolutists. What each has in common is that they are unwilling to allow political opponents the opportunity by way of *free and fair* elections to displace pre-existing governments. As a result of social and cultural influences, as much as political factors of ideology, 'Islam' is the slogan *and* the programme: 'Trust in Islam, God will provide' is the message. When Islamists appear to be set to win elections, as in Algeria in early 1992, then the state prevents victory by raising the spectre of 'Islamic fundamentalism' and dealing with it accordingly. 'Islamic fundamentalism', it is argued, would utilize the electoral system in order to win power and then abolish all secular political parties, only allowing Islamic movements. Such a process of removing the wheels from the democratic vehicle is viewed with both embarrassment and satisfaction by the West: the former because of the belief in the popular will expressed through the ballot box; the latter because of the welcome thwarting of the political aspirations of the Islamists. It would be most unwelcome from a Western point of view that there should be 'any more Irans'.

What perhaps stands out most clearly is the widespread apparent absence of faith in secular alternatives to religion as facilitators of aspirations. This is not only the case in Muslim countries, but also among Christian communities in the Third World. It is as though at the current historical juncture neither vanquished communism nor victorious capitalism (and its political vehicle, liberal democracy) has the ability to appeal politically. Why is this the case? The simple answer is that neither of the previously hegemonic secular ideologies has been seen to 'deliver the developmental goods' in the Third World. Governments in secular and capitalist Nigeria and Indonesia have been as unsuccessful as regimes in secular and socialist-oriented India in satisfying popular socio-economic aspirations. A result has been that each country experienced religio-political resurgences, which obviously encompassed differing religions (i.e. Islam, Christianity, Hinduism) but had in common a serious dissatisfaction with the political status quo.

I commented briefly in the first chapter on the importance of the dichotomous realms of the theatrical and imaginary in politics, and noted their importance and commonality in all cultural settings. This book has, it is hoped, underlined their analytical appropriateness in the context of religion in Third World politics. Rulers care most about their continued rule, about their personal prosperity and about 'their' state holding together. They will often do virtually anything rather than freely allow genuinely competitive elections in order to maintain their regimes' continuity, except under the most serious internal and external pressures. To justify the capriciousness of their governance everything is vindicated by the four icons: order, stability, continuity and development. Huntington, writing 25 years ago, articulated many Western governments' concern from individual as well as systemic perspectives with international socio-political stability above all else. After all, unless a system is stable and (to a degree) predictable it is not possible for state decision-makers to attempt to make definitive foreign policy decisions. It is only recently (i.e. after the Cold War from about 1989) that Western governments and international financial agencies have sought overtly to link foreign aid and other economic support to certain internationally acceptable standards of governance. Yet it is clear that there is also a theatrical and imaginary realm in international politics. The systemic rulers (i.e. Western governments) have a certain conception of how and to what ends governments should govern. The less powerful Third World rulers, on the other hand, have different conceptions of what governing is about, as noted above. As the recent cases of Algeria, China, Zaire, Haiti, Peru and elsewhere indicate, the West (led by the United States) demands that its notions of democracy, human rights and social pluralism should predominate. Yet, just as with the rather arrogant presumptions and prescriptions of modernization theory a generation ago, Third World peoples and governments stubbornly refuse to conform to Western stereotypical expectations.

Religion and nationalism in the Third World

Religion encompasses a body of ideas that may form the basis of a way of political thinking. Politics is always and everywhere about power, and concerns 'the process by which groups make collective decisions' (Hague and Harrop 1987: 3). As we have seen, it is more frequent, perhaps, that politics is the mechanism by which they *fail* to make decisions peacefully. Contemporary religio-politics involves the interaction of religious and political issues, sometimes, but by no means always, allied to ethnic or regional concerns. This book has indicated that religion is significant, in varying ways under different conditions, in helping to build or maintain ethnic or nationalist consciousness (Warhola 1991: 259). As Brass (1985: 55) puts it: 'religion [is] a persisting force in the development of many nationalist movements up to contemporary times'. Yet religion is but one cultural component of the ethnic or nationalist mindset. Others of importance are language and history, as both offer avenues towards ethnic or nationalist consciousness. In additions, owing to specific sets of historical circumstances, region may be a focus of allegiance. A number of Sub-Saharan African countries contain regional divisions that may have religious and/or ethnic overtones. For example, northern Nigeria, which is mainly but not exclusively Muslim, regards the south and east of the country, which is mostly Christian, with both envy and suspicion owing to the latter's relative economic prosperity. Religion is the *cause célèbre* setting community against community both in the north of the country and between that region and the south and east.

Although the actually very rare 'nation state' is generally held to be the basic building block of the international system (especially in the postcolonial era), 'the simple political fact is that few if any *states* preside over one *nation* in any significant ethnographic sense' (Warhola 1991: 260). Even when they do, there is no guarantee of political stability or of the absence of challenges to political rulers. Both Thailand and Somalia, two of the very few examples of (near) mono-ethnicity and mono-religiosity among Third World states, experienced serious political upheavals in the early 1990s. In the former case the context was popular anger at the presumptions of unelected leaders in the context of a desire for democracy, while in the latter it was the (re-)emergence of localized clan rivalries at the end of the Cold War that led to serious political strife. In neither of these cases was religion or ethnicity of importance *per se*, whether taken singly or together.

At the same time, other civil political conflicts testify to the salience of religion-ethnicity in political disputes. For example, in the early 1990s Christian Serbs fought (mainly) Bosnian Muslims in what was once Yugoslavia; Muslim Hausas battled with Christian Katafs in northern Nigeria; the Indian government continued its struggles to defeat Sikh separatism; and the rulers of Buddhist-hegemonic Myanma (Burma) sought to crush the attempts by both Christian Karens and Muslim Rohingyas for a degree of self-government. Such was the ferocity of the military-dominated Myanman state in the assault against the Rohingyas that by February 1992 over 50,000 refugee Rohingyas had fled to the haven of their co-religionists in neighbouring Bangladesh (Mahmud 1992). But while religion is a central characteristic of each of these conflicts, it is not the defining quality. That is to be found in the challenge of minorities for a greater say in the government of the states they find themselves in as a result of the drawing up of an international system where states are both ubiquitous and *de rigeur*. In this context religious differences reinforce rather than define ethnic or national strivings for self-government or autonomy. Thus religion (re-)assumed an important position in political developments globally, at a time when ethnic and nationalist pressures on the constituent units of the largely post-1945 colonially created international state system threatened to bring about serious and widespread changes.

Religion, politics and foreign policy

For the West collectively there is a considerable dilemma. What if Third World peoples do not seek the road of liberal democracy towards the promised land of politically plural, orderly polities? What if they pursue the fragmentation or balkanization of their post-colonial states along religious or ethnic lines, with scant regard for either domestic or international stability and restraint. If these developments occur, what should be the West's response? This is, of course, both over-simplifying and over-generalizing in a number of respects. Yet it also encapsulates one of the foremost contemporary international dilemmas from the point of view of the states that exercise a leadership role: how far should peoples be allowed to change their own socio-political and economic realities if this not only has a deleterious effect upon indigenes but also threatens to spill over into the wider international theatre? The cynic might respond that it depends on how far such developments threaten fundamental Western interests. The response of the West to Saddam Hussein's attempt to annex Kuwait was obviously of a qualitatively different nature from its muted reaction to the massacre by Indonesian troops of Timorese in East Timor in early 1992. Yet, arguably, both were crimes that demanded an even-handed response from the international community, if it was serious about the creation of a New World Order in the wake of the demise of communism as a dynamic international(ist) ideology.

This is by no means to argue that religio-politics are always manipulated (or indeed manipulable) by external interests. At the same time, the support by Western governments of the military-backed government under the High State Committee (HSC) in Algeria, after the determined attempt to crush the Islamist Salvation Front during 1992, was clear indication of its intention to make or break regimes (*Friends for Democracy in Algeria Bulletin* 1 March 1992). At the same time, the HSC had great difficulty in persuading Algerians that stability had been restored. Official attention focused on the arrest of thousands of FIS supporters and the execution of a number of the Front's zealots (*Africa Confidential* 8 May 1992).

The reasons for the growth and electoral support of the FIS and other Islamist parties in Algeria and elsewhere in the Muslim world were examined in Chapter 4. Apart from relatively minor differences, it was noted that declining living standards, burgeoning populations, decreasing authority and increasing corruption of incumbent governments were the key to their growth. Such support was especially noticeable in urban areas. A linked issue was the diminishing status and stature of women in many Muslim societies. Their removal from paid employment and retreat back to the privacy of the home was seen as both a religious and an economic priority in order to release employment for the huge numbers of unemployed and under-employed young men.

The resounding electoral victory of the FIS in the first round of elections in late 1991 forced Western governments to reassess their North African regional policies. Increased financial support for the Mahgreb was written into the European Community's (EC) fourth financial protocol (1992–6). It was fundamental to its 'Redirected Mediterranean Policy', Community jargon for trying to block Islamism in North Africa. EC policy in this respect had three interlinked aims: to prevent the type of socio-political instability apparent in Algeria from manifesting itself elsewhere in North Africa; to counteract potential waves of immigration to France and elsewhere in Southern Europe from the region; and to seek to undermine the chances of the creation of another regime along the lines of Gadaffi's in Libya.

While such foreign policy aims could be described as anti-Islamic, as we saw in Chapter 5, Muslim states had their own foreign policies which sometimes included Islamic goals. It is frequently argued that the international impact of Iran's revolution would be limited because of religious and ethnic factors: the vast majority of Iranians are both non-Arab and Shiite. Yet the wide-ranging internationalist foreign policy of Iran since 1979 led to the exporting of its Islamic revolution to geographically contiguous areas in the (Arab) Middle East and beyond, to Sudan, Nigeria and elsewhere. As with Libya's foreign policy guided by a long-term vision of world, anti-imperialist revolution, Iran's international outlook is moulded by an ideological vision of Islam's supremacy. In this context Islamist opposition groups, regardless of their position on the question of the Sunni–Shiite division, welcome Iran's financial and ideological solidarity.

Foreign policy goals are always fundamentally dominated by national security considerations even when a state's policy is proclaimed to be dominated by ideological (including religious) concerns. United States policy in Central America and other important geo-strategic areas was dominated by security concerns (i.e. anti-communism), yet, as we saw, sub-state actors, including fundamentalist, politically conservative Christian missionaries, had their own foreign policy agenda which dovetailed neatly with state concerns. It would be difficult to describe US policy as a religiously oriented policy if we take that to mean attempts to further Christian values by foreign policy means. Nevertheless, the rise of Christian fundamentalism in the USA was closely linked to the state ideology of anti-communism; indeed, the latter was perceived as literally evil-inspired: to root out secular Marxism and liberation theology were seen as the two sides of the same coin. Such an idea was used to justify all means to undermine the Sandinista government in Nicaragua and keep the economic screws tightened on Cuba.

Religio-politics in the future

It is 30 years since the modernization literature predicted the demise of traditional religions. Contrary to the then conventional wisdom innumerable religio-political agendas and movements have since emerged in the Third World; some of them have been examined in this book. Generally, it has been argued that in many Third World countries religion has featured as one of the most important socio-political factors. At the same time this should not be taken to imply that the world is on the threshold of a new religious era. Among Muslim countries only a handful have Islamic governments. In others, such as Syria, Iraq and Morocco, more or less secular governments maintain a tight grip on the reins of power. Nevertheless, in each of these states Islamist groups are of lesser or greater socio-political salience. Sometimes foreign states aid and abet them for their own ends. This does not imply of course that Muslims in these countries are less religious than their counterparts in Iran or Sudan. It points to the fact that the success or failure of Islamist movements is directly related to the strength or weakness of incumbent governments. In addition, the very lack of Islamic governments serves to reinforce the Islamic message of the opposition. In Iran, more than a decade of clergy-led government did not lead to a sustained or widespread increase in living standards. Separate riots in the Iranian cities of Mashhad and Arak in mid-1992 were directed against symbols of oppression: government buildings, banks and shops (Imam-Jomeh 1992). In other words, once Islamic governments assumed power and were seen to be not necessarily more successful than their secular counterparts the move towards such regimes elsewhere might not enjoy the same momentum as before. Unless something unexpected happens, such as the linking up of Islamic regimes across state boundaries – which seems unlikely as an upsurge in nationalism is ubiquitous and often linked to the growth of religio-politics – there is little threat in the short term to the established pattern of generally secularized government.

This is not to argue that the current period is just another cyclical manifestation of religious resurgence. As I have tried to make clear there are a number of qualitatively different characteristics of the current period, especially in relation to the decline of secular ideologies other than nationalism. The separation of state and religion in the Christian context was of singular importance in arriving at an assessment of its role in Third World countries. As was noted in Chapter 4, two strands of Christianity are of particular political salience: socially progressive liberation theology and Protestant conservatism. The rapid growth of the latter, especially in Latin America, has paralleled the rise of Islamism. Yet if Islamism challenges rulers in Muslim countries, conservative versions of Protestantism do not. The move away from the political arena which many converts to conservative Protestantism demonstrate indicates the unlikelihood of a challenge to state power emanating from such a position in the future.

In conclusion, it would not be advisable to replace a wholesale rejection of the importance of religion in politics in the Third World with an equally general assessment of religion's overwhelming political salience everywhere and for all time. There is no reason to doubt that the current wave of religion-oriented political ideas and movements will in time give way (or at least be joined by) an at least partial resurrection of secular ideologies. This may happen within a relatively short time, given the porous nature of states' supposedly 'hard' frontiers, the inability of their governments to keep out external ideas and the expected failure of religious ideologies when used by governments as part of development policy. If the cyclical nature of politics is accepted – and this in the context of an expected lack of change for the better in most people's lives in the Third World – then we may well see a reversion to currently marginalized ideologies such as socialism, communism, populism or even fascism, by both ruling governments and opposition groups. Most people in the Third World will continue to understand by the term 'politics' something quite different from what is understood by their rulers and other political leaders. This is to underline that religion will remain an intensely personal experience for millions, as it has for thousands of years. Political ideologies may wax and wane but religion will maintain its position of personal salience for many.

Bibliography

Abasiattai, M. (1988) The Oberi Okaime Christian Mission: towards a history of an Ibibio Independent Church, *Africa*, 59 (4): 496–516.

Agyeman, O. (1984) Pan-Africanism versus Pan-Arabism: a dual assymetrical model of political relations, *Middle East Review*, 16 (4): 5–30.

Alexander, S. (1982) Religion and national identity in Yugoslavia, in S. Mews (ed.) *Religion and National Identity*, Oxford, Blackwell.

Alvarez, C. (1981) Latin American Protestantism, 1969–78, in S. Torres and J. Eagleson (eds) *The Challenge of the Basic Christian Communities*, Maryknoll, NY, Orbis.

Ammah, R. (1984) New light on Muslim statistics for Africa, *Bulletin on Islam and Christian-Muslim Relations in Africa*, 2 (1): 11–20.

Anderson, E. (1984) *Messianic Popular Movements in the Lower Congo* (Uppsala, Studio Ethnographica Upsaliensia 14: 244–5), quoted in T. Hodgkin, 'Mahdism, messianism and Marxism in the African setting', in J. Bak and G. Benecke (eds) *Religion and Rural Revolt*, Manchester, Manchester University Press.

Anderson, L. (1991) The Tunisian National Pact of 1988, *Government and Opposition*, 26 (2): 244–60.

Asad, M. (1980) *The Principles of State and Government in Islam*, Gibraltar, Dar al-Andalus.

Ashraf, A. and Banuazizi, A. (1985) The state, social classes and modes of mobilization in the Iranian revolution, *State, Culture and Society*, 1 (3): 25–45.

Ayubi, N. (1991) *Political Islam. Religion and Politics in the Arab World*, London, Routledge.

Azzam, A. (1979) *The Eternal Message of Muhammad*, London, Quartet.

Azzam, M. (1991) The Gulf crisis: perceptions in the Muslim world, *International Affairs*, 67 (3): 473–85.

Banuazizi, A. (1987) Social-psychological approaches to political development, in M. Weiner and S. Huntington (eds) *Understanding Political Development*, Boston, Little, Brown.

Barreiro, A. (1982) *Basic Ecclesial Communities*, Maryknoll, NY, Orbis.

Brass, P. (ed.) (1985) *Ethnic Groups and the State*, Manchester, NH, Barnes and Noble.

Brittain, V. (1991) Drought, death and donor fatigue, *The Guardian*, 18 April.

Brown, D. (1989) Ethnic revival: perspectives on state and society, *Third World Quarterly*, 11 (4): 1–17.

Bruce, S. (1990) Protestant resurgence and fundamentalism, *The Political Quarterly*, 61 (2): 161–8.

Cammack, P., Pool, D. and Tordoff, W. (1989) *Third World Politics*, Harlow, Longman.

Capitanchik, D. (1986) Terrorism and Islam, in N. O'Sullivan (ed.) *Terrorism, Ideology and Revolution*, Brighton, Wheatsheaf.

Cardenal, R. (1990) The martyrdom of the Salvadorean Church, in D. Keogh (ed.) *Church and Politics in Latin America*, London, Macmillan.

Choi, S.-D. (1986) A comparative study of two new religious movements in the Republic of Korea: the Unification Church and the Full Gospel Central Church, in J. Beckford (ed.) *New Religious Movements and Rapid Social Change*, London, Sage/UNESCO.

Chamberlain, G. (1991) Right backs communist in Haiti, *The Guardian*, 23 December.

Christian Students' Social Movement of Nigeria (1983) Prayer Bulletin, 1983, quoted in M. Ojo (1988).

Clapham, C. (1989) Ethiopia, in S. Mews (ed.) *Religion in Politics*, London, Longman.

Cooper, J. (1988) Liberation theology, human rights, and US security, in R. Rubenstein and J. Roth (eds) *The Politics of Latin American Liberation Theology. The Challenge to US Policy*, Washington, DC, Washington Institute Press.

Cruise O'Brien, C. (1990) God and man in Nicaragua, in D. Keogh (ed.) *Church and Politics in Latin America*, London, Macmillan.

D'Antonio, M. (1990) *Fall From Grace. The Failed Crusade of the Christian Right*, London, Andre Deutsch.

Darwish, A. (1991) Religious rift in Saudi Arabia, *The Independent*, 29 May.

Das Gupta, J. (1990) India: democratic becoming and combined development, in L. Diamond, J. Linz and S. Martin Lipset (eds) *Politics in Developing Countries. Comparing Experiences with Democracy*, London, Reinner.

Davies, J. (1971) *When Men Revolt and Why*, New York, Free Press.

Dawisha, A. (ed.) (1983) *Islam in Foreign Policy*, Cambridge, Cambridge University Press.

Deeb, M. (1978) Islam and Arab nationalism in Al-Qaddhafi's ideology, *Journal of South Asian and Middle Eastern Studies*, 2 (2): 12–26.

Deeb, M.-J. (1989a) Algeria, in S. Mews (ed.) *Religion in Politics. A World Guide*, Harlow, Longman.

Deeb, M.-J. (1989b) Tunisia, in S. Mews (ed.) *Religion in Politics. A World Guide*, Harlow, Longman.

Deeb, M.-J. (1991) *Libya's Foreign Policy in North Africa*, Boulder, CO, Westview.

Del Aguila, J. (1990) Cuba, in H. Wiarda and H. Kline (eds) *Latin American Politics and Development*, Boulder, CO, Westview.

Desanti, D. (1971) The Golden Anniversary of Kimbanguism, *Continent 2000*, April: 7–19.

Dessouki, A. (1982) The Islamic resurgence: sources, dynamics and implications, in A. Dessouki (ed.) *Islamic Resurgence in the Islamic World*, New York, Praeger.

de Tocqueville, A. (1969) *Democracy in America, Volume One*, New York, Anchor Books.

Diamond, L., Linz, J. and Lipset, S. M. (eds) (1990) *Politics in Developing Countries. Comparing Experiences with Democracy*, Boulder, CO, Reinner.

Dietz, H. (1990) Revolutionary organization in the countryside: Peru, in B. Schutz and R. Slater (eds) *Revolution and Political Change in the Third World*, Boulder, CO, Reinner.

Digan, P. (1984) *Churches in Contestation: Asian Christian Social Protest*, Maryknoll, NY, Orbis.

Dobbelaere, K. (1981) Secularization: a multi-dimensional concept, *Current Sociology*, 29 (1): 11–12.

Dodson, M. (1979) Liberation theology and Christian radicalism in contemporary Latin America, *Journal of Latin American Studies*, 11 (1): 203–22.

Doornbos, M. (1991) Linking the future to the past: ethnicity and pluralism, *Review of African Political Economy*, 52: 53–65.

Durling, A. (1989) *Action at the Grassroots*, Washington, DC, Worldwatch Papers 88, Worldwatch Institute.

Eckstein, S. (1989) Power and popular protest in Latin America, in S. Eckstein (ed.) *Power and Popular Protest. Latin American Social Movements*, Berkeley, University of California Press.

Esposito, J. (1990) Presidential Address, 1989. The study of Islam: challenges and prospects, *Middle East Studies Association Bulletin*, 24 (1): 1–11.

Evans, K. (1990) Bhutto loses control of her base in Sind, *The Guardian*, 29 October.

Evans, K. (1991) Signals cloud hostage issue, *The Guardian*, 30 September.

Faksh, M. (1990) Concepts of rule and legitimation in Islam, *Journal of South Asian and Middle Eastern Studies*, 13 (3): 21–36.

Farouk-Sluglett, M. and Sluglett, P. (1989a) Syria, in S. Mews (ed.) *Religion in Politics*, Harlow, Longman.

Farouk-Sluglett, M. and Sluglett, P. (1989b) Iraq, in S. Mews (ed.) *Religion in Politics*, Harlow, Longman.

Farouk-Sluglett, M. and Sluglett, P. (1989c) Saudi Arabia, in S. Mews (ed.) *Religion in Politics*, Harlow, Longman.

Fathers, M. (1991) Revolution in paradise, *The Independent on Sunday*, 21 July.

Ferdows, A. (1983) Khomeini and Fadayan's society and politics, *International Journal of Middle Eastern Studies*, 15: 241–57.

Fineman, M. (1987) Cult wages holy war on Philippines' communists, *Los Angeles Times*, 3 April.

Fisher, A. and Fisher, H. (1971) *Slavery and Muslim Society in Africa*, New York, Doubleday.

Foltz, W. (1990) External causes, in B. Schultz and R. Slater (eds) *Revolution and Political Change in the Third World*, London, Adamantine.

Foster-Carter, A. (1985) The sociology of development, in M. Haralambos (ed.) *Sociology: New Directions*, Ormskirk, Causeway.

Frank, A.G. (1971) *Capitalism and Underdevelopment in Latin America*, Harmondsworth, Penguin.

Freire, P. (1970) *The Pedagogy of the Oppressed*, New York, Seabury.

Gelber, G. (1989) Haiti, in S. Mews (ed.) *Religion in Politics*, Harlow, Longman.

Ghosh, S. (1987) *Communal Riots in India – Meet the Challenge Unitedly*, New Delhi, Ashis.

Gifford, P. (1989) Zambia, in S. Mews (ed.) *Religion in Politics*, Harlow, Longman.

Goldthorpe, J. (1975 and 1984) *The Sociology of the Third World. Disparity and Involvement*. Cambridge, Cambridge University Press.

Green, J. (1985) Islam, religio-politics and social change, *Comparative Studies in Society and History*, 27: 312–22.

Gutiérrez, G. (1973) *A Theology of Liberation*, Maryknoll, NY, Orbis.

Hadden, J. and Shupe, A. (1986) *Prophetic Religions and Politics: Religion and the Political Order, Volume One*. New York, Paragon House.

Hague, R. and Harrop, M. (1987) *Comparative Government and Politics: an Introduction*, Basingstoke, Macmillan.

Hall, S. (1985) Religious ideologies and social movements in Jamaica, in R. Bocock and K. Thomson (eds) *Religion and Ideology*, Manchester, Manchester University Press.

Halliday, F. (1987) The Iranian revolution and its implications, *New Left Review*, November–December: 29–37.

Halliday, F. and Alavi, H. (1988) *State and Ideology in the Middle East and Pakistan*, London, Macmillan.

Hart, N. (1985) The power of medicine in society, in M. Haralambos (ed.) *Sociology, New Directions*, Ormskirk, Causeway.

Haynes, J. (1989) Ghana, in S. Mews (ed.) *Religion in Politics*, Harlow, Longman.

Haynes, J. (1992) Islam and politics in West Africa. Paper presented at the Political Studies Association Annual Conference, Queen's University, Belfast, April.

Hehir, J. (1990) Papal foreign policy, *Foreign Policy*, 78: 26–48.

Herring, H. (1968) *A History of Latin America*, New York, Knopf.

Hewitt, W. (1987a) Basic Christian communities of the middle classes in the Archdiocese of São Paulo, *Sociological Analysis*, 48 (2): 158–66.

Hewitt, W. (1987b) The influences of social class on activity preferences of Communidades Eclesias de Base (CEBs) in the Archdiocese of São Paulo, *Journal of Latin American Studies*, 19 (1): 141–56.

Hewitt, W. (1990) Religion and the consolidation of democracy in Brazil: the role of the Communidades Eclesias de Base (CEBs), *Sociological Analysis*, 50 (2): 139–52.

Holsti, K. (1972) *International Politics: a Framework for Analysis*, Englewood Cliffs, NJ, Prentice Hall.

Hooglund, E. (1989) Iran, in P. Schraeder (ed.) *Intervention in the 1980s: US Foreign Policy in the Third World*, London, Reinner.

Hooper, J. (1991) Street violence forces Chadli to resign party post, *The Guardian*, 1 July.

Huntington, S. (1968) *Political Order in Changing Societies*, New Haven, CT, Yale University Press.

Hussein Razi, G. (1990) Legitimacy, religion and nationalism in the Middle East, *American Political Science Review*, 84 (1): 69–91.

Ibrahim, J. (1991) Religion and political turbulence in Nigeria, *Journal of Modern African Studies*, 29 (1): 115–36.

Imam-Jomeh, S. (1992) Thousands go on protest rampage through Iranian Holy City, *The Guardian*, 1 June.

Imasogie, O. (1983) *Guidelines for Christian Theology in Africa*, Achimota, Ghana, Christian Press.

Imobighe, T. (1981) Security implications for Nigeria (1), *New Nigerian*, 27 February.

Ingham, K. (1990) *Politics in Modern Africa. The Uneven Tribal Dimension*, London, Routledge.

Islam, N. (1981) Islam and national identity: the case of Pakistan and Bangladesh, *International Journal of Middle Eastern Studies*, 13: 55–72.

Kaba, L. (1976) Islam's advance in Tropical Africa, *Africa Report*, March–April: 37–41.

Kautsky, J. (1972) *The Political Consequences of Modernization*, New York, John Wiley.

Keogh, D. (ed.) (1990) *Church and Politics in Latin America*, London, Macmillan.

Kirk, G. (1959) *A Short History of the Middle East*, London, Methuen.

Kornbluh, P. (1989) Nicaragua, in P. Schraeder (ed.) *Intervention in the 1980s: US Foreign Policy in the Third World*, London, Reinner.

Laitin, D. (1978) Religion, political culture, and the Weberian tradition, *World Politics*, 30 (4): 563–93.

Lannon, F. (1982) Modern Spain: the project of national Catholicism, in S. Mews (ed.) *Religion and National Identity*, Oxford, Blackwell.
Lapidus, I. (1988) *A History of Islamic Societies*, Cambridge, Cambridge University Press.
Laquer, W. (1984) International terrorism, *Washington Post*, 29 April.
Lawson, F. (1989) Bahrain, in S. Mews (ed.) *Religion in Politics*, Harlow, Longman.
Lernoux, P. (1988) The fundamentalist surge in Latin America, *The Christian Century*, 20 January.
Levine, D. (1986) Religion and politics in comparative perspective, *Comparative Politics*, October: 95–122.
Levine, D. (1990) The Catholic Church and politics in Latin America: basic trends and likely futures, in D. Keogh (ed.) *Church and Politics in Latin America*, London, Macmillan.
Linden, I. (1991) Review of Paul Gifford, 'The New Crusaders: Christianity and the New Right in Southern Africa', *Review of African Political Economy*, 52: 118–20.
Livingstone, W. (1917) *Mary Slessor of Calabar. Pioneer Missionary*, London, Hodder and Stoughton.
Lowry, S. (1991) Eight killed in Algiers violence, *Daily Telegraph*, 27 June.
McBeth, J. (1989) Critical solidarity, *Far Eastern Economic Review*, 1 June: 30–1.
McWilliams, W. and Piotrowski, H. (1990) *The World Since 1945*, Boulder, CO, Reinner.
Mahmud, A. (1992) Burmese Muslims fight army assault, *The Guardian*, 13 February.
Mallia, J. (1991) Fundamentalists rejoice but Sudan's millions starve, *The Guardian*, 15 July.
Manor, J. (ed.) (1991a) *Rethinking Third World Politics*, Harlow, Longman.
Manor, J. (1991b) Introduction, in J. Manor (ed.) *Rethinking Third World Politics*, Harlow, Longman.
Marishane, J. (1990) *Prayer, Profit and Power: American Religious Right-wing and Foreign Policy*, Amsterdam, Govan Mbeki Fund, University of Amsterdam.
Marishane, J. (1991) Prayer, profit and power: US religious right and foreign policy, *Review of African Political Economy*, 52: 73–86.
Martin, D. (1969) *The Religious and the Secular*, London, Routledge.
Martin, D. (1989) Speaking in Latin tongues, *National Review*, 29 September: 31.
Martin, D. (1990a) Fundamentalism: an observational and definitional tour d'horizon, *The Political Quarterly*, 61 (2): 129–31.
Martin, D. (1990b) *Tongues of Fire. The Explosion of Protestantism in Latin America*, Oxford, Basil Blackwell.
Mbiti, J. (1969) *African Religions and Philosophy*, London, Heinemann.
Medhurst, K. (1981) Religion and politics. A typology, *Scottish Journal of Religious Studies*, 2 (2): 115–34.
Medhurst, K. (1989) Brazil, in S. Mews (ed.) *Religion in Politics*, Harlow, Longman.
Medhurst, K. (1991) Politics and religion in Latin America, in G. Moyser (ed.) *Politics and Religion in the Modern World*, London, Routledge.
Mews, S. (ed.) (1989a) *Religion in Politics. A World Guide*, Harlow, Longman.
Mews, S. (1989b) Vatican City, in S. Mews (ed.) *Religion in Politics*, Harlow, Longman.
Milton Yinger, J. (1967) Religion and social change: functions and disfunctions of sects and cults among the disprivileged, in R. Knudten (ed.) *The Sociology of Religion: an Anthology*, New York.
Mitra, S. K. (1987) Desecularizing the state in India. Paper presented at the annual conference of the Political Studies Association, Aberdeen, April.

Mitra, S. K. (1991) Competing modes of the state in Indian political discourse, *Comparative Studies in Society and History*, 33 (4): 755–77.

Modood, T. (1990) British Asian Muslims and the Rushdie affair, *The Political Quarterly*, 61 (2): 143–60.

Montgomery Watt, W. (1990) *Islamic Fundamentalism and Modernity*, London, Routledge.

Moyser, G. (1991) Politics and religion in the modern world: an overview, in G. Moyser (ed.) *Politics and Religion in the Modern World*, London, Routledge.

Munson, T. (1988) *Islam and Revolution in the Middle East*, New Haven, CT, Yale University Press.

Murphy, C. (1991) Islamic challenge to Saudi royalty, *The Guardian*, 11 June.

Naipaul, V. (1981) *Among the Believers: an Islamic Journey*, Harmondsworth, Viking.

Newman, S. (1991) Does modernization breed ethnic political conflicts? *World Politics*, 43: 451–78.

Norton Moore, J. (1985) The secret war in Central America and the future of world order, *World Affairs*, 148: 75–130.

Ochsenwald, W. (1981) Saudi Arabia and the Islamic revival, *International Journal of Middle Eastern Studies*, 13: 271–86.

O'Connell, J. (1989) Nigeria, in S. Mews (ed.) *Religion in Politics*, Harlow, Longman.

Ojo, M. (1988) The contextual significance of the charismatic movements in independent Nigeria, *Africa*, 58 (2): 175–92.

O'Shaughnessy, L. (1990) What do the evangelicals want? in E. Sahliyeh (ed.) *Religious Resurgence and Politics in the Contemporary World*, Albany, State University of New York Press.

Palmer, J. (1992) Turkey offers EC delays in return for regional role, *The Guardian*, 9 March.

Parpart, J. (1988) Women and the state, in D. Rothchild and N. Chazan (eds) *The Precarious Balance*, Boulder, CO, Westview.

Parrinder, G. (1976) *Africa's Three Religions*, London, Sheldon.

Parry, G., Tran, M. and Pallister, D. (1991) Irangate's arms conspiracy ensnared Waite's delicate mission of diplomacy in Middle East, *The Guardian*, 19 November.

Pendle, G. (1976) *A History of Latin America*, Harmondsworth, Penguin.

Perry, G. (1991) The Islamic world: Egypt and Iran, in G. Moyser (ed.) *Politics and Religion in the Modern World*, London, Routledge.

Pipes, D. (1983–4) Understanding Islam in politics, *Middle East Review*, 16 (2): 3–16.

Piscatori, J. (1980) The roles of Islam in Saudi Arabia's political development, in J. Esposito (ed.) *Islam and Development: Religion and Sociopolitical Change*, Syracuse, NY, Syracuse University Press.

Rajgopal, P. (1987) *Communal Violence in India*, New Delhi, Uppal.

Randall, V. and Theobald, R. (1985) *Political Change and Underdevelopment. A Critical Introduction to Third World Politics*, London, Macmillan.

Rashid, A. (1991) Founder's mission to rival the West, *Independent on Sunday*, 14 July.

Reid, M. (1990) Centre-right ahead in Guatemala, *The Guardian*, 13 December.

Roberts, H. (1988) Radical Islamism and the dilemma of Algerian nationalism: the embattled Arians of Algiers, *Third World Quarterly*, 10 (2): 567–75.

Robertson, R. (1988) Liberation theology, Latin America, and Third World underdevelopment, in R. Rubenstein and J. Roth (eds) *The Politics of Latin American Liberation Theology*, Washington, DC, Washington Institute Press.

Robertson, R. and Chirico, J. (1985) Humanity, globalization and worldwide religious resurgence: a theoretical exploration, *Sociological Analysis*, 46: 219–42.

Rocha, J. (1991) Catholicism falls from grace as Indians seek alternative salvation, *The Guardian*, 24 April.

Roelofs, H. (1988) Liberation theology: the recovery of biblical radicalism, *American Political Science Review*, 82 (2): 549–66.

Rosberg, C. and Nottingham, J. (1966) *The Myth of 'Mau Mau': Nationalism in Kenya*, New York.

Rostow, W. (1959) *The Stages of Economic Growth. A Non-Communist Manifesto*, Cambridge, Cambridge University Press.

Rostow, W. (1991) *Theories of Economic Growth from David Hume to the Present with a Perspective on the Next Century*, Oxford, Oxford University Press.

Rubin, B. (1990a) *Islamic Fundamentalism in Egyptian Politics*, London, Macmillan.

Rubin, B. (1990b) Religion and international affairs, *The Washington Quarterly*, 13 (2): 51–63.

Sahliyeh, E. (ed.) (1990) *Religious Resurgence and Politics in the Contemporary World*, Albany, State University of New York Press.

Samudavanija, C.-A. (1991) The three-dimensional state, in J. Manor (ed.) *Rethinking Third World Politics*, Harlow, Longman.

Sardar, Z. (1985) *Islamic Futures: the Shape of Ideas to Come*, London, Mansell.

Searle, C. (1991) The Muslimeen insurrection in Trinidad, *Race and Class*, 33 (2): 29–43.

Serra, L. (1985) Ideology, religion and class struggle in the Nicaraguan revolution, in R. Harris and C. Vilas (eds) *Nicaragua: a Revolution Under Siege*, London, Zed.

Shaikh, F. (1986) Islam and the quest for democracy in Pakistan, *Journal of Commonwealth and Comparative Politics*, 24 (1): 74–92.

Shaikh, F. (1989a) Iran, in S. Mews (ed.) *Religion in Politics*, Harlow, Longman.

Shaikh, F. (1989b) Pakistan, in S. Mews (ed.) *Religion in Politics*, Harlow, Longman.

Shaikh, F. (1989c) Afghanistan, in S. Mews (ed.) *Religion in Politics*, Harlow, Longman.

Shepperson, G. (1954) The politics of African church separatist movements in British Central Africa, 1892–1916, *Africa*, 24: 233–45.

Sivan, E. (1985) *Radical Islam. Medieval Theology and Modern Politics*, New Haven, CT, Yale University Press.

Smith, B. (1982) *The Church and Politics in Chile*, Princeton, NJ, Princeton University Press.

Smith, D. E. (1970) *Religion and Political Development*, Boston, Little, Brown.

Smith, D. E. (1990) The limits of religious resurgence, in E. Sahliyeh (ed.) *Religious Resurgence and Politics in the Contemporary World*, Albany, State University of New York Press.

Stoll, D. (1990) *Is Latin America Turning Protestant? The Politics of Evangelical Growth*, Berkeley, University of California Press.

Sundkler, B. (1948) *Bantu Prophets in South Africa*, London, Oxford University Press.

Swift, R. (1990) Fundamentalism, *New Internationalist*, August: 4–6.

Tekle, A. (1989) The determinants of the foreign policy of revolutionary Ethiopia, *Journal of Modern African Studies*, 27 (3): 479–502.

Thapar, K. (1990) Pride and the political fall-out, *Sunday Correspondent*, 28 October.

Tibi, B. (1990) *Islam and the Cultural Accommodation of Social Change*, Boulder, CO, Westview.

Tisdall, S. (1991) US keeping alive option of intervention in Haiti, *The Guardian*, 15 November.

Torres, S. and Eagleson, J. (eds) (1981) *The Challenge of the Basic Christian Communities*, Maryknoll, NY, Orbis.

Urena, H. (1949) *Literary Currents in Hispanic America*, Cambridge, MA, Harvard University Press.

van Binsbergen, W. (1981) *Religious Change in Zambia. Exploratory Studies*, London, Kegan Paul.

van der Veer, P. (1987) 'God must be liberated!' A Hindu liberation movement in Ayodhya, *Modern Asian Studies*, 21 (2): 283–301.

Vanhanen, T. (1991) *Politics of Ethnic Nepotism. India as an Example*, New Delhi, Sterling.

Vatikiotis, P. (1991) *Islam and the State*, London, Routledge.

Vatin, J. (1982) Revival in the Maghreb, in A. Dessouki (ed.) *Islamic Resurgence in the Arab World*, New York, Praeger.

Vines, S. (1991) Birthday bash for man who has it all, *The Guardian*, 25 July.

Voll, J. and von der Mehden, F. (1990) Religious resurgence and revolution: Islam, in B. Slater and R. Schultz (eds) *Revolution and Political Change in the Third World*, London, Adamantine.

von der Mehden, F. (1989a) Philippines, in S. Mews (ed.) *Religion in Politics*, Harlow, Longman.

von der Mehden, F. (1989b) Indonesia, in S. Mews (ed.) *Religion in Politics*, Harlow, Longman.

Walshe, P. (1991) South Africa: prophetic Christianity and the liberation movement, *Journal of Modern African Studies*, 29 (1): 27–60.

Waltz, K. (1979) *The Theory of International Politics*, Reading, MA, Addison-Wesley.

Warhola, J. (1991) The religious dimension of ethnic conflict in the Soviet Union, *International Journal of Politics, Culture, and Society*, 5 (2): 249–70.

Wiebe, V. (1989a) Guatemala, in S. Mews (ed.) *Religion in Politics*, Harlow, Longman.

Wiebe, V. (1989b) Jamaica, in S. Mews (ed.) *Religion in Politics*, Harlow, Longman.

Wilson, B. (1985) A typology of sects, in R. Bocock and K. Thompson (eds) *Religion and Ideology*, Manchester, Manchester University Press.

Wright Mills, C. (1959) *The Causes of World War Three*, London, Secker and Warburg.

Wuthnow, R. (1986) Religious movements and counter-movements in North America, in J. Beckford (ed.) *New Religious Movements and Rapid Social Change*, London, Sage.

Index

African Independent Churches, 61,
112–14
African Orthodox Church, 61
Algeria
Islamic Salvation Front (FIS),
81–2
Islamic Society Movement
(HAMAS), 82
status of Islam, 18, 27, 80–2
apartheid, 61–2
Aristide, J.-B., Fr., 19, 108–9
Ayubi, N., 70–1

Bruce, S., 116

Catholicism, 54–6, 62, 97
Chilembwe, J., 60
Christian base communities
(Communidades eclesiales de
base)
characteristics, 18, 103–7
in Haiti, 107–8
in the Philippines, 107–8
Christian fundamentalism
characteristics, 4, 34–7, 41–2, 96,
109–10
in Ghana, 19, 110
in Nigeria, 18–19, 110–11
political impact in Africa, 111–12
Christianity
in Africa, 57–8
historical expansion, 54

missionaries, 57–8
separation of church and state, 27,
53–4
in South America, 54–6
Christian-Muslim conflict, 2–3
communism in Ethiopia, 123–4

democracy, 11–12
dependency theory, 23–5
de Tocqueville, A., 18
Doornbos, M., 38

Egypt, 18
Esposito, J., 39–40
ethnicity, 7–8

Frank, A.G., 23–5
Freire, P., 101–2
fundamentalism, *see separate entries
for* Islamic *and* Christian
fundamentalism

Garvey, M., 58
Goldthorpe, J., 36
Gramsci, A., 34
Gutierrez, G., 98

Hadden, J., 31
Holsti, K., 122
Huntington, S., 6, 11

Iran
    international impact of 1978–80
        revolution, 40, 144
    Islamic state, 65–6
    revolution, characteristics of, 12–13,
        18, 35–6, 72–80
    Shah Pahlavi, 40
Islam
    in Africa, 50–2
    historical expansion, 44–53
    mainstream, 40–1
    political opposition, 64–8
    popular, 68
    radical, 40–1
    resurgence, 37, 39, 93–4
    revival movements, 50–1
    Sunni-Shiite division, 30, 46
    traditionalist, 40–1
Islamic fundamentalism, 3–4, 34–7,
    70–2
Islamic state, 64–7
Islamists, 70
Israel, 4–5, 19, 37

Jehovah's Witnesses, 60–1

Khomeini, Ayatollah, 12, 35, 46,
    65
Kimbangu, S., 60
Korea, 19, 141–2

Laitin, D., 9–10
Lakwena, A., 113
liberation theology
    in Brazil, 102–3
    characteristics, 30, 42, 98–103
    in Chile, 103
    in Haiti, 19
    and Marxism, 100–1
    in Philippines, 19, 140–2
Lumpa Church in Zambia, 112–13

Manor, J., 32
Martin, D., 34, 110
Medhurst, K., 146
Mitra, S.K., 32, 38
modernization, 21–3
Muhammad, Prophet, 45–6
Muslim East Asia
    Brunei, 92–3
    Indonesia, 90–2
    Malaysia, 92–3

Muslim Brotherhood, 69
Muslims
    categories, 69
    in India, 49, 51–2
    minorities, 69
    Shiite radicals, 27
    in South-East Asia, 52–3

naparamas (Mozambique), 113–14
Nicaragua
    role of religion in politics, 19, 27
    US support for Contras, 117,
        142–3

Pakistan
    Bhutto, Benazir, 87–8
    status of Islam, 19, 84–8
politics, imaginary and theatrical
    dimensions of, 32
Protestantism
    as conservative doctrine, 56, 95–6
    and fundamentalism, 96–7
    in Guatemala, 118
    in Honduras, 118
    in Latin America, 114–21

Rastafarianism, 58–9
religio-political movements, 13, 30,
    147–9
religion
    characteristics, 32
    definition, 28–9
    global resurgence, 28
    and nationalism, 150–2
    in pre-modern societies, 29
    role of women, 113
religion and foreign policy
    Iran, 132–4
    Libya, 129–32
    national interest, 123
    Pakistan, 134–6
    realpolitik, 123
    religious heterogeneity, 136–8
    significance, 122–7, 152–3
    United States, 126–7, 139–40
    the Vatican, 127–9
religious
    fundamentalism, 33–7
    revivalism, 14
Rida, M., 66–8
Rostow, W., 21–2

Sardar, Z., 65–7
Saudi Arabia, 19, 41, 88–90, 124
sects
  Ethiopian, 58
  Zionist, 58–9
secular ideologies, 29–30
secularization, 31
Sudan, 19, 84
Sundkler, B., 58

Swift, R., 36
syncretic religions, 14, 39

terrorism, 37–8
Tunisia
  An Nahda, 82–3
  status of Islam, 18

Wilson, B., 59, 115